TRANSFORMING INDIC

Urbanization and Language Revitalization in the Brazilian Amazon

Transforming Indigeneity is an examination of the role that language revitalization efforts play in cultural politics in the small city of São Gabriel da Cachoeira, located in the Brazilian Amazon. Sarah Shulist studies how discussions and practices aimed at providing support for the Indigenous languages of the region shed light both on global issues of language revitalization and on the meaning of Indigeneity in contemporary Brazil.

São Gabriel is characterized by a high proportion of Indigenous people and an extraordinary amount of linguistic diversity, with nineteen Indigenous languages still spoken there today. Shulist explores the effects of urbanization, multilingualism, and state intervention in this setting, and how they relate to understandings of Indigeneity and the use and transmission of Indigenous languages. Drawing on perspectives from Indigenous and non-Indigenous political leaders, educators, students, and state agents, *Transforming Indigeneity* provides insight on the revitalization of Amazonian Indigenous languages in a context of major social change.

(Anthropological Horizons)

SARAH SHULIST is an assistant professor of Anthropology at MacEwan University.

ANTHROPOLOGICAL HORIZONS

Editor: Michael Lambek, University of Toronto

This series, begun in 1991, focuses on theoretically informed ethnographic works addressing issues of mind and body, knowledge and power, equality and inequality, the individual and the collective. Interdisciplinary in its perspective, the series makes a unique contribution in several other academic disciplines: women's studies, history, philosophy, psychology, political science, and sociology.

For a list of the books published in this series see page 243.

SARAH SHULIST

Transforming Indigeneity

Urbanization and Language Revitalization in the Brazilian Amazon

UNIVERSITY OF TORONTO PRESS
Toronto Buffalo London

© University of Toronto Press 2018
Toronto Buffalo London
www.utppublishing.com
Printed in Canada

ISBN 978-1-4875-0287-4 (cloth)   ISBN 978-1-4875-2219-3 (paper)

♾ Printed on acid-free, 100% post-consumer recycled paper with vegetable-based inks.

Anthropological Horizons

Library and Archives Canada Cataloguing in Publication

Shulist, Sarah, 1979–, author
Transforming indigeneity : urbanization and language revitalization in the
Brazilian Amazon/Sarah Shulist.

(Anthropological horizons)
Includes bibliographical references and index.
ISBN 978-1-4875-0287-4 (cloth). – ISBN 978-1-4875-2219-3 (paper)

1. Language revival – Brazil – São Gabriel da Cachoeira. 2. Indigenous peoples – Brazil –
São Gabriel da Cachoeira – Languages. 3. Language and languages – Brazil – São Gabriel
da Cachoeira. 4. Urbanization – Brazil – São Gabriel da Cachoeira. 5. Multilingualism –
Brazil – São Gabriel da Cachoeira. 6. Social change – Brazil – São Gabriel da Cachoeira.
7. São Gabriel da Cachoeira (Brazil) – Ethnic relations. 8. São Gabriel da Cachoeira
(Brazil) – Social conditions. I. Title. II. Series: Anthropological horizons

P40.5.L3572B73 2017   306.440981'13   C2017-906088-0

This book has been published with the help of a grant from the Federation for the
Humanities and Social Sciences, through the Awards to Scholarly Publications Program,
using funds provided by the Social Sciences and Humanities Research Council of Canada.

University of Toronto Press acknowledges the financial assistance to its publishing
program of the Canada Council for the Arts and the Ontario Arts Council, an agency of
the Government of Ontario.

Canada Council for the Arts   **Conseil des Arts du Canada**

ONTARIO ARTS COUNCIL
CONSEIL DES ARTS DE L'ONTARIO
an Ontario government agency
un organisme du gouvernement de l'Ontario

Funded by the Government of Canada   Financé par le gouvernement du Canada

Contents

Figures and Tables

Acknowledgments

This book is the product of about seven years of planning, research, writing, and revision. Portions of Chapters 1 and 6 constitute revised versions of material previously published as "Collaborating on Language: Contrasting the Theory and Practice of Collaboration in Linguistics and Anthropology," in *Collaborative Anthropologies*, and permission has been granted for this revised reprinting by the University of Nebraska Press.

As with anything that occupies such an expanse of time and mental energy, it could not have been completed without an entire team of people and institutions to support it and, perhaps more importantly, its author. I received an incredible amount of help that has taken many forms, and I am overwhelmingly grateful for these contributions to the work produced here.

First, I must thank those who have guided this work intellectually. They include colleagues, friends, and mentors who have offered me suggestions, advice, and conversation that have guided both the questions I have asked in this research and the analysis I present here. Tania Granadillo brought to my attention the possibility of working in São Gabriel and, essentially single-handedly, turned me from a cautious person who preferred to remain closer to home into a much more confident fieldworker and Amazonian traveller. She has seen this research through from its inception to its publication here, and to this day it is hard for me to think of her role in my work and my life without tearing up, because without her guidance and unwavering confidence in my abilities I would never have taken the risk of exploring this fieldsite. I have no doubt that this risk greatly improved the scholarly insight I have been able to generate in this work.

Kristine Stenzel and Janet Chernela, who have been working in the Northwest Amazon for many years, have also been instrumental throughout this research. When we three first met in São Gabriel in 2011, Kris introduced me to the Kotiria people, with whom I would become deeply involved, and Janet helped guide me through the morass of regulations involved in helping AIPOK become formally registered. Both women have continued to provide comments and extremely generous encouragement regarding the research that has resulted from this, and their deep knowledge of the region, its peoples, and its languages has greatly enriched this work.

Others have provided feedback on this work and its various drafts. Here, I single out Kim Clark, Karen Pennesi, Regna Darnell, and Julie Byrd Clark. Kim and Karen helped me deal with the new challenges of being a fieldworker with a family in tow. Their warmth and kindness were matched only by their rigorous critiques of my ideas and theoretical perspectives, and their absolute commitment to my success is certainly among the reasons why this book exists at all. Every young scholar should have a team like this on their side.

Various sections of this book have benefited from discussions, commentary, and suggestions provided by a wide range of scholars at conferences, in classrooms, over coffee, and even over Facebook. Jenny Davis, Jenanne Ferguson, Aimee Hosemann, Anthony Webster, Jocelyn Ahlers, Luke Fleming, Christian Español, Jordan Levy, Jordan Lachler, and Zoe Todd have all contributed to this work and to my intellectual growth as a linguistic anthropologist. The students in my Winter 2017 Language Revitalization class at MacEwan University did me the immense kindness of offering constructive feedback regarding how this book would work for an undergraduate audience.

I am hardly the only scholar who has been drawn to the Northwest Amazon. I encountered many travellers in the field who shared pizza with my family and I and helped shape this work as it progressed. These discussions helped me untangle my ideas, consider new approaches, and understand important aspects of living and conducting research in this unique place. Frantomé Pacheco de Oliveira, Elise Capredon, Wilson Silva, Simeon Floyd, and Erick Souza were among these people. Fabiana Sarges deserves additional thanks not only for exchanging ideas about language policy but also for providing me with a place to stay in Manaus that made my visits to the big city much less stressful.

This work would never have been possible without the strength and commitment of the Indigenous people of São Gabriel, whose passionate and effective struggle for recognition of their rights and for the sustainability of their languages was the ultimate motivation for my work.

I am deeply grateful to the Federação das Organizações Indígenas do Rio Negro (FOIRN) and to the individual members of the 2008–12 board of directors, most notably Abrahão de Oliveira França and Maximiliano Correo Menezes. In addition to helping me gain formal approval to conduct this research, these men were constantly available to offer suggestions, guidance, encouragement, and advice about my work and its potential relevance to their own efforts. In addition, the staff of FOIRN's Department of Education, especially Denivaldo Cruz da Silva and Tarcísio Luciano dos Santos, were available for countless exchanges of ideas and discussions about language in the city. The Kotiria people of São Gabriel, through their openness to working with me and their embrace of my collaborative goals, shaped not only this book but also ongoing engagements that I hope will continue to generate productive results. I am honoured to have met this passionate group of people, most particularly Miguel Cabral, Franssinete Ferraz Henrique, and Flávio Ferraz. We could not have thrived during our time in Brazil without the joy that was brought into our lives by those who offered us friendship and who counselled me on the basics of early parenthood, a circumstance in which I felt perhaps even more lost than I did in the new cultural context of the Upper Rio Negro. Here I must single out Franssinete (again), Angelina Lima, Marcivânia Massa Menezes, Claudia and Gabriela Ferraz, Rosane Cruz, Roberlina Vargas, Braulina Baniwa, and Arlene Lima.

My trips to São Gabriel have been funded by grants and scholarships from the Social Sciences and Humanities Research Council of Canada, the University of Western Ontario Department of Anthropology, MacEwan University's Centre for the Advancement of Faculty Excellence, and the individual scholarship donation of Dr Regna Darnell. In addition to this material support, my visits would not have been possible without the administrative support of the Instituto Nacional das Pesquisas Amazônicas (INPA) and, specifically, the tireless efforts of Ana Carla Bruno, who navigated institutional hurdles to help me obtain the necessary permits and documentation.

I have also been very well served by the University of Toronto Press. The anonymous reviewers of this book offered excellent suggestions that have undoubtedly improved the work as a whole, and for that I have to thank not only them but also the excellent editorial support provided by Douglas Hildebrand.

I have, of course, saved the most important people for last. My partner, Peter Gore, had never been on a plane until he embarked on a journey of several months to the Brazilian Amazon, and his only concern and question for me before he committed to coming was "Can I fish there?" (for the record, yes). He has uprooted himself for the sake of my research and my career many times over, and he has done so with nothing but a joyful attitude and one piece of oversized luggage shaped like a fishing rod. Our son, William Gore, has no idea how many doors were opened to us because of his big eyes and toothless smiles, and both he and his baby sister Maggie Lou Shulist continue to remind me of why my work matters. With any luck, they will be able to accompany me on, and actually remember, another trip to São Gabriel as I continue the research I've begun here.

TRANSFORMING INDIGENEITY

Urbanization and Language Revitalization
in the Brazilian Amazon

1 Playing Indian: The Politics of Language, Identity, and Culture in Urban Amazonia[1]

One afternoon, as my family and I pulled up in a taxi at the home of my friends Patricia and Mateus,[2] their four children, along with several of the neighbours' kids (many of them cousins), ran towards the road to meet us. Their youngest daughter, Caroline, about two and a half years old at the time, was wearing a skirt and headband made from toilet paper. "Look, Dona Sarah," one of the older girls said, "she's playing Indian."[3] When we went inside, their father, who was also laughing, repeated this phrase and asked me if I had seen how she could "play Indian," encouraging her to perform a few steps in an Indigenous dance style.[4] Patricia is a Tuyuka woman who has been active in efforts to preserve and promote her language and traditional practices, and her husband Mateus is a Nheengatú-speaking Baré man. Both express great pride in their Indigenous cultures, speak their languages (Patricia is fluent in her mother's language, Tukano, in addition to Tuyuka), and often articulate the need for stronger promotion of Indigenous cultures within the urban area. But for their daughter, Indigeneity – or at least, Indianness – has become something she can *play* at, not necessarily something she understands as being the basis for her daily life.

This short interaction captures several important points about the changing nature of Indigenous identity within a multilingual, multi-ethnic, Amazonian town. On the one hand, Caroline's relationship to "Indianness" is obvious – as the child of two Indigenous Amazonians, she is a young Indigenous girl. On the other hand, her parents' and siblings' perceptions of her actions point to a distinction between a stereotypical, idealized version of how "Indians" behave and the reality of the context in which she is being socialized – the small city of São Gabriel da Cachoeira, Amazonas, Brazil. Like many contemporary

Amazonian people, Caroline is learning about her identity in an urban setting rather than in the "traditional" context of Indigenous settlements (*aldeias*). Though the popular imagination continues to construct Amazonia as a vast, unpopulated space, and its inhabitants as remote forest dwellers, more and more of the region's people are making their homes in cities.[5] Some of these people are non-Indigenous and have settled in large centres like Manaus and Belem; but others, including Indigenous families like Caroline's, have moved from interior *aldeias* to towns like São Gabriel over the past few decades. The implications of this migration for children like Caroline are only beginning to be explored.[6] Her mode of play, and her family's reactions to it, demonstrate aspects of the process of socializing her into a particular identity – Indigenous, to be sure, but a form of Indigeneity that is transformed by its urban setting. Though she is clearly familiar with many of the idealized markers of Indigenous identity and practice (including clothing, dance, and some linguistic elements), the characterization of her actions as "play" reflects how urban Indigenous people are both revitalizing and transforming Indigenous identity.

As Patricia became one of my closest friends in Amazonas, I came to know her four children quite well. All of them were born in the city, and all were monolingual Portuguese speakers. The older three, ranging in age at the time from eight to twelve, rushed towards us every time they saw us in an effort to be the first to carry away my infant son, William, and the eldest, Mário, the only boy, was invariably caring and responsible as he watched over his younger sisters, cousins, and even my baby when he was there. During a short return visit in 2014, I visited Patricia and she laughed as she talked about how Mário had gone behind her back to dye his hair with blonde streaks so that he looked like the Brazilian soccer star Neymar. Her concerns for her children were familiar to me – that they stay away from drugs and alcohol, that they not be victimized by violence (either directly or as a result of exploitation by drug-trafficking rings, which are active in São Gabriel because of its proximity to two international borders), that they continue to trust in their parents for guidance, that they stay in school. She was committed to retaining and promoting her culture, but that was rarely a part of how she talked about her goals as a parent. Much to her chagrin, at one point during my main field visit, she realized that Mário (then twelve years old) could not even correctly identify his mother's Tuyuka ethnicity. The relationship between language and cultural identity in the multilingual Northwest Amazon is a complex one, and while the pre-teen knew that she spoke both Tuyuka and Tukano, he didn't know which of them was "her language." "I think she's Tukano, because she speaks that most often," he told me. Patricia, who had been listening in on our conversation from across the room, hid her face in her hands dramatically and laughingly asked, "My God, what kind of Indian are you, if you don't even know?"

This book seeks to offer an answer, of sorts, to that question. What *kind* of Indigeneity do these children experience, and what does it mean, for them, to be Indigenous? How are their parents and educators, and other adults in their lives, teaching them about their Indigenous identities, through both their everyday cultural practices and their periodic discursive references to how their children manifest (or don't) and "play" with these identities? Clearly, their Indigeneity is different from that of their parents and is changing so rapidly that Mário's relationship to his identity may be different from that of Caroline, his baby sister. To address these questions, in this book I will be examining these changes as they manifest themselves specifically in efforts to revitalize and maintain the nearly two dozen Indigenous languages spoken in and around São Gabriel.[7] By considering the politics and activism surrounding Indigenous languages and their use in the city, I will illustrate how these processes inform Indigenous peoples' understandings of themselves and their ways of being, as well as reveal how the city constitutes a central site for anthropological research on the politics of culture. In a place that has dubbed itself "the most Indigenous city in Brazil," this quantification of "Indigeneity" is multifaceted and polysemous, encompassing relationships to territory, economy, and political structure, as well as to cultural property, knowledge, and practices – including, most importantly for this research, language.

Context

The city of São Gabriel da Cachoeira is situated on the Upper Rio Negro in the Northwest Amazon. It is the administrative centre of a huge municipality (*município*[8]) (109,182 km^2) bordering on both Venezuela and Colombia. Most of that municipality is comprised of formally designated Indigenous territories (*Terras Indígenas*). It is one of the largest municipalities by area in Brazil, as large as all of Portugal. Brazilian census figures report that in 2010, São Gabriel was home to about 13,000 people, and growing rapidly[9] – a large town by Amazonian standards. It is around 1,000 kilometres from the state capital of

Figure 1.1. Map of Northwest South America showing São Gabriel in context.

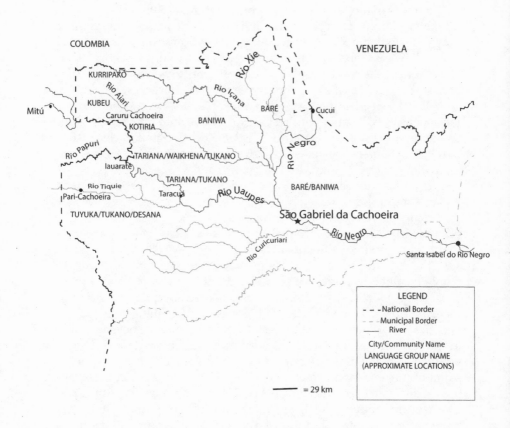

Figure 1.2. Map of the municipal area of São Gabriel da Cachoeira, with relevant settlements, language groups, and river systems shown. Language group locations are approximate and simplify overlaps and areas in which multiple language groups claim settlements.

Manaus and is accessible only by air or by boat. Commercial flights to and from Manaus arrive at and depart from the small airport just outside the city a few times per week; fluvial transportation options include a 24 to 30 hour "express" boat or the regular boat service, which takes 3 or 4 days to make the trip. For most residents of São Gabriel, the regular boat is the only affordable option, and even that often presents a hardship.

The municipality as a whole reports that almost 95 per cent of its residents identify themselves as Indigenous. However, this number drops somewhat in São Gabriel itself, which is home to almost all of the non-Indigenous migrants from other parts of Brazil. Even so, around 85 per cent of the residents of São Gabriel identify themselves as Indigenous, which makes it by far the most Indigenous city in Brazil. In fact, with 11,918 self-identified Indigenous people, it is second only to the metropolis of São Paulo with respect to the absolute number of Indigenous urban dwellers (Instituto Brasileiro de Geografia e Estatística 2010). This remains true even though the number fails to consider the many Indigenous people who keep permanent homes in the rural territories of the municipality, but who periodically come to the city to sell goods, conduct administrative business with government agencies, or obtain medical care, nor does it count those who spend parts of each year participating in educational or vocational training programs and living with urban-dwelling relatives.[10]

In the city, the cultural norms of non-Indigenous Brazil dominate daily life, albeit in ways that are infused with Indigenous social practices. The physical infrastructure is much like that in any town in Brazil: there is a downtown core filled with grocery and clothing stores, Internet cafés, snack bars, and by-the-kilo buffet restaurants. The main roads in the downtown area and in the *bairros* (specifically defined neighbourhoods, many of which have community associations that organize social events and small weekly marketplaces) are paved, but they are fed by dirt side roads through steep hills that can be very difficult to traverse, especially during heavy rains, which are common in the Amazon rainforest. One cannot walk far in São Gabriel without passing a church – there are four or five large Catholic churches in various parts of the town, including the cathedral on the hill overlooking the beach and the island that is home to "Sleeping Beauty," a mountain that figures in many regional histories and narratives. Various evangelical Protestant denominations have also established places of worship. Many of these have opened only recently in otherwise unremarkable storefronts; they are marked with homemade banners and furnished with nothing more than a podium, a few plastic chairs, and a microphone. Two banks sit almost kitty-corner to each other at one of the town's main intersections, and three small hotels are within a few blocks of one another in the downtown core. Important spaces of social contact include the farmer's market, opened by the municipal government in 2010, the beach, where a stage and street vendors are set up during *Carnaval* and other major events, and a gymnasium that hosts sports and cultural events, as well as large meetings or speeches by government figures. Most of the city's non-Indigenous people, including those temporarily posted to the area for military or medical service, live in the downtown area or near the beach, where the houses are a bit larger and are sometimes surrounded by gates and stone patios. In the other *bairros*, inhabited mainly by the Indigenous majority, one finds houses on dirt plots that the residents have built for themselves out of brick, concrete blocks, and wood. Many of these houses are at various stages of construction or disrepair; their inhabitants build or maintain them only after saving for months or years.

São Gabriel is not a large city in terms of population, but it is physically large, somewhat spread out across multiple *bairros*, with new ones sprouting up on the outskirts of town as migrants continue to arrive. The downtown is on the riverbank, and the town is expanding like a fan, with newer *bairros* farther and farther from the river. Patterns of settlement in the outlying *bairros* are based more on when the families arrived in the city than on things like ethnicity or linguistic affiliation, though sometimes several members of an extended family will construct houses on the same plot. Transportation within the city is not particularly easy, especially for those in the outlying areas. Very few Indigenous people have cars, and many take the one bus that runs back and forth from downtown at the beginning and end of the workday, as well as before and after the two-hour closure for lunch. Otherwise, people have to walk, and the hilly, winding roads mean that a trip downtown can take up to an hour from the closer *bairros*, and more than two hours from the more distant ones. This becomes additionally challenging because of the climate, which is oppressively hot and humid with sudden, intense downpours. Nonetheless, many Indigenous people do walk to work, and low wages and the need to support large, extended families mean that it is not unusual for individuals to work two or three jobs, or to work during the day and attend school at night. Many people, then, spent most of their day working, studying, and walking.

Figure 1.3. "Sleeping Beauty" (Bela Adormecida), in the Indigenous community of Curicuriari, pictured from downtown São Gabriel, outside the Cathedral. This mountain informs many of the narratives and myths of the region.

Figure 1.4. Cathedral of the Catholic diocese of São Gabriel da Cachoeira, constructed in the early twentieth century by Salesian missionaries.

In almost all local families, many needs are met through commercial exchange – one or more members of the household may earn money in wage labour positions or receive government benefits, and they purchase goods at the market or in stores – but this is supplemented with food grown on swidden plots just outside of town, as well as with fish and small game.[11] If their family has a plot, they travel periodically to tend to it, either by boat or on foot. The staple food for the region's Indigenous people remains bitter manioc root, which is used to make *farinha*, a thin stew called *xibé*, and, for celebrations, the alcoholic beverage *caxiri*. When available, this is supplemented with fruit – pineapple, *tucumã*, *papunha*, banana, and, most nourishing, *açaí*, which sustains many people during the rainy season. Indigenous people's houses – generally a few rooms in which several members of an extended family live – are furnished with a few beds as well as several hammocks in which to sleep.

Symbols of Indigeneity are incorporated into the city's crest. Indigenous craft products are sold in several stores and booths at the municipal market. Reminders that the city is predominantly and uniquely Indigenous persist in public addresses. Important festivals on the annual calendar include not only celebrations of various Catholic saints, but also Indigenous Peoples' Week in April. For several years, another important gathering place was a thatch-roofed structure behind the gymnasium, built in the basic style of the *malokas* that were, until very recently, the main buildings in Indigenous settlements. This *maloka* was centrally located and highly visible within the city, and hosted weekly gatherings as well as special events during which Indigenous people sold their agricultural products, drank *caxiri*, and performed music and dances. In 2014 this structure, and the Indigenous crafts store owned by the most important local NGO, Federação das Organizações Indígenas do Rio Negro (FOIRN), were destroyed by arsonists. The region's people and their Indigenous organizations suffered heavy financial losses from these acts, which also reminded them of the ever-present threat of physical and symbolic violence against them, even in a town where they are in the majority.

In addition to the distinction between "urban" and "rural," there is a meaningful difference in local discourse between those who are "from the region" (*da região*) and those who are "from outside" (*da fora*). Essentially, this is a division between local Indigenous people and outsiders. Indigenous people often describe these outsiders as *brancos* (white people) even though many of them are of Afro-Brazilian descent. The region's boundaries encompass not only the municipality of São Gabriel but also much of the Middle Rio Negro region, as well as the municipality of Santa Isabel do Rio Negro, located just downriver. Mobility between the city and the surrounding settlements is a prominent facet of daily life. On any given day, one will almost certainly encounter many people who are there temporarily, having come from the rural interior to obtain medical or government services, attend meetings, or pursue educational credentials (this latter reason is especially inflated during school holiday seasons). But this mobility is by no means easy: travelling to the city presents a significant hardship for most Indigenous people. Almost all of the *aldeias* are accessible only by river, and the journey to São Gabriel is measured in terms of days, rather than hours, of boat travel. For example, residents of the Upper Uaupés, near the Colombian border, require up to seven days to make a one-way trip, on a small and uncomfortable boat suitable for navigating the boulder-strewn rivers. The cost of gasoline – around US$2 per litre, with the longest journeys requiring several hundred litres[12] – must be added to the cost of the labour involved in making these journeys. Most travellers cannot afford this expense and require reimbursement from the government or from FOIRN. If accommodations are unavailable in relatives' homes or are not provided by one of these agencies, people construct makeshift shelters along the riverfront, in which they must sometimes live for months as they resolve concerns or try to acquire enough to pay for the return trip. Thus the urban/rural divide is highly permeable, but that mobility comes at a heavy cost and is highly disruptive to people's lives.

The Indigenous people of the Upper Rio Negro region belong to several different ethnolinguistic groups. Languages from five different families (Tukanoan, Arawakan, Yanomami, Nadahup, and Tupi-Guarani) are spoken within the municipality's territory, though speakers of the Yanomami and Nadahup languages have little presence within the urban area (where they rarely establish permanent homes). It is not uncommon to hear three or four Indigenous languages being spoken among friends and family members during a short walk around town or a trip to the market. Three of the most widely spoken Indigenous languages – Tukano (from the Tukanoan family), Baniwa (Arawakan), and Nheengatú (Tupi-Guarani) – were granted official status at the municipal level in 2002. This language policy, which has complex implications and ideological motivations, forms the backdrop of much of the analysis presented here.

It is in this environment that children like Caroline and her siblings are learning what it means to be Indigenous. Indigenous identities and politics are at the surface of life in this city, and these children are being raised by parents who are acutely aware of their identity, both as members of particular ethnolinguistic groups and as Indigenous people. The children, however, are developing an understanding of themselves primarily in relation to the latter identity. As Mário's comments reveal, he knows himself to be *Indigenous*, but he is much less sure of what that means in a specific sense. Caroline, at a much younger age, is developing an understanding of how to perform Indigeneity, but it's unclear to what extent she is learning to be a Baré or Tuyuka girl. In contrast to these specific cultural identities, "Indigeneity" is a recent construction that builds on existing localized identities in ways that make those identities legible to outside actors – from governments to environmental activists to international human rights organizations (cf. Jackson 1995; Niezen 2003). Although it functions primarily at a national or global scale, it also plays out in intimate interpersonal and domestic encounters (Graham and Penny 2014). At the same time, performances of Indigeneity, which can be used to acquire particular kinds of political and social capital, are subject to near constant examination of their "authenticity" (Conklin and Graham 1995; Graham 2002; Shulist 2016a). Living in the city, in and of itself, is often seen (both by outsiders and by local, Indigenous people) as a threat to this "authenticity," especially as territorial claims and land-based practices have been placed at the centre of global narratives of what it means to be Indigenous.[13] These questions are more than theoretical; they have immense material significance, as the state enters into debates about whether and how they will recognize the rights of Indigenous people to their lands and cultural autonomy. The idea that Indigenous ways of being are difficult to maintain or even locate in urban areas is one of several themes that characterize the ways in which many people (including local Indigenous activists and academic supporters) discuss Indigenous issues in São Gabriel, and that inform much of the analysis in this book. In contrast to these discourses, however, I suggest that the work that urban Indigenous people are doing is essential to (re)defining the meaning of Indigeneity in the contemporary Amazon.

When Caroline was "playing Indian," then, the small, offhand nature of her dance hid a multifaceted significance. She has been exposed to these types of performances enough to be able to mimic the dance steps and create a makeshift version of the clothing worn, but these events have not been made a part of her everyday life. The reactions of the adults and other children around her confirm that although her Indigenous identity is verbally emphasized, they don't fully expect her to inhabit these associated practices. At the same time, her older brother's inability to identify his mother's ethnolinguistic identity – initially the cause of some minor embarrassment – ultimately became an opportunity for him to learn about these ideas more directly. In both of these examples, the symbols of Indigeneity, from dance steps to language, are infused with meaning not only directly but also with regard to how they are interpreted and understood as manifestations of "play" or as diagnostic warnings about cultural knowledge. Both of these illustrations were unplanned: Caroline's dance took place at a time when it was not expected that outsiders would see it (since my arrival was spontaneous), and Mário's conversation with me took place when I turned to ask him a few questions after his mother briefly stepped out of the room. These meanings, then, are created not only in public, highly visible spheres, but also in private, intimate, and exclusively Indigenous ones (Graham and Penny 2014). The predominance of Indigenous people in the city, and in the region as a whole, means that these two small personal instances are not isolated incidents but rather microcosms of ongoing debates and discussions about Indigenous identity and culture. Municipal politics in São Gabriel revolve almost exclusively around how best to represent the interests of Indigenous people, how to create spaces of inclusion for Indigenous cultural practices, and how, basically, to Indigenize the city itself. At the same time, Indigeneity continues to function as a form of alterity, a deviation from the norm, especially for an urban space. An "Indigenous city" or even "Amazonian town" remains a marked category, and the city's residents are continually performing in ways that work to claim it as such.

Indigenous people are responding to, as well as creating, changes to their social worlds and identities; these processes form the backdrop for this book. The title *Transforming Indigeneity* refers to these vital forms of change while at the same time drawing on a core local theme of "transformation." Among Indigenous people from the Uaupés (Vaupes) River, which enters the Rio Negro just north of São Gabriel after winding its way down from the Colombian border, change is built into understandings and practices of identity. The Tukanoan inhabitants of this region have called themselves "the People of Transformation," making use of tellings and retellings of an origin myth that is predicated on establishing differences among them (Azevedo and Azevedo 2003; Cerqueira 2008). Each of the Tukanoan peoples makes use of a specific version of the narrative, but all of them recount how a sacred anaconda-canoe travelled from the spiritual world along the "Milk River,"[14] rose to the surface, and turned its head to face the waters of the Amazon. During its journey, various body parts split off and transformed themselves into humans – the founding ancestors of the Tukanoan peoples. Through the order of emergence, a hierarchical and specialized role relationship was created among the groups. Cultural identities were created through this transformative journey, and the relationship that each of the groups has to its founding ancestor forms the anchor of each identity, a sense of stability in relation to a world of change and difference (Chernela 1993; Lasmar 2005). These stories are forms of everyday linguistic practice that produce meaning and construct "culture" and identity (Urban 1993). Telling and retelling this origin story, using specific elements that belong uniquely to each of the subgroups, functions as a vehicle for information but more importantly as a discursive performance that creates and transforms both the storyteller and the learning listener.

The orienting principle of transformation provides a powerful anthropological metaphor for understanding the contemporary experiences of the inhabitants of the Upper Rio Negro (Andrello 2006; Lasmar 2005). Activism aimed at preserving or revitalizing languages and cultures works as a contemporary manifestation of a transformation narrative – indeed, one proposal for creating a cultural resource and educational centre in the city has brought this theme to the surface by suggesting that this site for language learning and cultural performances be called "The House of Transformation." In the politics of revitalization, then, the idea of "transformation" relates both to "traditional" understandings of culture and identity in the Rio Negro region and to contested visions for the future. Stories, and the origin myth in particular, have long been used among the Tukanoan peoples to enact and understand relevant social categories; contemporary revitalization activism makes use of a set of discursive resources that perform much the same function, but oriented towards the construction of a shifting set of relevant categories. Primary among these categories is the conceptualization of opposition between Indigenous and non-Indigenous peoples and worlds.

Indigenous and Non-Indigenous Worlds

Although I have described the social and institutional spaces of the city as fundamentally "non-Indigenous," the line between an "Indigenous" and a "non-Indigenous" world is not clear-cut. Indigenous people make up most of the city's population and occupy positions in every area of administration, politics, and service. In the electoral period from 2008 to 2012, for example, the mayor and deputy mayor (*prefeito* and *vice prefeito*) were both Indigenous, as were many sector directors in the municipal and local branches of the federal government. In many ways, the sense of a divide between Indigenous and non-Indigenous interests serves as a symbolic point of comparison (and one that is often invoked in political discourses in São Gabriel) more than as a description of reality.[15] Performance is what creates the distinction, rather than a pre-existing apparent set of boundaries (Graham and Penny 2014; see also Avineri and Kroskrity 2014 on boundary-making in revitalization work). At the same time, this binary is part of a broad symbolic system in which a range of practices, including linguistic forms, map onto a widely recognized set of symbolic practices, including linguistic forms, that map onto specific social meanings; in this case, as in many others, the colonial language is identified as the means of manifesting modernity, thereby justifying exclusion and inequality with regard to rural, Indigenous people who speak primarily oral languages (Bauman and Briggs 2003). The result is a division that marks the Indigenous as inherently "other" from the modern citizenry (Ramos 2003; French 2010).[16]

Understanding politics in São Gabriel involves understanding how these two broadly defined sets of interests are invoked and grouped together in opposition to each other. With the exception of the military, state institutions – most notably FUNAI (the Fundação Nacional do Índio, which is the federal Indigenous affairs office) and the various branches of state and municipal administrative agencies – function in direct consultation with representatives of Indigenous political organizations. Most of this consultation is mediated by FOIRN, an umbrella group for more than thirty smaller entities that have been formed based on both regional/ethnic associations (e.g., the Indigenous Peoples of the District of Iauaratê, the Association of Baniwa People) and specific interests (e.g., the Association of Indigenous Teachers, the Association of Indigenous Artisans). Each of these groups selects its leaders from among the relevant constituencies, and these representatives in turn select the five directors of FOIRN, one of whom is then elected "director-president." The directorate rotates every four years, and each body of five directors also selects a team to staff the administrative departments of FOIRN (which include education, communications, and women's issues).

This well-organized structure of representation works in a kind of symbiotic power relationship with local government. Consultation with "Indigenous representatives" is explicitly built into decision-making policies for many of the state institutions that operate within the city, and FOIRN's organizational structure facilitates the identification and provision of representatives for such consultative practices. References to the Indigenous side of this binary division almost always use the expression "the" Indigenous movement, eliding the wide range of debates that occur among various Indigenous groups and interested parties with regard to establishing the political positions and orientations of these bodies. FOIRN exerts an influence over municipal elections, party politics at the local level, and the selection of, for example, FUNAI representatives. This influence is, of course, shaped by extensive debate among FOIRN representatives and often remains controversial for those Indigenous people who sit outside of the FOIRN power structures. Even non-Indigenous organizations (such as the municipal government, FUNAI, and health and educational institutions) are staffed and sometimes run by Indigenous individuals, and many policies are implemented only with the involvement of political processes grounded in this Indigenous movement. By the same token, although FOIRN was born out of a desire to ensure the representation of Indigenous peoples' interests within the power structures of the state, its organizational practices mimic the structures of non-Indigenous organizations in order to translate Indigenous ways of being into contexts that the state can grasp. The binary between Indigeneity and non-Indigeneity at the institutional level is thoroughly blurred.

Also, this binary is complicated by the degree to which neither Indigenous interests nor non-Indigenous interests can be considered homogeneous concepts, especially given that the former group comprises so many languages and social groups. The theme of alterity and differentiation plays a vital social role in the Upper Rio Negro, both in creating and highlighting distinctions among the various Indigenous peoples of the region (for whom exogamous marital exchanges inform almost all aspects of social life) and in establishing and expressing their relationship to non-Indigenous society. The idea of a pan-Indigenous consciousness – of a relationship to identity in which the Other is primarily recognized as the non-Indigenous outsider – has become an important theme in recent ethnographic work in the Northwest Amazon (Andrello 2006; Lasmar 2005). As I discuss in later chapters, language in particular serves as a theme around which many people express an anxiety that this unified, pan-Indigenous identity will result in some of the more powerful ethnolinguistic groups of the region coming to dominate, ultimately leading to the disappearance of other smaller groups and their languages.[17]

The Politics of Language Revitalization

Because my training is in linguistics and linguistic anthropology, concerns surrounding Indigenous language use in the city constituted my point of entry into this conversation. São Gabriel's location on the Upper Rio Negro, near the mouth of the Uaupés (Vaupes) and Içana rivers, places it in the heart of the Northwest Amazon, a region that has attracted substantial anthropological attention with a specific focus on the social meaning of languages (Sorensen 1967; Jackson 1983; Gomez-Imbert 1991; Stenzel 2005). Language and multilingualism construct the social world of the Upper Rio Negro, though the ways in which they are able to do so are changing radically as a result of colonial practices (Aikhenvald 2003b; Bruno 2010). It was the rich picture of multilingualism and Indigenous cultural strength presented in this literature that first drew me to São Gabriel as a place to conduct long-term fieldwork.

Local linguistic practices and experiences, however, tell only half the story about what language means in the Rio Negro. The second component comes from the globally circulating discourses about the prospect of language loss and efforts to reverse this trend. Over the past thirty years, this threat has come to be understood as increasing both in scope and in speed as a result of economic and political globalization, and as having reached a crisis point with the potential to cause great harm both to small-scale societies and to humanity as a whole.[18] Since the early 1990s, linguists and anthropologists have become deeply invested in these battles (Hale et al. 1992). Methodologies for documenting and teaching minority languages, and for increasing their use – as well as fostering the cultural practices with which they are associated, such as rituals, songs, narratives, myths, and traditional knowledge – are now discussed and debated regularly in academic publications, at conferences, and through various types of training programs. Several academically affiliated non-governmental organizations, such as Survival International, Cultural Survival, the Hans Rausing Endangered Languages Project, the Endangered Language Fund, and the Foundation for Endangered Languages, issue grants to scholars and community organizations doing this type of research, and work to promote the cause beyond the limited fields of the academy, where it has become a mainstream concern. Linguists who are dedicated to language documentation and conservation emphasize the need to move beyond the tradition of "salvage linguistics," and to work not only to document languages before their disappearance but also to engage more fully with the needs of the speech communities that have been their research subjects for generations (Rice 2006; Czaykowska-Higgins 2009). As I will discuss throughout this book, my own research project developed out of this collaborative impulse, as did my sense of concern about the implications of language loss for minority and marginalized communities.

The causes of language shift are easy to oversimplify, and paradoxically, the "discourses of endangerment" that define the problem and propose solutions to it may perpetuate Western colonial ideologies (Heller and Duchêne 2007). Communities themselves are often blamed for failing to transmit the language to their children (committing, as it were, "linguistic suicide"), but this fails to account for the long-term and ongoing practice of colonial violence directed at the elimination of language ("linguistic genocide"). Likewise, the interests of various involved parties are often presumed to be transparent – the economic need to master the dominant language is assumed to be the central motivating factor in the linguistic decisions made by parents, for example – when in fact any given situation of language endangerment is built on a much more complex set of interests, actions, and ideologies.[19] Rhetorics of advocacy for languages tend to universalize what are in fact complex relationships between language and identity; they also invoke legalistic frameworks of "rights" and rely on an essentialized equation of language loss to cultural death (Hill 2002; Whiteley 2003; Silverstein 2000). The challenges posed by this mindset are not insurmountable, but recognizing the specific ways in which different communities experience and relate to language endangerment is central to addressing them. At the same time, as Urla (2015: 5–6) points out, the scholarship on social movements, collective protest, and multiculturalism – topics of broad interest in political anthropology and political theory – rarely includes or engages with language revitalization activism. Because of these gaps, the wide range of practices surrounding language revitalization are undertheorized as part of a broader set of social changes. Ethnography, because it can draw attention to the social processes and meanings that both create and result from the conditions of language shift and change, remains an important and underutilized tool for understanding how academics can best apply their skills in support of Indigenous and minority languages and their speakers (Franchetto 2006; Hill 2006; Granadillo and Orcutt-Gachiri 2011).

Given the amount of attention (both activist and academic) that the issue has received in recent decades, it is not surprising that the way in which it is discussed and labelled has itself become a topic of controversy. "Revitalization," "revival," "reawakening," "reclamation," and, more prosaically, "maintenance" are all terms in circulation for talking about the work being done by linguists and Indigenous people to ensure that these languages are remembered, transmitted to, and used by future generations (Garcia 2003; Hinton 2003; Leonard 2012). While I have chosen to use the term "revitalization" in this book, I am aware that it has both positive and negative connotations and implications. This book contributes to the scholarship on how best to support the efforts of Indigenous people in their language-related efforts, and with that activist goal in mind, I find that "revitalization" best captures the aims of those living and working in the city of São Gabriel. Indigenous languages – like Indigenous people themselves – are increasingly associated with the past and seen as "out of place" in the modern city (Peters and Andersen 2013).[20] "Revitalization," then, connotes the effort to breathe new life into these languages. In this way, it effectively invokes the kind of transformative effort that Anthony Wallace (1956) was referencing in his classic description of "revitalization movements" as "efforts to create a more satisfying culture" in periods of stress and pressure. These language planning endeavours function, then, not independently, but rather as part of a debate about what kind of a culture is being, or should be, created.

Language revitalization is never *only* about language; it is also about a language's connections to other social and political phenomena, as well as its role in the complex lives of the affected populations (Meek 2011; Ahlers 2012; Nevins 2013; Urla 2015). Advocacy for language revitalization hinges on the belief that language plays a deep and meaningful role in people's social and material well-being, yet most studies of these projects focus their discussion of outcomes on the language itself – number of speakers, domains for use and transmission, or production of materials. These studies rarely look beyond the polemics to consider what these projects do for the extra-linguistic factors of life to which they are discursively connected.[21] I raise this critique not because I believe that language revitalization efforts are misguided or potentially destructive, but because my observations in the complex social environment of São Gabriel reveal that failure to address these aspects of programs consciously and self-critically may be limiting the ability of revitalization advocates to achieve both their direct (language-based) goals and their indirect goals of supporting improvements to the social conditions in which Indigenous people live.

The complex meanings associated with language and languages are often understood, within linguistic anthropology, in terms of language ideologies. While this concept is amorphous, generally speaking it relates to a way of discussing "shared notions of commonsense ideas about the nature of language in the world" (Woolard and Schieffelin 1994: 55). Language ideology helps frame language in terms of its multifaceted social roles and situate it within local political economies (Irvine 1989); it also serves as a means to articulate the "mediating link between social structures and forms of talk" (Woolard and Schieffelin 1994: 55). The explicitly political, activist nature of language revitalization means that language ideology serves as a vital theoretical tool for improving our understanding of the processes involved. In general, language endangerment manifests itself in situations characterized by deep inequalities among different groups. This reinforces the need to consider how these power differences are played out in linguistic interactions, as well as the many meanings that are created in particular situations of multilingual contact (Hornberger 2000).

Conflicts among language ideologies often remain below the surface in contexts of language endangerment, and as such, some scholars and activists have advocated for "prior ideological clarification" as an important step in language revitalization planning (Fishman 2001). Rhetorical support for these projects does not necessarily translate into concrete action, and unstated fears and anxieties continue to manifest themselves in actions that tip towards language loss (Dauenhauer and Dauenhauer 1998); similarly, ideological "disjunctures" emerge as support for language revitalization entails different associated beliefs and actions for different actors, some of which may inadvertently undermine Indigenous language planning endeavours (Meek 2011).[22] These disputes and contradictions emerge as a result of overlapping understandings of "threats" to a specific type of social order, and connect both to additional ideological constructs – including nationalism and Indigeneity, as well as the management of diversity, for example – and to the particular interests of various stakeholders. While recognition of these conflicts is important in itself, the role that "ideological clarification" can play in improving language planning efforts is, ironically, unclear. Paul Kroskrity, in calling for an effort to invigorate this notion by more thoroughly theorizing its role, notes that it "seems to float on ambiguous assumptions of cognitive consensus and inappropriately monolithic conceptions of contemporary communities" (2009: 72). He highlights two key points with regard to better employing ideological clarification in revitalization contexts: first, language ideologies must be understood in relation to the political, economic, and social interests of the groups or individuals who hold them; and second, language revitalization inevitably co-occurs with conflicts and collisions among multiple language ideologies (73). The process of ideological clarification, then, is one through which "issues of language ideological contestation ... that can negatively impact community efforts" can be identified, discussed, and ultimately, resolved, at least to a "tolerable level of disagreement" (Ibid.). My analysis of language revitalization efforts in São Gabriel points to several ideological conflicts and disjunctures and, in bringing them to the surface, is intended to contribute to just such a process of clarification.

This form of language planning plays multiple and often conflicting roles in ongoing processes of identity and community formation. My attempt to read the ideological map that has created these connections, and to follow the trajectory it presents for this city and its people, is central to this book. In the Upper Rio Negro, language is central to culture; this, and the sheer number of languages spoken, has made it one of the most significant symbols of Indigenous identity. Thus, academic work in the region has generated a variety of linguistic grammars, dictionaries, and other analyses.[23] Many of these efforts have been produced after extensive consultation with community members, who have emphasized that these researchers need to support their efforts to preserve and promote their languages and cultural practices. This discussion is not merely about loss and endangerment, for the processes surrounding documentation and revitalization, while related, are separate. In other words, the dictionaries and grammars mentioned above are not simply detached descriptions of languages absent a social context, but rather responses to fears about language loss – fears that mask for other threats, which have been ideologically mapped onto language (Errington 2003; Heller and Duchêne 2007). Similar ideologies about conservation have been examined in relation to environmentalist movements, which Amazonian peoples have interacted with in complex ways (Conklin and Graham 1995; Conklin 2002; Dove 2006). Urban Indigenous people in particular exist in a relationship to a "nostalgic image of … 'wilderness,' 'tradition,' locality, and social and ecological embeddedness"; and in communities involved in ecotourism, for example, discourses about local identity, culture, and history are dictated by an international market for tourists (Peluso and Alexiades 2005: 9). In São Gabriel, which remains ill-equipped to receive such tourists but highly welcoming to anthropologists and language researchers, the same discursive field is, at least in part, dictated by the language revitalization market.

As happens so often in colonial situations, Indigenous peoples of the Rio Negro have experienced prohibition of their languages. In part, this has been a strategy for assimilation; in part, it has been the result of discriminatory beliefs about the "inferiority" of their speech and mental capacity. As a result, they have internalized a sense of shame about using their languages.[24] Efforts to document the languages, promote their transmission to younger generations, and increase their contexts of use, then, are simultaneously efforts to "valorize" the identities of the individuals and groups who speak them. These identities are symbolically associated with and represented by material artefacts (such as artisanal crafts and musical instruments), cultural performances (dances, rituals, and rites of passage), and complex social arrangements, including communitarian living arrangements and an economic system based on swidden horticulture. In discussions of revitalization, language is a part of this broader system of cultural practices that people wish to preserve as well as a symbolic index of the strength of Indigenous identity as a whole.

The process of language revitalization, then, is directly connected to contestation and debate about the type of community or nation that is being produced, and the role of different types of citizens within those communities (Avineri and Kroskrity 2014; Shulist 2016b). This process occurs across multiple scales of community and identity formation, from the local to the global, and from the ethnolinguistic to the national or transnational pan-Indigenous. Activism around language involves not only creating materials for language use, but also imagining contexts in which they will be used and future publics that will speak them. Because a community of speakers must be created (or at a minimum, reshaped), that community's make-up and nature become matters of constant negotiation (Swinehart and Graber 2012; Shulist 2016b). One question this book takes up is what this community looks like and how it involves establishing an Indigenous presence in public spaces – or indeed, imagining an explicitly Indigenous public sphere. Examining language revitalization as a political act of cultural "preservation" reveals the involvement not only of Indigenous political organizations, but also of state agents, and of anthropologists and linguists, in the definitions of Indigeneity, culture, language, and change. This book is as much a discussion of language and culture in a specific time and place as it is a reflection on the challenges of doing engaged, collaborative fieldwork on language revitalization. It also considers how such fieldwork is embedded in politics and power disputes that only rarely are explicitly addressed in literature on these efforts (French 2010; Perley 2011; Urla 2015).

Indigeneity and Urbanity

The construction of Indigenous identities in urban settings requires analysis and consideration in and of itself. Questions of authenticity in the face of cultural change are inevitably fraught aspects of Indigenous lives in the twenty-first century; colonial settler-states such as Brazil continue to employ strategies of recognition and legitimation to grant or deny these identities to individuals and groups in ways that reinscribe the violence of assimilation.[25] These political processes render significant the fact that "cultural innovations in cities are often not viewed as central to the production of contemporary Indigeneity" (Peters and Andersen 2013: 1). Examinations of urban Indigenous lives must attend to several important and interrelated facts. First, the construction of Indigenous people as rural – and this includes the creation of particular "homelands" located outside of cities – is itself a colonial project, based on the powerful notion that Indigenous people are connected to "nature," as distinct from the controlled and dominated "civilization" of cities (Ibid., 5). Second, how are Indigenous cultural practices reconstituted and reconceived within the heterogeneous social spaces of cities? The central question that scholars of urban Indigenous populations pose continues to be the most basic one – when the two terms have so often been defined in direct opposition to each other, what does it mean to be both *urban* and *Indigenous*? (Virtanen 2010; Gagné 2013; Alexiades and Peluso 2015).

Urban Indigenous people make sense of their own Indigeneity and form communities through specific social practices. Natacha Gagné's (2013: 63) analysis of Māori living in Auckland, New Zealand, emphasizes that the Māori people experience the city as an inherently non-Indigenous space, in which they feel disempowered by its unfamiliarity. She goes on to illustrate, however, how these spaces are reinscribed with meanings that reinforce Māori sociality, including through the use of different linguistic practices that allow urban residents to move between two conceptual worlds. She points out that "city dwellers necessarily situate themselves in relation to the family, subtribe, and tribe in the countryside, which still represent a very important ontological foundation and serve to situate urban dwellers and the urban whanau (extended family) or urban networks in the larger Māori system, whatever the changes that city life has brought about" (213–14). Similarly, Virtanen (2010; 2012) illustrates that youth in the city of Rio Branco, the capital of the Amazonian state of Acre, experience their identity as Indigenous people mediated through the lens of external expectations. They understand themselves as Indigenous people, but they also recognize that many of the clearly recognized symbols of Indigeneity have been rendered unavailable to them, including the languages they were never taught. Indigenous youth, in particular, constitute a relevant point of focus, both because they are the ones shaping their identities in relation to these new political and social formulations, and because they are frequently the targets of cultural revitalization movements. Even as they engage with discussions of language revitalization, however, they do not necessarily accept the terms of the debate, including the assumption that inability to speak Indigenous languages makes them "not Indigenous enough" to warrant recognition of their rights and identities.[26]

Also, Indigenous urbanization is not a uniform process, but one that occurs in situated ways in particular times and places. In many parts of Latin America, especially the Andean highlands, the proportion of the total population, including in urban areas, that identifies as Indigenous or "mestizo" is much higher, and the relationship between urban, "modern," nationalized practices and Indigenous identities is inherently a different one (cf. Postero 2013 on Bolivia; de la Cadeña 2010 on Peru). In lowland South America, the process has been much more connected to boom-and-bust extractive economic cycles, leading to "multilocational and multidirectional flows" (Alexiades and Peluso 2015: 5). "Indigenous urbanizations" in Amazonia are distinct processes, which include transformations that are "not only spatial and physical but also ideational, ideological, and aesthetic" (Ibid.). The Brazilian context also differs from other parts of Amazonia in that there is no highland group of Indigenous people informing the national conversation about Indigeneity; this has led to a different political context for interpreting urban populations and urbanization.[27]

A central component of my research and analysis involves discussing Indigenous language use and revitalization practices in an *urban* context as well as a multilingual one. International activist discourses tend to emphasize the importance of rurality and remoteness to "traditional" Indigenous identities and lifestyles, which they view as based on territoriality and a particular land base (Forte 2013). In urban spaces, where the options available to create Indigenous identities are different from those accessible to rural Indigenous populations, language, being highly transportable, becomes a distinctly powerful possibility (Patrick and Tomiak 2008; Graham and Penny 2014). Greater access and exposure to media technologies is another important factor to consider (both positively and negatively) in language revitalization (Eisenlohr 2004); the shaping of Indigenous identities and communication practices in relation to broadcast and social media demands further attention in this regard (Virtanen 2012: 182). There is very little literature that addresses, from either a pragmatic or an analytical perspective, the challenges and implications of implementing language revitalization programs in urban contexts, though a few scholars have drawn attention to the ways in which urban populations are excluded through the essentializing discourses of language revitalization advocacy (Errington 2003; Patrick 2007; Patrick and Tomiak 2008).[28] Given that language revitalization movements are self-conscious efforts to resist assimilation and assert the value of Indigenous cultural practices, they often make use of rhetoric and symbolic practices that reiterate assumptions about urbanization as assimilation. Such movements justify the preservation of Indigenous languages in Indigenous communities as part of a culture premised on its alterity to Western ones – and this includes promoting the desire to remain outside of and apart from cities (French 2010).

São Gabriel is no exception to ideologies of territorialized Indigeneity, including in relation to language. The use and visibility of Indigenous languages in this city must be considered in light of the specific relationship between the urban centre – the seat of the municipal government, as well as the site of most interactions between Indigenous people and non-Indigenous bureaucratic institutions representing the

Brazilian state – and the large, predominantly rural area that constitutes the rest of the municipality.[29] These rural territories are both legally and ideologically distinct from the city. They are made up entirely of federally demarcated Indigenous Territories, in which cultural and linguistic promotion, which includes the right to education in locally dominant languages, is constitutionally protected. They are also regularly held up as "another reality" in which Indigeneity predominates and cultural practices are easily maintained. In any Brazilian municipality the seat of governance is officially designated as an "urban" area and – by extension based on formal classification of territories in Brazil – as ineligible for inclusion in a demarcated Indigenous Territory. This political structure creates a context in which urban and Indigenous are inherently opposing rather than potentially concurrent classifications.

While the historical and ethnographic picture will be fleshed out more thoroughly in chapter 2, it is worth noting here that the patterns of settlement along each of the major rivers in the region mean that the area's smaller communities are much more linguistically homogenous than the city of São Gabriel: speakers of Nheengatú occupy the Rio Negro region as well as parts of the Içana; Baniwa-Kurripako speakers live mainly along the upper Içana; and the various Tukanoan languages are associated with communities along the Uaupés (with Tukano itself acting as a *lingua franca* for this part of the Northwest Amazon).[30] In discourses about language shift and Indigenous languages in São Gabriel, people often make the generalized claim that "in the communities, they have the language," even though some languages (e.g., Tariana, Siriano) are spoken by fewer than one hundred people, and others (e.g. Miriti-tapuya, Arapaço) are not currently spoken at all (see Table 1.1). The actual vitality of Indigenous languages, while undeniably stronger in rural areas than in the city, varies substantially; nonetheless, the symbolic reference to "another reality," and the idealized Indigenous presence that is invoked in the concept of "the communities," both play an important role in the discourses of Indigenous people in the city.

The creation of this binary dovetails with the Indigenous ideology of linguistic territoriality that is prominent in the area. This belief relates again to the Tukanoan practices of linguistic exogamy, as the traditional system involves the relocation of women into their husbands' communities upon marriage (Chernela 1993). The use of language as a marker of patrilineally defined identity also pushes these newly incorporated women to encourage their children to use their father's language as the language of public communication (Chernela 2004; Lasmar 2009). The

Table 1.1. Languages of the Upper Rio Negro

Tukanoan Family

- General information: Tukanoan languages are spoken in the Uaupés basin and its tributaries, including the Tiquié, Papurí, and Querarí rivers. Almost all of them are also present in Colombia.

Most significant languages (> 5,000 speakers)	• **Tukano**: Official language of SGC, lingua franca of the Uaupés basin. Total number of speakers includes both those who belong to the Tukano ethnic group and several thousand from other groups who have adopted it as a primary language (e.g., Piratapuya, Tariana) or as a secondary language that has continued to be used alongside their own. ISA (n.d.) estimates the total number of users at about 20,000. • **Kubeu**: The best estimate of speakers of Kubeu was developed by the linguist Simon Valência, who placed the total count at around 8,000 (Thiago Chacon, personal communication). The fact that Kubeu speakers do not practise language-based exogamy and remain somewhat apart from the social and cultural practices of either the Tukanoan or Arawakan societies may be supporting its continued transmission in both Brazil and Colombia, where other groups are moving to Tukano.
Additional prominent languages (500–2,000 speakers)	• **Kotiria[31](Wanano), Tuyuka**: These languages are spoken in territories that are among the most difficult to access in the Rio Negro region; this geographical situation may be among the reasons for their relative success (Stenzel 2005).
Smaller languages (100–500 speakers)	• **Dessana**: Estimated number of speakers c. 450 (Silva 2012). • Waikhana (Pira-tapuia)
Additional languages (< 100 speakers)	• **Karapanã, Bará, Siriano, Makuna**: Estimated number of speakers remaining of these languages is in the dozens, at most. Little documentation exists, and revitalization programs have not focused on these languages.
Languages not currently in use (sleeping)	• **Miriti-tapuia, Arapaço**: There is minimal, but some, available recording and documentation of these languages, and no active effort to revive them is under way.

Arawakan Family

- General information: The Arawakan (or Arawak) language family is one of the largest and most widespread Indigenous language families in Central and South America. Languages classed within this family are or were spoken in the Amazon basin, Paraguay and Argentina, along the northern coast of South America, in several countries of Central America, and in the Caribbean (Aikhenvald 2012: 32–3). Unlike Tukanoan languages,

Arawakan Family

whose speakers police the boundaries of language differences carefully and avoid borrowing to ensure well-marked kinship relationships (Aikhenvald 2003b), Arawakan languages exist in a continuum of dialects with some degree of mutual intelligibility; the number of distinct languages, as well as the speaker count of each one, is difficult to determine because of this (Michael and Granadillo 2014).

Most significant languages (> 5,000 speakers)	• **Baniwa**: Official language of SGC, widely spoken in the Içana region of Brazil as well as in Venezuela. • **Kurripako**: Closely related to Baniwa; what is called Kurripako in Brazil may incorporate what is called Baniwa in Venezuela (Tania Granadillo, personal communication). While the degree of mutual intelligibility makes the boundaries challenging, people who identify as Kurripako speakers in the Upper Rio Negro region express a clear sense of their language as distinct and different from Baniwa, as well as concern that the officialization of Baniwa will weaken their own language.
Smaller languages (100–500 speakers)	• **Tariana**: The Tariana people participate fully in the Tukanoan cultural system, which includes the practice of language-group-based exogamy; they have almost completely adopted Tukano as the language of communication. • Warekena: Language of the Upper Rio Negro region; communities of speakers have almost completely adopted Nheengatú as the language of everyday communication.
Languages not currently in use (sleeping)	• **Baré**: The Baré language was spoken along the Rio Negro and Içana rivers, as well as in Venezuela and Colombia, but began diminishing in use beginning with colonial contact; the point at which it ceased to be used entirely is unclear. Little documentation exists (Maia 2009).

Other Language Families

Most significant languages (> 5,000 speakers)	• **Nheengatú (Tupi family)**: Official language of SGC, estimated number of speakers 8,000 (da Cruz 2011: 16), belonging to the Baré, Warekena, and Baniwa ethnic groups. The history of the language as one introduced post-colonization places it in an ideologically and politically unique position, discussed throughout this book.
Additional prominent languages (500–5,000 speakers)	• **Maku family – Nadahup, Dâw, Hupdah, Yehupdeh**: Speakers of these languages are marginalized even among Indigenous populations. Before colonization they were enslaved by Tukanoan peoples. Documentation and revitalization efforts, including work designed to improve educational levels within this group, are relatively strong (Epps 2008).

(*Continued*)

Table 1.1. Continued

Arawakan Family
• **Yanomami family**: Classification of language boundaries is difficult to determine due to mutual intelligibility; the family as a whole is widespread across Brazil and Venezuela. Yanomami are prominently involved in activist resistance in general, though not necessarily in language revitalization.

Note: Information is, as much as possible, based on direct linguistic sources/ grammatical descriptions. Ethnologue is occasionally the only source available; this information is almost certainly outdated and inaccurate. The languages/ethnic identities listed are those listed by FOIRN/ISA (2006) as having a presence on the Brazilian side of the Upper/Middle Rio Negro region. Many of them have little or no significant presence in the city of SGC, either because of their small size (e.g., Siriano, Makuna), or because of cultural marginalization (e.g., Yanomami).

system of marital exchange helps sustain economic relations between communities, while the use of language in the public sphere marks not only the individuals as members of that ethnic group, but also the space as belonging to its speakers. In other words, the dominant language of a community acts to assert authority over and possession of the territory. By extension, however, Portuguese having inevitably become the *lingua franca* for communication in the city of São Gabriel, the city has been marked as non-Indigenous (Portuguese) space. The continuing discursive reiteration of a binary between urban and rural therefore contributes to a process of fractal recursivity (Gal and Irvine 1995) that supports the idea of a binary between Indigenous and non-Indigenous and, in turn, to an indexical link between the use of Indigenous languages and rurality. In this multilingual city, the political and social actions being invoked as a means of supporting and "revitalizing" Indigenous languages and cultures become sites of contestation, debate, and deliberation, as different types of identities are created, revived, challenged, and accepted in different contexts, often by the same actors.

There are undoubtedly barriers to implementing language revitalization programs in the urban area, though many of them are ideological rather than inherent to the pragmatic challenges of life in the city. This distinction is often erased from discussions about such efforts, especially with regard to the official language policy (discussed in detail in chapter 3), but also in reference to education (chapters 4 and 5).

Advocates for Indigenous languages often resort to arguments that come with additional ideological baggage, connecting Indigeneity with tradition, history, and rural communities rather than with urban "modernity." These "sociolinguistic disjunctures" create barriers to language revitalization that are at least as important as, if not more important than, the challenge of finding funding, creating infrastructure, and developing expertise. These questions and processes become still more complex as they arise simultaneously with shifts in the symbolic significance of language and in the make-up of social networks that take place in light of urbanization. Notwithstanding the prominence of Indigenous people in the city and in the surrounding municipality, language and cultural revitalization activities have been extremely difficult to sustain in the urban area. Debate persists not only regarding how to best bring Indigeneity into the urban area more fully, but also regarding whether this can (or should) be done at all. These relationships – among language, culture, and identity in particular – have been portrayed as stable and uniform in revitalization advocacy, when in fact they are subject to multiple, changing meanings under the influence of many different actors, including linguists and anthropologists. This was the situation in which my project took shape.

Establishing Collaboration

In February 2011, when I arrived in São Gabriel for my first preliminary field visit, I hoped to establish a collaborative research relationship with a group working on urban language revitalization. To prioritize collaboration and to most effectively allow the people engaged in these efforts to shape the project, I left a range of possibilities open. I did not make a predetermined decision about which language or group of languages I wanted to analyse, nor did I intend to examine the sites that inform most of the discussion in this book (language policy and education). In fact, in many ways, I worked to explicitly avoid those two topics, preferring to seek out some deeper areas in which language revitalization activism might be taking place, looking for the activism that, I presumed, existed beyond this surface-level valorization of Indigenous languages manifested in the on-paper policy. My reticence to engage in these topics was based in a prejudice against their effectiveness for addressing language maintenance and, admittedly, a somewhat closed-minded view of what counts as "revitalization." As the following chapters make clear, this presumption was ultimately worn down as I came to understand how it was that the Indigenous leaders and administrators in the city made connections between language, Indigeneity, and urbanity within these two domains.

The limitations that I did place on my project before my arrival – I was focusing on language revitalization and on the urban context – were clearly confusing to many of the people I met. Most of the time, when I approached different sites in the community – FOIRN, the Brazilian academic NGO Instituto Socioambiental (ISA), the municipal and state departments of education, or individual schools – to inquire about projects for language revitalization in the city, the initial response was "there aren't any." The first exception came when I met Kristine Stenzel, a linguist based at the Universidade Federal de Rio de Janeiro, at the ISA headquarters when she arrived to work on her Kotiria language documentation and sociolinguistic survey projects. She introduced me to Miguel Cabral, through whom I became involved with a group of Kotiria speakers who had been working to develop an association to support their language and culture (a process I discuss in depth in chapter 5). Eventually, in conversations with FOIRN, the directors and I agreed that it was worthwhile to pursue the question of how the official language policy could be made more effective in its support for Indigenous languages in the city. This second line of thought is the basis for the work presented in chapters 3 and 4.

As a whole, though, this period of extensive fieldwork was a frustrating one for me, since I continued to feel that I wasn't able to make any concrete contributions to improving language efforts in the city, or to participate on a daily basis in activities relating to language revitalization. The Kotiria group's work was occurring in fits and starts between periods of waiting for bureaucratic approval or negotiating the busy schedules of its members. Although FOIRN agreed that language revitalization in the urban area was worthy of concern, the organization's extensive involvement in Indigenous political issues of all types meant that quotidian activities rarely addressed language as a specific idea. For both of these groups, my limited funding also meant that I was unable to offer the financial basis for creating the type of project that both they and I recognized would be needed to really improve the situation in the urban area. Finally, my sense of frustration extended to my inability to find the time and space to learn one or more Indigenous languages; I felt like I was failing as a linguistic anthropologist by continuing to rely on Portuguese to communicate with my Indigenous collaborators on their linguistic projects.

I share these frustrations, disappointments, and anxieties here because those emotional realities became relevant to the research project as it played out, and because, in the end, they helped me understand the on-the-ground realities of how Indigenous identities are related to languages in complex and conflicting ways for various inhabitants of the city. As these challenges emerged, I came to understand the degree to which collaboration for language documentation warranted consideration as an object of study in and of itself, and how practices and discourses about it have shaped understandings of how, why, and importantly, where language revitalization should happen. São Gabriel presents a relevant case study for understanding how urban Indigenous realities force us to rethink both the theories and the strategies that we, as academic allies, have developed for describing and combatting language loss.

An unexpected element of the challenges I faced in establishing collaborations came from the impact that past collaborations have had on local understandings of the roles of researchers and academics working on language and cultural revitalization. Much of the current picture of language revitalization efforts that I discuss in this book – including the co-officialization law, differentiated schools, and language documentation projects – has emerged as a result of previous (and ongoing) collaborations with linguists and anthropologists. My consideration of the impact that these other academics – many of whom have decades of experience of deeply engaged collaborative fieldwork in the Northwest Amazon – have had is intended to expand on, rather than supersede, the insights they present. In focusing specifically on the city, and on the political and social practices involved in revitalization activism (rather than on documentary linguistic work itself), my observations suggest that additional conversation is needed to strengthen and deepen efforts related to language in the region. In this regard, I also want to highlight a topic of concern that is often elided from published discussion about language revitalization work, though it plays a role that is widely acknowledged in private conversations among scholars: the implications of social issues such as alcoholism and drug addiction, youth suicide, domestic and sexual violence, and the trafficking of young Indigenous women, all of which have a disproportionate impact on poor, marginalized communities. For many Indigenous people, urbanization has become synonymous with these issues, and the sense that they are increasingly encroaching into previously "safe" rural territories causes substantial fear among parents and leaders. On their face, these concerns have little to do with language, yet failing to mention them in any account of life in this region would be a major oversight.

I am suggesting here that it is possible to better understand the ideologies and social meanings related to language revitalization and urbanization through the lens of challenges to and implications of collaboration, and that furthermore, it is worth considering how the full picture of life in the city of São Gabriel motivates a rethinking of what types of projects are relevant for language-related work. Indeed, the experiences and observations I outline in this book lead me to conclude that an effective program for language maintenance in the Northwest Amazon will depend on better attention to the urban area specifically as a site for revitalization, and will need to engage directly with these additional threats associated with urbanity. Instead of drawing on language as a means of holistic healing, as some theorists of revitalization have proposed (Hallett, Chandler, and Lalonde 2007; McCarty, Romero, and Zepeda 2006; Iwasaki and Byrd 2010), I suggest here that a holistic model of what it is that is being revitalized, and what type of community structures are being created in which language can form a part, is needed. Underlying this analysis, then, is a methodological and theoretical question regarding how collaboration has functioned and *can* function in the disciplines of linguistics and anthropology. I revisit this topic in chapter 6 (see also Shulist 2013).

Chapter Breakdown

The ethnographic work presented in the following chapters addresses several aspects of how Indigenous languages are being incorporated into the politicized landscape of the city of São Gabriel. In chapter 2, I outline more of the ethnographic context of the region, describing both the main cultural features of the Indigenous groups present and the history of the relationships between Indigenous and non-Indigenous peoples that have shaped the present-day reality in which this research took place. Chapter 3 offers a detailed consideration of the municipality's official language policy, analysing what motivated the legislation as well as the discourses that have surrounded the limited implementation of its terms in the ten years between its passage and my period of intensive fieldwork. I examine the semiotics behind the policy's official status and the work that has since been done to increase the public presence of the three official Indigenous languages. I also consider the ways in which this policy embodies contestation over the city's identity and the meaning of Indigeneity in Brazil as a whole, and how it exemplifies an unacknowledged ideological debate about how Indigenous languages relate to these identities. Chapters 4 and 5 deal specifically with the education sector and with proposals for including Indigenous languages in the curricula of the city's schools. In chapter 4, I examine the existing ways in which language is taught, focusing on the limited time granted to Indigenous language classes and the use of Nheengatú as the sole Indigenous language represented in the classroom, despite the co-officialization of Tukano and Baniwa. Current language teaching practices, along with discourses about how to improve Indigenous-language presence in the schools, demonstrate the tensions among different types of identity and social mobility as they relate to urban students, situating the city of São Gabriel as a transitional space between the "Indigenous" interior and the "modern" world beyond the region. Chapter 5 considers the efforts of a group of speakers from one of the languages that was excluded from official status and is therefore marginalized not just as an Indigenous language but as a *non-official* Indigenous language. The formation of an organization of Kotiria speakers for the purpose of documenting and revitalizing their language – which includes efforts to establish a differentiated Kotiria school in the urban area – offers an additional lens for understanding the restrictions facing urban Indigenous advocacy under the existing policy framework. These efforts also tie in to the ways in which academic and non-governmental support for language revitalization has supported an essentialized vision of rural Indigenous identity. I highlight the ways in which ideological clarification could present a particularly powerful way of improving the efforts of this group. Finally, chapter 6 reflects on the development of this research program as a collaborative endeavour with language revitalization activists, building on the discussion initiated in this introduction. The challenges I experienced as I attempted to implement my vision of a fundamentally collaborative research program reflect a broader set of issues in relation to the conceptualization of language revitalization and documentation work as ethically engaged enterprises, and the ways in which urban peoples have so far been left out of these. As a whole, these chapters fit together to demonstrate the ways in which Indigenous languages and identities are being "played with" and how urban Indigenous people are using them, ultimately, to transform Indigeneity.

2 City of Transformation: Ethnography and History of a Multilingual Amazon Town

São Gabriel has always been a place of contact and change. It is a place that has been absorbed into imagined views of the Brazilian nation and its frontier zones, and of the past, present, and future of Indigeneity, into modernization projects, and into activism for the preservation of natural and cultural diversity. Literally and figuratively, it is a place that exists on the premise of transformation.

A significant amount of ethnographic attention has been given to the peoples of the Northwest Amazon, and São Gabriel often figures as a reference point within these examinations, yet the city itself has rarely been viewed as a site of interest in its own right (exceptions include Lasmar 2005; Fleming 2010). The background necessary to begin discussing language revitalization in this context includes not only an overview of the city's history, but also an account of the similarities and differences among the region's most prominent Indigenous groups. As the discussion throughout the rest of this book shows, the present reality facing Indigenous language revitalization advocates has been shaped by a heterogeneous set of interests and ideologies emerging not only from different Indigenous cultural belief systems (most prominently represented by three groups – Tukanoans, Arawakans, and Nheengatú-speaking Baré) but also from various social and institutional influences (the Catholic and Protestant churches, the Brazilian military, other state agencies, NGOs – Indigenous and otherwise – and businesses). This complexity emerges out of past and present-day disputes about control over the region, its resources, and its people.

Non-Indigenous Presence

In present-day São Gabriel, the influence of non-Indigenous people is felt primarily through the presence of three institutions – the Church, the military, and the civilian Brazilian state – as well as through the market economic interactions that characterize daily life. The relationships these social structures have to São Gabriel and its Indigenous inhabitants bear vestiges of the city's history, which dates back to the arrival of Portuguese colonizers in the mid-seventeenth century and the subsequent decimation and enslavement of the Indigenous population (Wright 2005).[1] The construction of the "savage" Indian engaged in constant intertribal warfare served to justify this violence (Ramos 1998); the need to impose order on the chaotic jungle (both natural and social) took root at this point of contact and would remain prominent in the discourses of non-Indigenous residents of the region. As a military captain told me, "Without us, this place has no order. It is hard to be here, hard to have the responsibility of holding it together, but it is necessary."

The municipality is located at the heart of the region known as the "dog's head" (Cabeça de Cachorro) because of the image formed on the map by the borders between Brazil, Colombia, and Venezuela; this bird's eye view manifests itself on the ground as a need, dating back to the 1759 Treaty of Madrid between the Portuguese and Spanish crowns,[2] to assert control over the territory and to ensure the clear recognition of its frontiers. For the nations that occupy them, the Indigenous lands through which these borders run remain sites that must be claimed. On one of my first mornings in São Gabriel, while I was taking notes on the balcony of the hotel where I was staying, I watched rows of uniformed men march down the streets chanting about the importance of Amazonia to Brazil's greatness. This performance was repeated several times a week throughout my fieldwork. Military officers would later tell me that their job, in the jungle territories they patrolled, was to ensure that the presence of the state remained visible and incontrovertible.

Another resonant historical theme is the degree to which legal restrictions promulgated in administrative centres (Lisbon and Belém when the Amazon region was part of the Portuguese colony of Grão-Pará, then Rio de Janeiro and Brasília after the Republic of Brazil was founded) did not take hold in actual fact in this distant region. Indigenous slavery was declared illegal in 1759, yet various forms of coerced labour, including indentured servitude and work obtained by threat of force, continued to characterize the relations between Indigenous people and white traders (regatões) (Wright 1992; Meira 1996). The threat of violence caused many Indigenous people to retreat to ever more remote parts of the Uaupés and Içana basins, where they were less likely to be confronted by these traders. These incursions intensified with the rubber boom in the 1870s, during which more white commercial traders arrived and the demand for Indigenous labour rose. Indigenous people now had to contend with the constant presence of sexual violence against young women and the trafficking of young men to work in larger centres (Lasmar 2009). Contemporary manifestations of these historical threads are common topics of conversation in São Gabriel, which, as a result of the power imbalance between the local Indigenous population and migrant *comerciantes*, is the most unequal city in Brazil (Programa das Nações Unidos para o Desenvovimento 2013). Young Indigenous boys and girls there are at serious risk of being coerced into the drug and sex trades. In 2013, three of the most prominent business owners in the city were arrested for running a pedophile ring, most of whose victims were Indigenous girls. The investigation and subsequent imprisonment of this group helped publicize and resolve concerns that up to that point had usually been discussed as something that "everyone knew" was happening, but that no one in power was interested in stopping. The movement of young Indigenous women into larger cities such as Manaus, where they find isolated and poorly paid domestic work, continues the pattern of exploitative economic relations between Indigenous and non-Indigenous people – a reflection of the migratory pressures created by the white marketplace (Chernela 2015).

The arrest of the prominent business owners for sex trafficking was facilitated by the activist efforts of the local Catholic diocese, which in recent years has made pursuing this type of social justice a central part of its mission. But the Church's positive influence with regard to these difficulties must be interpreted in light of the fraught relationship the Northwest Amazonian population has had in the past with missionaries. Many people in the area recount with considerable revulsion how the sacred instruments and masks of the Tariana people were destroyed and denigrated as objects of the devil by the Franciscan monk Illuminato Coppi in the late nineteenth century, and how the women of the community were traumatized by being forced to view these objects, which were intended for men's eyes only (Wright 2005). Yet other individual priests and monks are warmly remembered for the ways in which they adapted to Indigenous cultures, and the Catholic Church in general is praised for having brought education to the region. In most of the area, in the early twentieth century, it was the Catholic order of St Francis of Sales (the Salesians) that became most powerful, as their philosophical approach to evangelism and conversion was supported by the new Brazilian state. Salesians were (and still are) known for their focus on hard work and rigorous vocational training to learn how best to serve God and the Church. After arriving in São Gabriel and build- ing a mission centre there in 1913, the Salesians founded three addi- tional missions at Taracuá (1923), Iauaratê (1929), and Paricachoeira (1940) (now known as the "Tukano triangle") as well as farther down the Rio Negro, at Santa Isabel (1942), and along the Içana (1952). After the collapse of the rubber boom a few years after the Salesians arrived in São Gabriel, these missionaries, alongside the agents of the newly formed Serviço de Proteção ao Índio (SPI), became the most significant Western influence on the lives of the Indigenous people of the Upper Rio Negro (Meira 1996).

Soon after Brazil gained independence from Portugal in 1888, the SPI and the Salesian missions became its twin engines in the Upper Rio Negro. The SPI, led Marshal Cândido Rondon, was tasked with "pacifying" the Indigenous population of Brazil's Amazon and Panta- nal regions *without* the use of force and violence – organized under the famous Rondonian directive that SPI agents should die if necessary, but never kill (Ramos 1998). Similarly, the Salesian mission, with its emphasis on educating the population and bringing Indigenous people into the body of the Brazilian nation, was central to the SPI-era goals of state formation. To that end, each mission centre established a boarding school under the leadership of Salesian priests. The Indigenous people had a complex relationship with these evangelical missions: they came to appreciate the formal education and the knowledge they obtained in the mission schools, while simultaneously lamenting the prohibition of their languages and cultural practices (Rezende 2010; Luciano 2012). This prohibition, and the tactics of shaming and punishment that were connected to it, came to international attention during the Fourth Rus- sell Tribunal on the Rights of Indigenous People, held in Rotterdam in 1980. The testimony at that tribunal by Álvaro Sampaio, a Tukano man from the Iauaratê region, was an originating event of Indigenous activ- ism in the Rio Negro (Ramos 1998). He described the boarding schools as sites of cultural genocide, and his testimony led almost immediately to the closing of those schools. (The relationship of Indigenous people to the education provided in these schools, and the establishment of viable alternatives that allow for both educational advancement and cultural continuity, will be a central theme in the following chapters.) The tribunal was transformative for Indigenous political activism in the Rio Negro: up until then, any claims against the Brazilian state (at the time a military dictatorship) had been facilitated primarily by the

Catholic Church (in the form of the Conselho Indigenista Missionário, CIMI); after Sampaio's denunciation, an Indigenous-led political movement, allied with academic, non-governmental, and international environmental interests, began to take shape. The form this movement took has had an impact on today's politics of language and identity.

Developmental projects launched during the period of military government in Brazil (1960–84) were also vital in efforts to further incorporate the Amazon territory into the state. Such projects were implemented throughout the Amazon. They included the Northern Channel (*Calha Norte*) road construction project and the industrialization of the Northwest region. This project has continued, under different names and in different manifestations, well into the current period of redemocratization and has never been fully abandoned. The launching of these developmental projects in the 1970s sparked the transformation of São Gabriel from a barely populated mission outpost into the city it is today, as a result of the influx of migrants both from other regions of Brazil[3] and from Indigenous communities in the interior. Meanwhile, the SPI's inefficacy in either protecting Indigenous people or ensuring their assimilation led to its disbanding in 1970; it was replaced by a federal government body, the Fundação Nacional do Índio (FUNAI), which still exists as the nation's Indigenous affairs branch. FUNAI's responsibilities include controlling access to Indigenous territories, delivering services to Indigenous people, and acting as the state's representative in disputes with Indigenous groups. At the local branch of the FUNAI office in São Gabriel, there are often long line-ups of Indigenous people attempting to resolve administrative issues and navigate the bureaucratic structures through which they can receive the benefits that, for many families, constitute their primary engagement with a money-based economy.

The military maintains a constant presence in the region, given that the municipality is close to two international borders. The Colombian border, where confrontations between revolutionary guerrilla organizations (such as FARC) and the government sometimes spill onto Brazilian territory, is especially problematic for those whose task it is to assert control over both the territory and its Indigenous inhabitants. Colonialism rarely respects pre-existing boundaries between Indigenous groups when international borders are drawn; thus, many Indigenous people in the Rio Negro region have family members living on the Colombian side, and their alterity – their insecure incorporation into the body of the Brazilian nation – colours them as potential threats

(Fleming 2010). In addition, large quantities of illegal drugs cross these river and jungle borders and then flow through São Gabriel on their way to the international market, and this has led to dramatic acts of violence among participants in the drug trade. Drug violence is often a topic of conversation in and around São Gabriel – for example, immediately before my first field visit in 2011, a gruesome murder had taken place, and the recently discovered severed head of the victim was the topic of daily discussion on the streets and at the market. Because of the drug trade, the military has a highly visible presence in this city, and national-level interests supersede the local-level ones when security priorities are determined. That is to say, it is a well-known fact in São Gabriel that it is easy to sell a few grams of cocaine, because no one is interested in finding someone with a kilo – they're working to bust an organization with several hundred. State presence, in the form of policing and security, is simultaneously ubiquitous and out of reach of the daily lives of the population.

Because the military offers one of the few avenues for lucrative employment for young Indigenous men, many of them are now serving; but they are strongly concentrated in the lower ranks and do not continue beyond a basic service period of seven years (Fleming 2010). The higher-ranking non-Indigenous personnel are usually stationed in the region for two to four years and tend to live in military-exclusive neighbourhoods that demonstrate the obvious class disparities between them and the majority of the local population. And the military's influence on the city's social life is not limited to its official goals. The spouses of military personnel often have formal credentials in nursing, social services, or education that are difficult for local Indigenous people to obtain, which means they are relatively well-qualified to take on service positions in the city. This has exacerbated the racialized power imbalance in employment rates; it has also badly weakened the continuity of government services. This is especially true of health services; the local hospital falls within the purview of the military and is staffed by a combination of career military officers and young medical residents, who enter the military for one or two years to complete their training while providing care to an underserved population. Health care is also provided through municipally funded clinics, but it is hard for them to pay salaries high enough to attract permanent doctors to this remote area, so these clinics are usually staffed by military doctors from the hospital, who must work extremely long hours at a combination of jobs and then leave after one to two years. Whether specialists are available depends entirely on the pool of doctors that arrives in a given year. For example, during my preliminary field visit (February–April 2011), I heard several people complain that no pediatrician had arrived. The following year (2012), two pediatricians were available, but no obstetricians.[4] Many Indigenous people in the area express the hope that they will start to see Indigenous youth being trained as doctors and returning to occupy these positions. This would improve service continuity and establish an approach to health care that is more informed about local cultural practices, but it hasn't happened yet.

Indigeneity in the State

The role of non-Indigenous interests – especially those of the state – cannot be examined without reference to Indigenous engagement with those actors. These relations are at the core of local politics, and Indigenous people have worked for decades to organize means of bringing their interests to the table. Several Indigenous organizations are headquartered in São Gabriel, often under the umbrella of FOIRN, and this factor is important to understanding local social and political life. FOIRN was formed in 1984, after the Russell Tribunal, just as the military dictatorship was collapsing. As with many similar organizations throughout Latin America that emerged in the 1970s and 1980s, FOIRN's primary goal has been to secure protection and economic sustainability for Indigenous territories, as well as some degree of cultural autonomy for them (Warren and Jackson 2002; Wright 2005). Across the continent, the status of languages – more specifically, their use in education programs – has been closely intertwined with the experiences and construction of Indigenous citizenship. At the same time, the nature of that citizenship has been directly impacted by new legal understandings of what it means to be Indigenous.

In Brazil, since the promulgation of the 1988 constitution – a product of the country's redemocratization – Indigeneity has been recognized as a permanent identity rather than a transitional, "pre-civilized" stage of development that entails state wardship (Ramos 1998; Wright 1992). The notion that Indigenous people are "relatively incapable" has had strong repercussions; as just one example, when Sampaio travelled to Rotterdam in 1980 to give his testimony against the Salesians, a non-Indigenous Brazilian was required to accompany him, because his passport was equivalent to that of a young child. Only in the past thirty years have Indigenous people in Brazil been treated, even at a formal level, as adults with the capacity to represent their own interests. The legacy of this wardship model still resonates and can be seen especially in the anger and frustration that Indigenous leaders express about their continued dependency on outside funding – including from the state itself – to both advocate for and meet their people's needs. Autonomy and economic sustainability are, at best, distant goals.

At the same time, the state has been reluctant to codify the rights that have been granted to Indigenous people by the constitution (i.e., turn those rights into specific laws). The process of determining which territories should be officially demarcated as Indigenous lands is ongoing in many parts of the country. Many Indigenous people feel that this is the result of the state's stalling rather than any inherent legal complications. Since the Temer government has taken power, that process has not only slowed, but also runs the risk of being reversed, as this president has made it clear that even constitutional protections are sacrosanct. This ongoing battle received a rare piece of national (and limited international) attention during the 2014 World Cup, when the young Guarani boy who had been selected to represent Brazil's Indigenous people during the opening ceremonies (alongside the two other people understood to make up the mixed racial identity of the country: a European-descended and an African-descended child) unexpectedly unveiled a banner reading "Demarcation now!" The Rio Negro region is, in many ways, ahead of other parts of the country in that regard: FOIRN successfully pressured for the demarcation of the entire contiguous territory of the municipality (with the exception of the city itself) (FOIRN/ISA 2006).

The issue of land demarcation unified the region's Indigenous people in the 1990s; they were able to agree that the most important priority for Indigenous politics was the terms according to which it should take place. Other concerns and needs, however, have not enjoyed such a sharp focus. It is clear that culture, language, and education are important; not so apparent is the form that protections and supports should take. One example of the ongoing challenges and conflicts relates to the municipal policy that recognizes three local Indigenous languages (Tukano, Baniwa, Nheengatú). This policy reform was driven by the efforts of Indigenous people and academic advocates but has been difficult to implement, and many people in the city remain unaware of its intentions or tenets (Oliveira and Almeida 2007; Sarges 2013). In and of itself, though, the existence of these "co-official" Indigenous languages emphasizes one of the themes I explore throughout this book: the changing relationship that Indigenous peoples have to the state. Institutional recognition for their languages is now not just imaginable but immediately realizable. The impact of such changes is multifaceted and still being negotiated, as I will show.

Indigenous Diversity and Interrelationships

Considering the history of São Gabriel only in terms of relations between Indigenous and non-Indigenous people would present a very limited view of the town's contemporary social and political make-up. The city functions as a meeting place for a diverse set of Northwest Amazonian Indigenous cultures and peoples, who coexist according to social relationships with one another that have come about through circumstances existing both before and since the arrival of European colonizers (Wright 1992). Alongside some practices shared among the groups and characteristic of lowland South America in general, each of the area's main Indigenous groups demonstrates particular ethnographic features that shape their role in the urban area's social system. The region's Indigenous peoples share a reliance on swidden horticulture, with bitter manioc root serving as the dietary staple in a region where the acidic black water system makes for extremely poor growing conditions. Hunting and fishing supplement the diet depending on the season, and among all of the region's peoples, an understanding of cosmologies, seasonal patterns, and growing cycles is linked to ritual actions and shamanic knowledge (Hill 2008). My effort here to discuss the politics of culture in São Gabriel – and in particular, to treat that city as a community of practice in its own right, rather than as a contact zone between disparate, migratory Indigenous communities with one another or with mainstream Brazil – should also be contextualized in relation to the existing ethnographic analyses of each of these peoples.

Tukanoans

The umbrella term "Tukanoan" serves as the best way to capture the people of the Uaupés (Vaupes) basin, as it is best understood not as a confluence of several bounded "cultures" but rather as a single, multilingual cultural system (Jackson 1983). The social practices of Tukanoans destabilize and disrupt the idea of a one-to-one equation between "language" and "culture" that has dominated European thought since Herder (cf. Bauman and Briggs 2003). In describing the Tukanoan system, Jackson (1995: 4) uses the metaphor of "members of a symphony orchestra – each playing a different instrument" to describe how "the members of different language groups together produce a coherent and often harmonious performance." The various instruments within the Tukanoan system include the Tukano, the Dessana, the Tuyuka, the Kotiria (Wanano), the Waikhena (Piratapuya), and the Barasana. The term "Tukanoan" resorts to the name of the language family to describe the cultural system; note, however, that speakers of Tariana, an Arawakan language, participate fully in the marital and economic exchanges that have created this system. A full analysis of Tariana language and cultural practices in relation to the Tukanoan and Arawakan societies is beyond the scope of this book;[5] I have elected to consider this group within the Tukanoan category. As I show throughout this analysis, the Tariana people play a significant role in the cultural politics of São Gabriel, and especially as most of them are now speakers of the Tukano language (rather than their own), they do so in ways that demonstrate their own adoption of this categorization.[6]

Tukanoan society is organized around exogamous marriages and patrilineal descent groups. A person's language group affiliation is established by the group affiliation of his or her father, and potential marriage partners must be selected from outside that group, since other members are considered kin. Group affiliation is most clearly represented by and constituted through linguistic performance. The complex system of hierarchical relationships includes subgroups of sibs[7] within the language groups, as well as phratries that unite two or more language groups into agnatic relationships that discourage marriages between members of groups that are too closely related. The language group, however, works as the core determiner of identity, and an individual when identifying him- or herself will immediately ensure that language group membership is communicated (either through the linguistic performance itself or, when interacting in Portuguese, by appending it to his or her name). The nature of the interaction between language and identity makes it difficult to select an appropriate term for the Tukanoan subgroups. Although "language group" is probably the most common, Christine Hugh-Jones (1979: 16–17) disputes the term, preferring instead "Compound Exogamous Group," since, she argues, its status as "a language-bearing unit" constitutes the ideal situation but by no means the only possible one; this ideal has become even more rare in light of language shift (Fleming 2010). Despite the problematic conflation of language and "culture," the latter term also circulates as a gloss for "language group," while many Tukanoans themselves have adopted the Portuguese term *etnia* to refer to their language groups. This multiplicity of labels itself demonstrates that the way that language, culture, and identity interrelate among Tukanoan peoples is neither simple nor easily translatable into conventional anthropological terms. Throughout this work, I use the shorthand term "language group" as much as possible, while also drawing on the Portuguese term to articulate particular points about Indigenous peoples' self-conceptualizations.

Because exogamous marriages create multilingual households, multilingualism is extremely common among Tukanoan people (Sorensen 1967). While the system is often summarized as one in which a person must marry a speaker of a different language, it would be more accurate to say that he or she must marry a member of another language group (though the assessment of speaker status is directly tied to this group membership; see Chernela 2013; Chernela and Shulist 2014; Shulist 2016a). Language group membership is patrilineally defined – a person is automatically considered to be a member of his or her father's language group, though mastery (if not use) of one's mother's language is common (Chernela 2004). The idea of language group membership as the primary exogamous determiner has been retained despite the "linguistic reality" that has emerged as a result of colonization. Indeed, the influence of the Salesian missionaries has helped establish Tukano as a regional *lingua franca*; and especially within the larger mission settlements of Iauaratê, Paricachoeira, and Taracuá, for example, the pattern of this shift is such that many people of various language group affiliations are speakers of Tukano *instead of* their patrilect. This is especially the case among the Tariana, but it also occurs among members of other groups. It is not prohibited, then, for Tukano-speaking Tariana to marry people from the Tukano language group. The patrilineally determined group membership remains in place, though some Tukanoans are clearly uncomfortable with the idea that one can be a member of a group without an ability to speak the language (Shulist 2016a). This brings up an additional terminological challenge I faced when writing this book – while it is convenient shorthand, and fits with local descriptive choices, to talk about a person's "primary language" as the one belonging to his or her language group (the patrilect), this does not necessarily refer to the Indigenous language in which the person is most fluent (or even, in many cases, to a language that the person knows at all). "Primary language," then, refers more to its cultural and social significance for the person's identity than to degree of linguistic ability.

Language, of course, is not the only marker of membership in each of these groups. Each Tukanoan subgroup is defined by a particular role in the origin myth about the emergence of the peoples of the region. That myth involves the journey of a sacred anaconda-canoe, from whose body the first ancestors of each of the language groups emerged. Shared descent from these ancestors is the feature that defines members of each language group as kin, and further subdivision into sibs within each language group helps shape the social functions within each of these communities. Within these groups, ranked roles emerge according to sib (Christine Hugh-Jones 1979; Chernela 1993), while each language group also shares a set of common, distinguishing characteristics, which Jackson (1995: 4) enumerates as follows:

> (1) language and name; (2) separate founding ancestors and distinct roles in the origin myth cycle; (3) the right to ancestral power through the use of specific linguistic property such as sacred chants; (4) the right to manufacture and use certain kinds of ritual property; (5) a traditional association with certain ceremonial objects; and (6) a symbolic association with a territory whose boundaries are unspecified.

Individuals also fit into specialist roles in a spiritual context. However, the practical functioning of all of these roles has eroded to the extent that contemporary anthropological accounts have only been able to discuss descriptions of its full complement, which is no longer functional among any of the Tukanoan societies (Christine Hugh-Jones 1979: 54). Shamanic practices have been increasingly difficult to maintain and transmit. The Indigenous inhabitants of the Uaupés continue to believe that magic and evil intent play a role in creating disease and killing their people, and they often lament the loss of those who are able to cure illness (both physical and social) by applying shamanic knowledge. Some language groups have no remaining shamans; others have very few. The arduous training involved discourages many young people from acquiring shamanic knowledge. As intergenerational transmission of these specialist roles has been disrupted, knowledgeable shamans are left with few appropriate potential trainees from within their own lineages, while interested apprentices whose lineages have no shamans are left with no possible mentors.

Prior to the interventions of non-Indigenous Brazilians – and specifically, of the Salesian missionaries – Tukanoans lived in longhouses called *malokas*, which ideally housed several extended family members and in-married wives. This pattern persisted, at least to some extent, well into the twentieth century, and it remains part of the living memory of many Tukanoan people today. Stephen Hugh-Jones's (1979) ethnographic study of the Barasana devotes substantial attention to the meaning of *maloka* construction patterns and to the ways in which this structure shaped the social practices and beliefs of the Tukanoan peoples. The Salesian missionaries targeted the *maloka* for destruction for two reasons: first, they saw these living arrangements, in which adult men and women lived together with other unmarried adults or the spouses of other family members, as immoral; and second, each *maloka* was several hours' canoe travel from the next, which created a sparse population distribution that made evangelism more physically arduous than might be ideal. The destruction of many of the *malokas* in favour of single-family homes and the consolidation of these families into larger settlements had a significant and likely irreversible impact, and clearly illustrates how the arrival of Christianity has led to major changes to the cultural practices of the Indigenous peoples of the Uaupés.

Tukanoans play a dominant role in contemporary Indigenous politics, both because they are demographically among the largest groups (with a total population, in Brazil, of around 11,000, with another 18,000 living in Colombia [Instituto Socioambiental 2010]) and because they have – whether by necessity or as a result of affinity for this type of political practice – embraced the idea that active engagement with the state is the best way to ensure protection of their material and cultural needs (Andrello 2010). Tukanoan cultural practices – including multilingualism, patrilineal descent, and material products – have come, then, to stand as clear markers of alterity and of prototypical Indigeneity in discussions of the Rio Negro region. This status permeates conversations about language revitalization in ways that become complicated, both for speakers of Tukanoan languages and for members of other groups whose understandings of language are different from the one discussed here.

Arawakan Culture

North of São Gabriel, along the Rio Negro and Içana rivers and their tributaries and across the Colombian and Venezuelan borders, live several groups of speakers of Arawakan languages, including Baniwa, Kurripako, and Warekena, along with Tariana (discussed above). In several settlements the ancestral Arawakan language has been replaced by Nheengatú. The most prominent example of this relates to the Baré – the Arawakan Baré language, once widely spoken, is not currently in use at all, and the cultural features of Baré peoples have been particularly affected by this shift (see the following section). These Arawakan peoples are, in some ways, similar to their Tukanoan neighbours (indeed, to the general pattern in lowland South America), with their emphasis on ritual and myth (Hill 2008), their holistic understanding of health and healing (Garnelo 2003), and their patterns of material production and subsistence (Wright 1992). At the same time, a few key social elements differentiate this group from others in São Gabriel, especially in terms of the relationship between language and identity.

First, the Arawakan groups do not rely on language affiliation when determining marriage partners, though clan-level exogamy is important to their social organization (Hill 1984). While some Baniwa-speaking communities living near the Tukanoans on the Colombian border have engaged in marriage exchanges with these neighbours (notably the Kotiria), the definition of other Baniwa as kin is not present, and marriages between two Baniwa are quite common. As a result, the need to carefully police linguistic boundaries that characterizes Tukanoan ideologies (to ensure the clear ability to manifest and differentiate the linguistic groups) is absent from Arawakan cultures, and the labels for and borders between the various linguistic subgroups are much less clearly established (Aikhenvald 2003b). Scholars of Arawakan linguistics have debated just how many separate Arawakan languages are spoken in this region, citing a high degree of intelligibility among several of the groups as well as self-identifications that differ in Brazil from those in Venezuela or Colombia (Granadillo 2006). In São Gabriel, most Arawakan speakers identify themselves as Baniwa, though a smaller group of Kurripako insist that their language is distinct from this more dominant cousin.

The Baniwa and Kurripako are among the most recent migrants to the urban area, a fact that is often highlighted in general commentaries about why they have been more able to retain and transmit their language to children, even in the city. This focus on timing of arrival, however, elides another important difference between this group and the Tukanoans (and the Nheengatú-speaking Baré) – the Salesian missionary influence did not arrive in the Içana region until the 1950s, and

Christian evangelism took a very different form among the Baniwa, most of whom are Evangelical Protestants. The New Tribes mission, and especially the frequently discussed missionary Sophie Muller, were responsible for bringing this form of Christianity to the region; the existing apocalyptic stories that were present in Baniwa culture proved to be rich soil for planting the seeds for their conversion (Wright and Hill 1986; Wright 1998). Core elements of the New Tribes' religious practice included the prohibition of many cultural symbols, including dances, rituals, and songs, which were viewed as a form of devil worship. Catholic missionaries in the Uaupés basin also demonized and prohibited these practices; that said, the Arawakan peoples of the Içana subregion absorbed and accepted these shifting understandings of God and salvation more thoroughly. Alcoholic beverages and hallucinogenic drugs – some of which were traditionally used in various rituals, ceremonies, or celebrations – were also strictly prohibited. This component, too, of evangelical religious practice has sharply distinguished the Protestant Baniwa from their Catholic neighbours.

But unlike the Salesian missionaries, Sophie Muller and her followers did not prohibit the use of the local language; instead, they subscribed to the Protestant ideology that emphasizes the translation of God's word into the Indigenous vernacular (Hill and Santos-Granero 2002). As a result, a New Testament translation exists in both Baniwa and Nheengatú (spoken by some of the Baniwa population on the Negro and Lower Içana rivers), and Baniwa-Kurripako speakers do not experience or relate the same type of anxiety about the use of their language in formal contexts (such as in church services or schools) that is reported by many Tukanoan peoples. While this religious framework may support the maintenance of language, cultural revitalization efforts must take into account the prevalent beliefs among many Baniwa and Kurripako people that the practices targeted for revival are immoral or demonic, albeit others feel more comfortable continuing to identify as Evangelical Christians while readopting many of the old Baniwa ritual practices.[8]

These religious dynamics influence the ways in which the Arawakan peoples inhabit the space of São Gabriel. While no neighbourhood in that city can be considered ethnolinguistically homogenous, the Baniwa are more likely than nearly any other group to live in close proximity to their own; this is largely because of the timing of their arrival, as well as their links to specific Protestant denominations and the nearby churches. There is only one church in which the language of service is Baniwa, and it is located in a neighbourhood populated mainly by Baniwa speakers. Along with the higher likelihood of linguistically endogamous marriages, this grouping together facilitates the continued use of Baniwa in a variety of domains and contexts in the urban area. Despite the similarities between the Baniwa and other Northwest Amazonian peoples (primarily the Tukanoans), and the long history of relations between the two, the Arawakan Baniwa maintain a different form of engagement with language and the politics of culture, and this informs their role in the social life of São Gabriel.

The Baré

Even a brief description of the population that identifies as Baré involves wading into some complex and contested anthropological territory. The Baré are one of the largest population groups in São Gabriel – while a breakdown of the city's population by ethnic group is unavailable, preliminary surveys reasonably suggest there are several thousand of them. Baré communities of varying sizes, from a few dozen to a thousand individuals, can also be found up and down the Rio Negro from São Gabriel. Yet in contrast to the other two main groups described here, the Baré have received little ethnographic attention, and indeed, they were treated as extinct or as entirely enculturated in ethnographic work conducted in the region in the mid-twentieth century (e.g., Nimunedajú 1982; Galvão 1979). Koch-Grünberg's (2005) early-twentieth-century descriptions mention the Baré but suggest that their presence was minimal even during that era. This presumed extinction and anthropological erasure relates directly to the framing of Amazonian Indigeneity as dependent on marked alterity from mainstream Brazilian culture, and on the legally enshrined vision of a degree of "acculturation" seen to render a group no longer Indigenous. These ethnological perspectives were, in fact, reflected in a report produced by the SPI that described the Baré as almost entirely assimilated (Maia 2009: 14).

The Baré have a long and intensive history of contact with non-Indigenous society, have intermarried with non-Indigenous Brazilians extensively, and no longer manifest many easily identifiable symbols of Indigenous alterity (rituals, clothing, craftwork, etc.). Most significantly, the Arawakan language from which the group gets its name is no longer spoken at all, having been replaced mainly by Nheengatú. Until relatively recently, many Baré, especially those residing in the urban area, did not see themselves as Indigenous. This population historically referred to itself as *caboclo* – that is, as peasants of mixed Indigenous and non-Indigenous ancestry. They took pride in being less "backward" than the other residents of the region and sought to distance themselves from the "Indians" of the Uaupés and Içana basins. The transition to viewing and representing themselves as Indigenous has come about primarily in relation to the shifting terrain of political capital that comes with this ascription – in particular, that ascription's salience in terms of claiming protection for territories they have been living on for generations (Fleming 2010). Maia (2009), however, has presented a powerful analysis of Baré symbolic practices that demonstrates the degree to which this adoption of the colonizers' practices has occurred within a framework of Arawakan cultural meanings – including, for example, the structural patterns surrounding the celebration of Catholic saints' days, which build on a substrate of Indigenous references. Thus, while the Baré's self-conscious practice of identifying as "Indigenous" may be recent and politically driven, Maia's work helps contextualize the continuity of Indigenous traditions among this group and emphasizes the extent to which colonial powers have enforced "acculturation" as a tool for denying the identity of this population.

Maia does not deal explicitly or in great detail with the feature that most centrally embodies the discussion of Baré "extinction," though it is the one that, of course, forms the foundation for my own analysis in this book – language. The Nheengatú language has generated an ideological debate that underpins many of the political issues discussed in the following chapters. That language, of Tupi origin, is also known as Língua Geral Amazônica (or regionally, simply Lingua Geral) and is descended from a variety introduced to the region by Jesuit missionaries (Freire and Rosa 2003; Rodrigues and Câmara Cabral 2011). Although it originally functioned as a *lingua franca* facilitating communication with speakers of a variety of Arawakan and Tukanoan languages, it strengthened specifically in the middle Rio Negro region that was home to the Baré, where it has been spoken as a first language since at least the mid-nineteenth century (da Cruz 2011). While the language belongs to an Indigenous language family of the Americas, and even though it is the language of communication among these Indigenous communities, its colonial origins mean that it is regularly grouped differently by scholars when they discuss the languages of the region. Many publications (e.g., FOIRN/ISA 2006; Epps and Stenzel 2013) place the count of language families represented in the region at four – Tukanoan, Arawakan, Yanomami, and Nadahup – and either implicitly or explicitly group Nheengatú with Spanish and Portuguese as a colonial language rather than an Indigenous one. Indeed, the idea that speaking Nheengatú constitutes a loss of Indigenous identity and culture originated among those who *introduced* the language. The Jesuit missionaries who taught the population to speak it saw it as a means of enabling their transition from monolingual savage "Indians" to potentially literate, multilingual citizens who could be put to work (Freire 2004: 181). The pre-existing multilingualism in Indigenous languages was irrelevant in this conceptualization – Nheengatú was a means of civilizing this group and of *proving* they were civilized.

The Baré, however, view Nheengatú as the language of their Indigenous identity. It is also spoken as a first language among most of the Warekena people, as well as in many Baniwa communities along the lower Içana and Negro rivers, yet neither of these groups expresses the same type of ownership of the language. Presumably, this is at least in part because of the continued presence of their ancestral language, however minimal (the Warekena count only a few dozen speakers, for example). As I collected personal linguistic histories from various acquaintances and collaborators, I heard many Baré people stake a claim to the Nheengatú language – saying, for example, "I speak Nheengatú because it is my language" or "I am Baré, and I speak my language, which is Nheengatú" (both of these are translations from field notes, and these or similar phrases were often repeated). This equation was sometimes embedded so deeply in a person's self-concept that they referred to the language itself as Baré. But this was not necessarily an overtly conscious effort to claim the language. In at least one case, the person who said it was unaware there had once been an Arawakan language of this name. Himself a monolingual Portuguese Baré man, he called it Baré, he said, because the Baré speak it.

The reconceptualization of Nheengatú as an Indigenous language and as the language of Baré identity depends both on the romanticization of the history of the language and the relationship that people have to it (a process that da Cruz [2011] identifies as beginning during the late eighteenth and early nineteenth centuries), and on the material significance of a language/culture connection. According to Fleming (2010), this material significance emerged during the era of land claims, and he specifically highlights the inclusion of Nheengatú within the municipal official language policy as an example of the successful entextualization of this revised language ideology. In the context of the on-the-ground politics of language and culture in São Gabriel, however, the debate continues. The authenticity of Baré Indigeneity and the importance of the Nheengatú language as an identity marker and carrier of cultural knowledge – rather than as a simple communicative tool that could easily be substituted for Portuguese – are contested in subtle ways. Referring to the language as Lingua Geral, for example, emphasizes its colonial connection, while referring to it as Nheengatú – which translates as "good speech" in the Tupi tongue – indexes a reference to Indigeneity. The idea that the language does not carry the same weight of identification as the Tukanoan languages emerges throughout Tukanoan discourses. Members of these groups are inclined to point out the Baré people's acculturation as represented by their speaking Nheengatú, or to note the degree of borrowing present in this language as a marker of its inherently less "Indigenous" nature. Baré practices, including for example the adoption of Nheengatú-based "Indigenous names," are described as meaningless (Shulist 2016c). The Baré people have developed ways of manifesting and performing Indigeneity in such a way that it has been accepted by the state and external actors as authentic and politically valid; even so, local Indigenous people continue to question whether the Baré version of Indigeneity, manifested specifically in the colonially introduced Nheengatú language, should be counted as truly Indigenous, or whether the Baré represent a watered-down version of Indigeneity that ultimately detracts from the cultures these other groups are trying to preserve. This question becomes especially pertinent in the urban area, where Nheengatú has, in many ways, taken hold as the language representing Indigeneity (for example, it is the only Indigenous language taught in schools), and where the dispute about what it means to be Indigenous floats on the surface of nearly all political discussions.

Revitalization and Transformation

This historical and ethnographic background informs the ways in which the politics of language and culture are playing out in the city of São Gabriel. Although many Indigenous communities encompass diverse political, social, and ideological visions, this type of heterogeneity is often elided in the development of language programs and the identification of goals for revitalization politics (Meek 2011; Granadillo and Orcutt-Gachiri 2011; Nevins 2013). The diversity present in São Gabriel is not simply linguistic or cultural, but also generational, social, and political; it can be defined along lines such as type of employment (or, more radically, relationship to the formal market in general), length of time in the city, and reason for moving there in the first place. The features shared by the people and organizations with whom I was involved during the research for this book did not relate to language or culture; what mattered, rather, was social position. That is to say, I conducted my research in public and private spaces in which people were engaging with the question of language revitalization in the urban area, without specifically seeking out those who were working to document, maintain, or increase the transmission of a particular language or the practices of a particular cultural group.

Revitalization involves change. While this may seem basic, among some language activists the ideals of "preservation" and "maintenance" and ecologically influenced metaphors of conservation include a persistent note of cultural stasis, despite the emphasis on language being a "living thing" (Maffi 2005; Harmon 2001; Mühlhäusler 2001). In the Northwest Amazon, where transformation is a central ontological concept in identity formation, the tension between cultural preservation and incorporation of change serves as a useful way of engaging with this discussion.

The urban population is experiencing rapid social change, and in response, they are using activism around languages not only to ensure the continuity of the languages themselves, but also to construct and perform identities. Their discursive practices are shaping what it means to be Indigenous individuals living and working in an urban area, as well as creating an identity for the city itself, as various people play with and perform the "Indianness" of the city in complex ways. A dance is taking place in which some social actors in São Gabriel are working to incorporate Indigeneity into a non-Indigenous public sphere, while others are seeking to redefine the public space as inherently Indigenous, with the accompanying debates about what "Indigenous" means, both in general and in this specific context. These discussions raise the underlying question of what it means to be "Indigenous" and whether it is inherently incompatible with urbanity. The deep influence not only of colonialism, essentialist policies, and assimilationist pressures, but also of ideologies of tradition, purism, identity, and territory, have meant, so far, that the aspiration to establish an Indigenous city remains, at best, a long-term vision, though the framework of change-as-tradition (rather than the dichotomous model between these two points of Indigeneity and modernity that is often invoked), and the model of the Northwest Amazon as a "house of transformation," could serve as the cornerstone of a hopeful future.

Schools and discourses about education exemplify the complexity of the positions that language activists often occupy with varying degrees of self-consciousness. Educational institutions are potent means for creating and disciplining citizens, for constructing national identities, and for establishing or reinforcing linguistic power relations. In Brazil, this idea is on the surface of conversations about education and pedagogy, as the influence of Paulo Freire is visible among teachers, in schools, and in departments of education. In São Gabriel, where teachers and municipal administrators are predominantly Indigenous, and where (as I discuss in more depth in later chapters) education has been embedded in both colonial domination and Indigenous resistance and contestation since the advent of the Indigenous political movement, this means that schools become hotly contested grounds for reconfiguring understandings of Indigenous identity, the significance of language, and the importance of pluralist nationalism. They are also, however, state institutions, whose importance as recipients of public funds is rooted in the interests of the national body. The emphasis placed on education by the Workers' Party (PT, Partido dos Trabalhadores) governments of Luis Ignácio da Silva (Lula) (2003–10) and Dilma Roussef (2011–16),[9] for example, emerged not out of concern for social justice, but as a strategy for ensuring sustainable growth by strengthening Brazil's domestic economy. The degree to which language and cultural activism in São Gabriel has focused on schools and formal education, then, places the political advocacy movements in direct connection to broader processes of state recognition.

Indigenous peoples' attitudes towards state-supported and state-recognized institutional education are complex, and many aspects of the topic are sharply contested. Indigenous people in the Rio Negro, generally speaking, emphasize education as a force for liberation and as the fulcrum on which Indigenous autonomy rests. The questions become these: What form should education take? And by extension, what is the nature of the autonomy being sought?

As has been common throughout Latin America – and indeed, in colonial contexts around the world – the introduction of formal schooling into Indigenous people's lives demonstrated its power to dominate, assimilate, and control. Experiences of language prohibition in assimilationist boarding schools (*internatos*) form part of the living memory of many of the Indigenous people of the Upper Rio Negro, given that the Salesian schools were not closed until the 1980s. While the degree to which these schools were experienced as traumatic or oppressive varies among individuals, they performed a significant part of the state-building work of introducing the Portuguese language and non-Indigenous cultural practices to the Indigenous population (Fleming 2009). Bringing schools under Indigenous control, and securing the constitutional right to educate Indigenous children in culturally appropriate ways and in their own languages, has been a hard-fought battle, one whose goal has been not just to support Indigenous people as individuals but also to contest state structures that are premised on the eradication of cultural differences and group rights (Luciano 2012). Along with the demarcation of lands and access to health care, education has been central to Indigenous political activism in the Rio Negro, and in this context, it constitutes an indispensable and unquestionable part of self-determination (López and Sichra 2008; Rockwell and Gomes 2009).

As a result of this history, "differentiated education" is now seen as necessary if Indigenous people ever hope to transmit their own cultures and forms of knowledge to their children, while also ensuring that Indigenous children have access to the kinds of opportunities associated with formal education. Both linguists and anthropologists have been heavily involved in developing intercultural forms of schooling throughout Latin America; that said, local understandings of *why* autonomous control over these schools matters may clash with the emphasis on cultural survival that non-Indigenous academics, particularly linguists, have tended to advocate. Over the past decade, several "differentiated Indigenous schools" have been established throughout the rural territories in the municipality of São Gabriel. The opening of such schools has been viewed as a major victory for Indigenous people, because it means that families no longer have to relocate in order to educate their children, and because such schools allow a much higher degree of autonomy over the material taught, which opens the door to the use of locally relevant Indigenous languages (Cabalzar 2012). But for many Indigenous leaders in the Rio Negro specifically, the strongest motivation for high-quality, self-directed education is that it strengthens their ability to appropriate the dominant society's tools and to acquire the necessary social capital to fight for their peoples' economic and political needs (Luciano 2012: 46). Although these goals intersect with those of language preservation activists, they do not overlap completely – and the structures and discourses of differentiated Indigenous education situate the primary sites of language and culture within the rural territories, explicitly excluding the city of São Gabriel.

This erasure of the urban area relates not only to ideologies about schools but also to the relationship between language, culture, and territory. Indigenous people maintain that control over their land base is the single most important goal in their political struggles, since without that control, any possibility of autonomy or self-sustainability is at best difficult to imagine. The state's ongoing interest in maintaining control of the border zone and in accessing the region's extractive resources has led to heated political debates among Indigenous people – debates that are currently playing out in the question of whether to allow mining on demarcated Indigenous territories. The importance of land in this discussion, however, is as much spiritual as political. For many Indigenous groups of the region, territorial origin is foundational to identity. For the Tukanoans, for example, although there have been multiple relocations, reorganizations, and convergences into larger communities, each subgroup distinctly remembers and lays claim to specific territories within the Uaupés basin, regardless of whether they currently occupy those territories (Andrello 2006). These territorial origins are spiritually rooted in the emergence of each group from the body of the anaconda-canoe out of which they were formed. Furthermore, an individual's place of birth has a spiritual significance, and the place in which he or she received an ancestral name (Hugh-Jones 2006; Shulist 2016c) is a place to which he or she is inherently connected regardless of future travels.[10]

The importance of land both for contemporary political projects and for the construction of identities according to Indigenous ontologies, then, has placed Indigenous residents of the urban area in a precarious position (even more so if they were born in the city instead of having migrated from the rural territories). FOIRN functions based on a regionalized substructure that elects representatives from each of the various river systems of the municipality. The directorate consists of a representative from each of the Middle Rio Negro, the Upper Rio Negro, the Lower Uaupés, the Upper Uaupés, and the Içana. Although this body operates out of an office in the city, no representation exists for urban people except insofar as they can connect themselves to the interests and identities found in one of these subregions.

While Indigenous people (beginning with mostly the Baré, including those who once identified themselves as *caboclo*) have been trickling into the city in pursuit of economic opportunities for nearly a century, it was in the 1970s and 1980s that the "rural exodus" began in earnest. Two contributing factors were the expanded efforts of the military government to develop the Amazon and the closure of the Salesian boarding schools, which made it impossible for children to advance their education unless their families dislocated themselves. Over the past few decades, then, São Gabriel has been transformed from a tiny village inhabited almost exclusively by non-Indigenous residents of the region into a rapidly growing town with a very high proportion of Indigenous residents. As a result of this influx, it has become possible to talk about the place as an "Indigenous city." Andrello (2006) uses this same term to discuss the Uaupés settlement of Iauaratê, located on the Colombian border, and the contrast between these two "Indigenous cities" is a useful one. Iauaratê, which was founded by the Salesians as a mission centre, today is an emphatically Indigenous place, populated by Indigenous people and dominated by Indigenous languages and ways of being, and has grown to the size and function of a "city." São Gabriel, by contrast, was founded as a non-Indigenous place and has since incorporated Indigenous people – and in the perceptions of most people, it has become a site where they are transformed into members of non-Indigenous society. As I show throughout this book, the process of revitalizing Indigenous languages and cultures in this space, including through efforts to "Indigenize" the city itself, is pushing back against this history and discursive framework. The official language legislation, one of the most visible ways in which Indigeneity has been established in the city, serves as the starting point for this ethnographic examination of the complexities involved in these transformations.

3 Language Policy on Paper and in Practice

Prior to arriving in São Gabriel, I was aware that three Indigenous languages – Baniwa, Nheengatú, and Tukano – had been made official at the local level. The existence of this policy was a significant factor in motivating me to learn more about language planning efforts in the city. My hope – indeed, my expectation – was that the existence of this official language legislation reflected a strong commitment to language revitalization, including in the urban area. I did not, of course, discount the likely need for additional efforts to strengthen and expand the use of all of these languages, especially those that had *not* been granted official status, but the policy itself gave me a sense of optimism about language revitalization efforts in São Gabriel.

The legislation was first passed in late 2001, and further elucidated in 2006, with an additional law that outlined the steps to be taken to encourage the public use and recognition of these languages (the second law was to "regulate" the policy). Basic points included the requirement that all public services be provided, both orally and in written form, in all four of the official languages; the requirement that the municipal authority support the learning and use of the three Indigenous languages (with emphasis in that regard placed on schools and media outlets); and the prohibition of discrimination on the basis of language. Appendix A of this book provides the full text of the policies.

Immediately after arriving in the city for a preliminary field visit in February 2011, I realized that my impression from afar was not entirely accurate. The linguistic landscape – the ways in which language occupies the visual and textual space of the area (Landry and Bourhis 1997; Gorter 2006) – was marked almost entirely by Portuguese. Although I occasionally heard Indigenous languages being used in conversations among friends meeting on the street or families shopping at the market, the default language of public interaction was overwhelmingly Portuguese. During that visit, I found only one Indigenous-language text on a sign in a prominent, public location – the "welcome" sign that had been painted on the side of the city's gymnasium (Figure 3.1, below), at an intersection marking the entrance point to the downtown area coming from either the airport or the town's main river port. The sign makes use of the unofficial slogan "the most Indigenous city in Brazil," provides a list of local foods and traditional dances, and invites the reader to become familiar with these "parts of our cultural identity." The word "welcome" is written in six languages: Portuguese, Spanish, English, Nheengatú, Baniwa, and Tukano.

This sign exemplifies the role that the official language policy, and Indigenous languages in general, have come to play in the lives of the region's Indigenous population, as well as in shaping an identity for the city itself. It also initiates a discussion about language policy

Figure 3.1. "Welcome" sign on the gymnasium (February 2011). In addition to the word "Welcome" written in multiple languages, the Portuguese text of the sign says "The most Indigenous city in Brazil," provides a list of traditional foods, local fruits, and dances, then says "This is part of our cultural identity."

as a meaningful way of understanding how these languages and their speakers are relating to one another within this space. Studying language policy, of course, involves much more than analysing legal documents and their implementation (Spolsky 2012). Language policy is a complex and often contradictory set of social practices as well as a series of ongoing changes enacted and embodied through the actions of people on the ground. Although this chapter is primarily concerned with a piece of legislation and the granting of official status to three Indigenous languages, it is also a way of examining this legislation as a part of the broader picture of policy – what McCarty calls "a practice of power that operates at multiple, intersecting levels" (2011: 3). These relationships and practices of power are especially salient in contexts of language endangerment and revitalization, which are, as Woolard and Schieffelin (1994) put it, continuations of the colonial encounter that throw language ideology "into high relief." Formal language policy as a means to support endangered languages is relatively common, but never without complications emerging from the local legal, political-economic, and ideological framework in which the policies are enacted (Romaine 2002; Spolsky 2003; Patrick 2005). For the Indigenous people of São Gabriel, the granting of official status to three of their languages has constituted a symbolic point of transformation in their relationship to the state and to their public identities. In many ways, the creation of the official language policy can best be understood as a *performative* act, one that has marked and constituted the city as simultaneously Indigenous and Brazilian (Garcia 2012). The process involved in creating and working with this legislation reveals complex relationships among ideologies about language and identity, especially as conflicts emerge between traditional Indigenous understandings of these associations and the beliefs of powerful actors – Indigenous and otherwise – regarding the value of minority language maintenance in the context of larger political goals.

Origins of Co-officialization

The idea to create a law recognizing these languages as official came out of a class of Indigenous leaders and educators who were participating in the Magistério Indígena (MI), a program offering secondary education with a focus on Indigenous pedagogies to Indigenous teachers who had never completed this level of schooling.[1] In discussions about the importance of languages and the potential use of language policy as a means of protecting or promoting Indigenous languages, one student made an offhand joke about trying to make their languages official in Brazil. Another student suggested that, while it was useless to consider at the federal level (given the small proportion of Indigenous people in Brazil, in contrast to their more dominant presence in countries like Bolivia), the idea might actually become reality at the municipal level. Gilvan Müller de Oliveira, a linguist from the Brazilian Instituto de Política Lingüística (Language Policy Institute, IPOL), was present in the area during this course and offered to help the students design the policy and move forward with it.[2] The significance of language to Indigenous identity in the local context means that language loss and the threat of shifting completely to Portuguese are major concerns for the people of the area, and the significance of a law like this one for valorizing Indigenous identities was apparent to the group. Notwithstanding the high degree of linguistic diversity, the three languages chosen for official recognition definitely serve as *linguas francas* for the Indigenous population, and it seemed reasonable to limit the extent of legal recognition to these three, with the additional languages mentioned as being inherently official "within their own territories." After these discussions, the proposed legislation was developed by IPOL in consultation with FOIRN, which presented it to the municipal city council and saw it successfully passed in December 2001.

But the development of the law itself as well as the attempts to implement it since have suffered from a lack of ideological clarity about its purpose, about the intended role for both official and non-official Indigenous languages in public life, and about what types of planning measures will be required to ensure its effective application (most notably with respect to language standardization). As a result, the practical implementation of this law remains stalled, and people often talk about it as "never having left the paper." The 2006 legislation that outlined specific steps to be taken with respect to the newly declared official languages also set clear deadlines for each action; these deadlines have long passed, with essentially no change. Despite the strong presence of Indigenous people and speakers of Indigenous languages within the municipal government,[3] the state has demonstrated very little political will to promote or preserve these languages. This limited commitment to the recognition of Indigenous languages is usually cited by people in São Gabriel as the commonsense reason for the policy's failure. However, both the view that the law has had no impact because of the stalled implementation of its tenets, and the explanations for that stalling, are oversimplifications. In debates about the nature of Indigenous identity and its role in the urban area, the policy has become a point of contention (an object of concern in itself) as well as a symbolic tool for staking claims and shaping the space.

The primary aim of the official language legislation remains a matter of disagreement: Is it more important to serve the needs of the (relatively small) population of Indigenous people whose Portuguese language skills are very poor, or should the focus be placed on efforts that promote the use and teaching of the languages? Despite a surface-level complementarity in its two stated aims, this dual purpose provides preliminary insight into conflicts about its social and political significance. Both these goals are based on an overall desire to improve the material experience of marginalized people and to address historical and ongoing discrimination, but they differ with regard to their long-term vision of what this improvement should look like. As several scholars have pointed out (Kymlicka and Patten 2003; May 2003; Réaume and Pinto 2012), two possible responses exist for providing support to individuals who are uncomfortable operating in the dominant language. The first is to improve the availability of services in their own languages, and the second is to improve their capacity in the dominant language. The latter solution is, in many ways, much easier – and much cheaper – to implement, albeit to the detriment of the Indigenous and minority languages themselves. This point reflects a basic premise of language revitalization activism (Hinton 2003). These two arguments intersect, however, in efforts to advocate for the policy's implications – while "valorization" and revitalization were central goals in its establishment, the need to address the extreme marginalization of those who cannot speak Portuguese is sometimes seen as a more forceful argument. The surface-level similarity in these goals masks the degree to which the latter goal may in fact undercut the efforts of language maintenance activists, who operate from different ideological frameworks with regard to why Indigenous languages matter.

In further examining discourses and practices surrounding this official language policy, two important ideas come into view. The first is that, contrary to the perception that a general lack of political interest is the main factor that has restricted the implementation of its tenets, a larger role may be played by ideological contradictions, disagreements, and unacknowledged debates among the policy's supporters. The second is that even in the absence of "top-down" implementation, the official language policy has had a much more significant impact on the city than is often recognized in discussions of its limitations. Grassroots language activists have been able to carve out space for revitalization work in the urban area using the existence of the policy as an emotional and political framework. Here, the distinctions between "top-down" (state-level) and "bottom-up" (grassroots activist) actions are blurred, just as, in São Gabriel, what constitutes an "Indigenous" body and what constitutes a "non-Indigenous" one remains unclear. The policy was developed almost exclusively by a group of Indigenous organizers and subsequently passed by the state; and furthermore, the macro-level policy has been taken up by and transformed in the hands of individual actors. In fact, given the lack of top-down implementation of the policy's terms, this latter role played by the law may be even more important than its status as a framework within which government power functions. Thinking through that law's role in shaping the city, then, must begin with an examination of perceptions, reactions, and representations of its past, present, and future.

Ten Years Later: Marking the Tenth Anniversary of the Official Language Legislation

In late February 2012 a public discussion was held to commemorate the tenth anniversary of the co-officialization law and to debate future directions for municipal language policy. This event was organized by students and instructors from the Indigenous pedagogy class being offered at the São Gabriel campus of the Universidade do Estado de Amazonas (UEA) as part of a teachers' training program that runs during school holiday periods. The theme for the discussion was "Mudanças, Perspectivos e Desafios" (Changes, Perspectives, and Challenges). In and of itself, the fact that the tenth anniversary of a piece of municipal language legislation was seen as an occasion worthy of commemoration and public discussion demonstrates the law's significance for some members of the community. Some of the organizations and political bodies that were invited to send speakers chose not to do so. On the day, at the table of panellists sat Pedro Machado, a Tukano political leader who was instrumental in the establishment of FOIRN and in shaping the direction of Indigenous activism in the 1970s and 1980s; Edilson Martins Melgueiro, a Nheengatú-speaking Baniwa man and former FOIRN director with a master's degree in linguistics; Maximiliano Menezes, a Tukano leader and then FOIRN vice-president who is well-known for his passionate concern about Indigenous languages;

and Adi Nagel Júnior (known as Catarino), a non-Indigenous member of the town council, representing the municipal government. The discussion was moderated by Israel Pontes, a young Tuyuka political organizer who has a master's degree in anthropology and who is seen as an authority on local cultural practices.

The discussion was attended primarily by educators, who are often among the most acutely aware of how schools can use language to support the transmission of knowledge to the next generation of Indigenous children. A few representatives of municipal agencies came in response to the invitation from the class, though many departments were not represented, and several of those who did attend left early. One high-ranking (non-Indigenous) official from the health department later expressed to me her frustration about the time she had spent at the event, since in her view the language question had nothing to do with her work or her department.

Besides sending formal invitations and ensuring the presence of important voices in the conversation, the class arranged to have a banner printed professionally for the event, and decorated each of the four walls of the classroom with the word or phrase meaning "Welcome" in each of the four official languages of São Gabriel (Portuguese, Nheengatú, Tukano, and Baniwa). The discussion opened with three members of the class greeting the audience in each of the official Indigenous languages and offering a bit of personal information regarding their language and its importance. The Nheengatú speaker, for example, a Baniwa woman from the Lower Içana region, noted that although for her, Nheengatú is a "borrowed language," it is nonetheless important to her that she be able to use an Indigenous language in an official capacity. The Tukano woman nervously performed a traditional song along with her greeting, and expressed deep gratitude at knowing her language so that she could have access to the type of knowledge contained in songs like that one. The young Baniwa man spoke so briefly and so quietly that later on, I was unable to transcribe or translate my recording of his speech.

Each of the invited panellists offered information about the co-officialization law based on their role in or understanding of its development and implementation, and made suggestions about why they saw it as failed so far (the perspective that it had indeed been unsuccessful or ineffective was never questioned). The discussion lasted for nearly two hours following completion of the speeches. Questions and comments from the audience included expressions of passionate

Figure 3.2. Tukano language cut-out saying "Welcome" on one of the walls of the UEA classroom in which the 10th Anniversary event was held.

concern about the politics of Indigenous languages, education, and cultural revitalization in the region. In the following sections, the commentary made by speakers and questioners at this event provides a focal point for understanding the discourse about this official language policy, why it matters, and how it can be improved. These discussions shed light on the language ideologies in which the policy is rooted and on those that inform the "real" language policy that has been created and enacted by speakers in their day-to-day interactions.

The Semiotics of Officialization

An ethnographic examination of the language policy at work in São Gabriel reveals the limitations of considering the impact of the official language legislation solely by examining its practical manifestations.

Statements about the law's significance, both in the documents that led to its creation and in discourses about it around the time of the tenth anniversary, place much stronger emphasis on its status as an assertion of symbolic power (Bourdieu 1991). The effort to craft and pass the legislation emerged from a subset of ideas circulating within the Indigenous political movement regarding the importance of recognizing and valorizing Indigeneity in the context of the Brazilian state, as a specific response to the formalized nature of past disparagement. The tenth anniversary discussion opened with words from Pedro Machado, who acknowledged that although he had been asked to talk about language, while he was preparing for his presentation he had almost immediately forgotten about this focus, because the question was much more complex. As one of the central organizers involved in the founding of FOIRN and the Indigenous political movement in the region, he offered historical context about how he had come to recognize his identity both as Tukano and as a member of a unified body of Indigenous people. He recalled that

São Gabriel da Cachoeira, in the 70s, didn't have – any image, didn't have any identity – and no one talked about the Indian. Or about the Indigenous peoples. It was just a municipality with its people – that didn't have origins, histories, language families … In this gathering, at that time [1984], there still wasn't any imagination that we had to keep our languages alive.

Here, Machado was situating the discussion about the status of Indigenous languages with reference to the formation of Indigenous identity – specifically, of a unified, pan-Indigenous identity – as a political issue. This practice of historicizing the current conversation is a common feature of Tukanoan discourse patterns. Just as the origin myth of each of the peoples serves to ground individuals in their context and orient their statements (Chernela 1993), discussions of contemporary political and social events often begin with reference to the original claims around which the Indigenous movement was founded in the 1970s and 1980s and the changes that have taken place since then. Similarly, explanations of individuals' personal positions are often prefaced with an extended description of their life histories, whose relationship to the topic of conversation may not be immediately apparent. These discursive practices emphasize the need to constantly reorient towards personal, political, and spiritual origin stories in order to understand the meaning of what is happening in the present moment. Machado's speech, then, served to place this discussion about languages within the broader framework of the Indigenous movement, and specifically, to highlight the significance of the language policy with respect to the assertion – or creation – of particular types of Indigenous identity.

Similarly, in written documents submitted to town council in 2006 calling for the expansion and clarification of the terms of the official language act, FOIRN grounded its argument in the need to address the historical legacy of discrimination experienced by Indigenous peoples. The authors of these texts called attention to the role that the 2001 language policy had played in strengthening the languages – and by extension, their speakers – as they overcame the legacy of shame and stigmatization that was a consequence of the prohibition of their languages and cultures, and of the construction of an indexical relationship between Indigenous languages and "primitive savagery":

> But *today, primarily as a result of the co-officialization of the three Indigenous languages and other projects developed by FOIRN, the picture is reversing itself* ... The self-esteem of Indigenous people has gone up, because of the affirmation of the culture and the guarantee of the right to freedom of expression in the mother tongues of the Indigenous peoples of the Rio Negro *in the city,* and *indirectly contributing to the use of the rest of the Indigenous languages of the region.* [emphasis mine]

In this excerpt, the elevation of the languages' status is seen in terms of a concomitant elevation in the status of those languages' speakers, through the reduction of feelings of inferiority and humiliation. The officialization of three of the region's largest and most politically dominant languages is also construed as a symbolic action that has had an impact on *all* of the Indigenous languages spoken in the municipality, and suggests that this impact has been felt despite the limited implementation of the policy's formal articles.

FOIRN's focus on the symbolic significance of the legislation as it relates to the valorization of Indigenous identity in the urban area is echoed in a commentary made six years later at the UEA event. The ideological perspectives that emerge in these discussions, and how they inform the implementation (or lack thereof) of the on-paper policy, provide a particularly fruitful ground for understanding how the role of language is being reconceptualized – including through the policy itself – in the local political economy; furthermore, this illustrates the multiple levels of conflict and contention that emerge around the formation and re-formation of different types of linguistic identity.

Shame, Valorization, and the Creation of an Indigenous Public Space

The most common theme invoked in conversations about Indigenous language use, and about the legislation in particular, is the role that shame (*vergonha*) has played, and continues to play, in linguistic choices in the city. Indigenous leaders and the general public both express a perception that shame has diminished around the use of Indigenous languages and that this reduction has been a direct result of Indigenous advocacy, including the development of the official language legislation. At the UEA commemoration, Max Menezes reiterated this point, emphasizing the successful aspects of the legislation:

> I remember here, when I arrived ... we would always speak really quietly, right. So that no one would notice. Today, you speak openly, right – whether it be Língua Geral – which is Nheengatú, right, or Tukano, other languages are spoken – this, for us, is – is really important.

Historically, shame has been an important component of language shift in the Rio Negro region. As has been common in contexts of colonialism, the speaking of an Indigenous language has come to index a non-modern state of being, one that positions the speaker within a state of nature that is simultaneously childlike and savage. Many people in São Gabriel reflected on how weak Portuguese-language skills continue to mark someone as uncivilized. Twenty or thirty years ago in the city, teachers typically used the word "Indian" as a way of labelling someone stupid, uneducated, or unteachable.

Given these experiences of shame and shaming, the choice to self-identify as Indigenous is considered an important step among Indigenous political activists. One educational administrator and Indigenous activist (anonymous interview, 20 June 2012) observed that in the 1980s, when she was a student in the city of São Gabriel, several of her fellow students actively denied their identities, saying "I'm not Indian; I'm not Makú."[4] While she herself had never gone so far as to renounce her status as Indigenous, she admitted that she had refused to affirm it or to call attention to her Indigeneity. This denial of, and shame about, one's identity continues to inform the discourse about valorizing Indigenous languages in São Gabriel. The elevation of Indigenous languages to official status, making them formally equal to Portuguese, is a means of symbolically responding to these disparagements and to the continued internalization of shame.

This framing of the motivation for the official language legislation emphasizes its role as a revitalization strategy targeting the public sphere. The creation of public domains for using Indigenous languages has been highlighted as an important element in cases where the ideological connection between the private, domestic sphere and minority identities has historically been a part of the marginalization process (Dorian 1987; Eisenlohr 2004). In creating these contexts for use, however, an additional process of creating and establishing an Indigenous public space also occurs. Despite the prevalence of Indigenous people in São Gabriel, public environments continue to function as "White public space" (Hill 1998; Page and Thomas 1994). In this case, a more accurate term would probably be "non-Indigenous public space," as the difference between Afro-descended and European-descended Brazilians is remarkable only in its insignificance. The racialized "Other" in this context is Indigenous, in contrast to other parts of Brazil, where the Indigenous population has been almost completely invisible and the legacy of black slavery is the predominant reference point with regard to continued inequality (Warren 2001). Even though they are a demographic majority, then, Indigenous people must confront the default assumption that the public space is non-Indigenous. A principal way in which the language policy is discursively invoked is as a counter to this image – that is to say, it offers speakers permission to use their languages outside the home by defining them as legally belonging to that space. Indigenous people can regularly be heard speaking their languages to one another in the market, in the workplace, or in encounters on the street – something I was often told would have been impossible ten or fifteen years ago.

On the other hand, though they may have become more audible, Indigenous languages remain essentially invisible in the urban public sphere. Given that the language policy mandates that all signage and public written information (such as menus and price lists) should include all of the official languages, the relative *absence* of Indigenous language texts on the landscape is striking. The sign on the gymnasium referenced at the beginning of this chapter illustrates how the marginalization of Indigenous languages is accomplished not just through the selection of language but also through the visual resources available in the physical dimension of textual representation. The size and positioning of each of the languages marks the first indication of a hierarchy among two different types of languages on the sign (Jaworski and Thurlow 2010; Coupland 2012). The binary is based not on official status but rather on a clear distinction and differentiated priority between local, Indigenous languages and national/global, European languages. The text in Portuguese (the national language) is larger than for any of the official Indigenous languages; indeed, it is English and Spanish – which have no legislated presence in the area (and in the case of English, no locally based function or community of speakers) – that are placed on par with Portuguese through size and position.

In addition to the unequal distribution of semiotic space offered to the Indigenous languages, however, a further ideological stance is established on this sign through the bracketed labelling of the text in each of the Indigenous languages. This addition signals the assumption that the readers are unfamiliar with these languages, to the point that they would not necessarily even recognize the language itself, let alone be able to understand the content of the message that is written there. The languages are placed alongside pictures of local fruits and the names of local dances and grouped together with the announcement that "This is part of our cultural identity." These markers serve to exoticize the city through its Indigeneity, to establish the presence of Indigenous peoples and languages as quaint attractions for the visitor's observation and consumption. The relationship between the available Indigenous-language signage and the idea of an Indigenous public is also clear from the fact that, without exception, the text I saw in these languages was limited to this word/phrase meaning "welcome" – regardless of whether the signs were created "from above" or "from below." While expressing the idea that Indigenous languages and their speakers have a place in this environment, then, they did not go beyond that in any effort to communicate content to them in their own languages.

On several occasions during my field visits, the three co-official Indigenous languages were used by speakers making public addresses. These uses were explicitly politicized by the speakers, who conceptualized them as ways of making a claim about the right of Indigenous people and Indigenous ways to occupy the public space – invoking what Duranti (2006: 455) calls "ego-affirming agency" not only for themselves as speakers but also for their languages. The reduction of shame discussed above helps frame the more casual uses of Indigenous languages in public spaces. These may more accurately be described as semi-private interactions, for they take place among relatives and acquaintances in direct conversations. By contrast, the use of official Indigenous languages in formal addresses constitutes an effort to perform political work that is specifically related to the existence of the official language policy.

Two different types of formal speeches were used Indigenous languages in my observations. The first was exemplified by the three students at the UEA event who initiated the discussion about the language policy with brief comments in each of the official languages, and consisted of short, prepared, formalized greetings in one or more Indigenous languages by event organizers or invited speakers. The second type was much more rare and involved the delivery of a full address in one of the three official Indigenous languages. Patterns within each of these uses, and responses to them, help illustrate the challenges involved in Indigenizing the public space within the urban area.

The first category of use falls into the category of ritualized speech that is not designed to communicate referential content, but that uses the marked language to contest the default form of non-Indigeneity (for an additional example of this type of pattern, see Ahlers [2006]). Prominent political, social, and religious leaders within the community, including non-Indigenous individuals, often make use of this strategy as a means of affirming their predominantly Indigenous audience. The current Catholic bishop of the diocese, Dom Edson Damian, himself originally from the south of Brazil, has made this practice of symbolic valorization a priority since his arrival in the area in 2009, incorporating each of the three official Indigenous languages into the opening and closing of every public address, including masses that he leads. In each case, he opens with the word "welcome" in each language, following each one with a pause to allow small groups of speakers to offer the appropriate response, or, sometimes, for the entire audience to applaud. Because the Catholic population as a whole has an extremely strong respect for clergy, and given the wide variation in attitudes towards languages and Indigenous cultural practices that Church representatives have demonstrated, the bishop's actions are frequently lauded. Both the status of the speaker and the public spaces in which these greetings take place solidify the performative value of these acts.

By contrast, the opening greetings by the Indigenous students at the UEA events were positively received but did not receive the same amount of praise. Because the event was *about* the co-officialization of these languages, the fact that they were used in a primarily symbolic manner, and remained distinctly secondary to the default communicative language of Portuguese, is itself noteworthy. Max Menezes called attention to this fact in his own address, suggesting that ten years into a regime in which these three languages have official status, every public address in Portuguese should be translated into Nheengatú, Tukano, and Baniwa. This type of speech, in which an Indigenous language is used to deliver content to the audience, is relatively rare – during my fieldwork I heard, in total, fewer than ten examples, most of these at gatherings where almost all of those in attendance were Indigenous (events held by *bairro* organizations, for example, farther from the city centre). These actions assert a stronger claim for an Indigenous public space than the use of more purely performative greetings. While those expressions make a claim for the validation of Indigeneity in public, these communicative uses of Indigenous languages centre on an Indigenous audience. The difference between the two acts marks the difference between *Indigeneity in public* and an *Indigenous public space*. While the former has been generally accepted around the city, the latter remains a contested goal among Indigenous actors.

I observed only three instances of addresses made in Indigenous languages in environments that were explicitly coded as non-Indigenous and in situations where the audience included a mixture of Indigenous and non-Indigenous people. One of these occurred when the deputy mayor addressed town council using his native language (Baniwa), followed by Portuguese; the other two took place during political assemblies. These communicative uses were, of course, also political acts, and in all cases, they were discursively framed as such. During an Indigenous education assembly in May 2012, for example, Juscelino, a Nheengatú-speaking teacher from a community a few hours' boat ride from São Gabriel, was one of several speakers discussing the state of Indigenous education and present challenges faced in different parts of the region, and the only one to use an Indigenous language to deliver remarks. He opened with an apology in Portuguese to those who would not be able to understand, then stated that he would be presenting his comments "in my language, because it is now co-official and it is my right." The rarity of this decision was such that several people subsequently highlighted it in conversations both immediately after the event and a few months later, praising Juscelino for this act and claiming it as a moment of victory for proponents of Indigenous languages in the face of political apathy.

In all of the cases when such public addresses were given using Indigenous languages, the speeches were followed with a Portuguese translation by the speaker, or, as occurred following Juscelino's remarks, by a hastily procured summation by another speaker. Luiz Brazão, the Nheengatú-speaking FOIRN director who stepped up to translate Juscelino's fifteen-minute comments, prefaced his recollection of the content by stating that he wanted to reassure the audience that Juscelino had not been speaking ill of them. This point references a common technique used to discourage the use of Indigenous languages and to reinforce the default status of Portuguese; I often heard people switch a conversation into Portuguese after being teasingly castigated about saying bad things about others who might not understand their Indigenous language. The default to Portuguese and the distrust of Indigenous languages constitute barriers to the creation of an Indigenous public space, though they might allow for a much looser, much less threatening practice of Indigeneity in public.

The complex semiotics of using Indigenous languages in public must also take into account the degree to which they can be softened and made more palatable to the dominant social order. During an interview (27 July 2012), Max Menezes – one of the most consistent and dedicated advocates of Indigenous languages in São Gabriel – described his ideal view of Indigenous language use in public contexts:

MAX: Not to be afraid, we shouldn't be afraid to speak our language.
This policy has to be put into practice. If not, if I'm the mayor, I'm here serving my own relatives, from *my own* region, from *my own* community, in Portuguese, what kind of example am I presenting? ... So I have to show – that I want to strengthen my language, so I'm the mayor, I'm speaking in my language. I'm making *speeches* in my language ... **if the majority is Indigenous. Of course there would have to be translations for the non-Indigenous people**.
ME: **And for other Indigenous people, right?**
MAX: **And for other Indigenous people, right**, for the Baniwa, for other people who don't speak the language, that's right. Who don't speak Tukano. To have translations in the three languages.
[bold emphasis mine; italics represent emphasized words in the recorded interview]

While Max emphasizes the importance of speaking his language (Tukano) and increasing its public presence as a vital symbolic means of countering fear or shame, he is also careful to ensure that he does not advocate doing so in a way that would alienate or exclude non-Indigenous people. First, he notes that such public discourses should be limited to contexts in which Indigenous people are in the majority, and second, he emphasizes that "of course" translations would be offered for non-Indigenous people. Even though many of the non-Tukano-speaking Indigenous people would also require a translation, this population is mentioned only as an afterthought, following my interjection.

Patterns of translation and accommodation in these public addresses demonstrate that despite the claim of equality among languages embedded in the legislation, in practice, the relationship of colonial dominance and oppression remains a powerful orienting force for language use. Portuguese translation is required for Indigenous language use as soon as non-Indigenous people are present, but I did not encounter a single example of a Portuguese-language speech being accompanied by translation into any or all of the official Indigenous languages. While this type of translation was suggested as a long-term goal for implementation of the language policy, it never manifested itself in a public context, even when there were ample opportunities for speakers to enact this policy through their own actions.

Public Spaces, Revitalization, and Ideological Transformation

Thinking about Indigenous languages in public, and the creation of Indigenous public spaces as a revitalizationist strategy, raises several additional questions. What are the implications of this focal point of the language legislation for the goals of revitalization? To what extent has the official language legislation, and the focus placed on it in language revitalization discourses in São Gabriel, drawn attention away from private, familial domains in which intergenerational transmission might take place? And finally, to what extent is an ideological transformation involved in the invocation of legal terms and constructs, not the least of which is a public/private distinction?

The very idea of a divide between life within the home and life outside it, and the implication that there is a hierarchy between the two, is an ideological construction (Gal 2005). The traditional communitarian living space of the *malokas* of the Upper Rio Negro does not lend itself well to a straightforward divide between public and private; indeed, the Salesian missionaries who saw these structures as immoral *created* this distinction when they insisted on (private) single-family dwellings. Within the rural territories of the region, for example, the language legislation notes, with little clarification or expansion, that the dominant language of each community should be considered "official" within its own space. How to define the "dominant" language within the multilingual communities is never discussed; rather, that language is presumed to be obvious. Yet the idea of "officiality" in these cases does not reflect the type of formal legal arrangement that is normally associated with this concept. "Official" status in the rural communities is essentially created by the daily actions of the local population that embody a *de facto* language policy. By contrast, the legislation targeting the urban area much more explicitly invokes the notion of public life in its language planning endeavours, and becomes primarily a symbolic resource for increasing the use of these languages in higher-status environments.

As with the introduction of literacy practices and the production of written materials in Indigenous languages, the legislation's introduction of these languages in public, urban, and conceptually Western spaces serves as a transformational act that "civilizes" the languages and their speakers (Fleming 2009; Hugh-Jones 2010). The language itself is allowed to enter the public sphere, but at the same time, the very existence of a public/private distinction reflects a non-Indigenous conceptual frame that defines the conditions for allowing symbols of Indigeneity to enter. Again, it becomes a matter of bringing Indigeneity into the urban public space rather than of creating an Indigenous public akin to the rural communities.

In addition, to a large extent, revitalization in São Gabriel has become synonymous with the application of the official language policy and with other types of "valorization" efforts. The success of this revitalization strategy is further complicated because the process of valorizing Indigeneity and Indigenous practices does not take place along a linear trajectory. Indigenous leaders and their academic supporters emphasize the value of Indigenous languages not as communicative codes but rather as part of the essence of traditional Indigenous cultures, an essence that must be preserved; as a consequence, those languages come to be seen as performative of a social and political position that many Indigenous people – especially urban youth – do not want to accept in its entirety (Fleming 2010: 175–6). Arguing for language use as a means of countering shame through the performance of symbolic "Indigeneity" ultimately grounds the policy in an ideology that discourages everyday use. Several of the most passionate language activists in the city observe that, among their friends and neighbours, while shame has diminished and self-identification and pride have become common, real work to strengthen Indigenous practices and languages, including through the use of their languages, has not followed from these steps. As Denivaldo Cruz da Silva, former director of FOIRN's education department, put it:

> I think it's like ... yes it's changed, on the question of not being ashamed, right. But like, to really take things on, this hasn't changed. No one takes it on ... They don't have pride. They leave things as they are, you know. If you ask someone, are you Indigenous? – I am. But they don't do much beyond that. [interview, 21 July 2012]

Many of these language activists further scrutinize the idea of claiming Indigenous identity without embracing additional practices as potentially emerging from a desire to use the symbolic capital of Indigeneity for selfish personal gain (e.g., consideration for university admission under the affirmative action quota system) without contributing to the strength of the community that fought to have that identity revalued.

In addition, the continued attention that Indigenous political leaders draw to the idea of "shame" as a barrier to language use may not be accurate in identifying the nature of the current pressures to shift towards Portuguese in the urban area. Indigenous youth in particular were far less inclined to express a sense of shame about being Indigenous or about using Indigenous languages than they were to lament that they were unable to speak them better. Among youth, Indigenous identity was consistently claimed as a point of pride. In participating in several groups that were trying to improve the lives of young people in the city – for example, through the formation of theatre and dance clubs, or church-based youth groups – I saw, among urban Indigenous people who had been raised in an era of valorization and who had never experienced direct prohibition of their languages or cultural practices, an awareness that such shame existed among their parents, but little personal emotional connection to that concept. At the very least, the idea of shame no longer manifests itself in the lives of young people in the way that it did among their parents who are now the leaders of the Indigenous advocacy movement. The problem is that many of these young people are not speakers of the languages, and if they are, they are conscious that their friends are not, and they are unable to use

Indigenous languages for regular conversation with peers. While valorization and shame reduction have been effective in increasing the use of Indigenous languages, their effectiveness for revitalization is limited both by the additional performative baggage that is connected to these and by their inherent inability to produce new *learners* of the languages.

The City as Transformational Space

Making an Indigenous public space involves both welcoming expressions of individual Indigenous identity and establishing a vision of the city as an Indigenous one. The mural on the gymnasium pictured above (Figure 3.1), for example, not only used Indigenous languages to welcome visitors but also invoked the municipal government's frequent assertion that São Gabriel is "the most Indigenous city in Brazil." At the most basic level, this assertion is certainly true, given the extraordinarily high proportion of Indigenous people living in the urban space in contrast to their minimal numbers in the rest of the country. At the same time, the expression invokes questions about its deeper meaning: What does it mean for a city to be Indigenous? And is the mere presence of Indigenous people sufficient to make it so? In many ways, the symbolic practices surrounding the implementation of the language policy help constitute it primarily as a transitional space between the Indigenous world and the world outside – a binary distinction that is frequently invoked, as people are either from the Rio Negro region, or from elsewhere (*da região* or *de fora*). São Gabriel becomes a space that works to transform its inhabitants from members of Indigenous communities into members, first and foremost, of the national Brazilian community (this transformation, of course, never happens in the opposite direction). To be sure, for individuals, these identities are complicated, but in relation to the space itself, a transformational effect remains present. The language policy, both in its paper form and in its limited practical implementation, embodies this pattern.

In the view of many supporters and originators of the idea of officialization, the policy was specifically intended to support Indigenous languages in the urban area. In the constitution, protections for the right to use, teach, and preserve Indigenous languages and cultural practices already exist for residents of the rural territories. Those protections are applied, however, to *territories* rather than *persons* – a distinction that calls into question the meaning and implications of group rights (Réaume and Pinto 2012). An additional complicating point arises from the fact that these constitutional rights state simply that Indigenous communities have the right, for example, to educate children using "their own language," without regard for the possibility of multilingualism and with the assumption that it is a straightforward matter to define the community's language in these spaces. Ethnolinguistic identity in the Rio Negro, particularly among the exogamous Tukanoan groups, includes a distinctly spatialized dynamic, for patrilocal residence means that it is only the women of the community who belong to other linguistic groups, and the public use of the patrilect is emphasized not only as a way of articulating the identity of the resulting children, but also as a way of laying symbolic claim to the community space for members of that language group. That is to say, using the patrilect as the language of public communication works to ontologically connect the language with that place (Chernela 2003; Lasmar 2009). The origin myths of the Tukanoan peoples emphasize how each ethnolinguistic group came to occupy certain territories along the river as they emerged from the body of the anaconda-canoe. The knowledge of sacred places is especially vital cultural and linguistic information – something that is highlighted in conversations about what is being lost as a result of language shift (FOIRN/ISA 2006; Andrello 2010).

In the urban area, no Indigenous language has a clear claim to authoritative ownership of the space. In this context, the historical establishment of São Gabriel as the locus of settlement for migrants from other parts of Brazil (including missionaries, military personnel, and miners) has led to its conceptualization within the system of linguistic territoriality as belonging to the Portuguese language. In part, this is the result of the settlement story, and in part, this is a reversal of the conscious dynamic of using the patrilect to mark the space – as Portuguese became the default language of communication and the only possible language of public communication, these usages unconsciously worked to plant the flag of that language within the city. The official language legislation and the concomitant increase in the public use of Indigenous languages become necessary means of symbolically (re)claiming the urban area as part of the Indigenous territory.

At the same time, a dichotomous conceptualization of rural versus urban, which recursively maps onto Indigenous versus non-Indigenous, is central to understanding the challenge of urban language revitalization. At a very basic level, the existence of such a dichotomy serves to reinforce a position for Portuguese that is fundamentally different from that of any one of the Indigenous languages, which are grouped together as an undifferentiated mass that is contrasted most frequently against the single national language. This means that Indigenous competes with non-Indigenous overall in the central struggle for recognition, but that each Indigenous language must also compete with the other twenty in the subsequent struggle for revitalization. Furthermore, these indexical associations with rurality and tradition situate the Indigenous language as static in space and time, whereas Portuguese offers mobility into the rest of Brazil, and beyond that, Spanish and English offer movement into the future and around the world.

To a significant degree, the motivation for learning Indigenous languages continues to be expressed in terms of the potential for youth to live traditional Indigenous lifestyles and to be comfortable in the rural area. Donato Vargas, director of the municipal department of Indigenous education, spoke about the backlash that his proposals for Indigenous schools in the urban area have faced:

> At the beginning, just because it had the word "Indigenous," it was a crazy fight that we had to win. Youth, students, father, mother – "Geez, Donato, we're in the 2000s, you want to take the peoples *backwards*?" "How's that, what?" "*You want to take [us] back, go back to being Indian?*" No, man. That's not what we want. *On the contrary, we want to show them that we are peoples too. We have our language, our culture, all of that.* [interview, 20 June 2012]

Donato's comments emphasize not only the conceptualization of social mobility mapped onto non-Indigeneity (and restrictedness mapped onto Indigeneity), but also the ways in which the use of Indigenous languages in these modern spaces – educational centres, specifically those in the city – is tied to an assertion not of the value of traditional Indigenous ways, but of the possibility of civilizing the Indigenous, because they "are peoples too." The issue of mobility, both social and geographic, constitutes a major part of the challenge facing Indigenous language revitalization advocates. Pedro Machado made note of this in his speech at the UEA, during which he emphasized that strengthening Indigenous languages has to take place at the local level, because that is the only place in which they are important:

> I won't say take them outside, because it's very clear, the world is a white world, the world outside. The most sought-out languages, you know which ones they are? English, Spanish. These are two languages that – if

you speak English, you can go anywhere. Spanish, you go. Portuguese
you go almost nowhere, it doesn't matter in any place.

The question of whether Indigenous languages can be strengthened
in the city of São Gabriel therefore centres on whether the boundaries of their utility can be extended to include the city or whether they
should remain in the rural territories. The concern here is not merely
about the languages, but also about the city, for the question of whether
or not Indigenous languages are being publicly used and affirmed by
public institutions shapes views about whether the city is "Indigenous"
or not. The pushback against strengthening the Indigenous language
legislation, from Indigenous and non-Indigenous actors alike, can be
seen, in part, in the same terms as individuals' reluctance to perform
symbols of Indigeneity despite their willingness to identify themselves
as Indigenous. That is to say, people may be open to affirming the value
of Indigenous cultures and practices and strongly support the idea of
improving the sustainability of rural communities, but the implications
of constituting an Indigenous city are less easily accepted and adopted.

As the debate takes place around how much Indigenous languages
belong in the city – and how much the city belongs to Indigeneity –
a sense emerges that São Gabriel exists as a halfway point between
these two extremes (Indigenous and not). It is through this debate that
it becomes a transitional space between rural Indigeneity and non-
Indigenous Brazilian lifestyles, a place that provides access to both
sides of this equation. Youth residing in the urban area, in particular,
are encouraged to embody this transition, as various actors express the
desire for them to understand their Indigenous cultures and the legacy
that belongs most primarily to their parents and ancestors. This understanding and awareness is intended to help them move through a non-
Indigenous world; so the Indigenous world with which it is associated,
then, will accompany them but will never really be theirs.

Differentiating the Three: Creating an Indigenous Linguistic Hierarchy

In the deterritorialized, diasporic urban space, the officialization of
three representative languages acts as part of the reification of a political Indigenous identity rather than an ethnolinguistic one. Proponents
of the official language legislation draw attention to the traditional
significance of language for ethnic identity in arguing for the need

to protect these languages, but their political and performative acts ultimately reveal ideologies that construct new types of language/identity relationships. In the urban centre, Indigenous identity is immediately recognizable as different. The official language policy works to counter the dominant perception that the city – and indexically, modernity and urbanity in general – are not Indigenous, but it does so by transforming the nature of Indigeneity more than by questioning the terms of modernity. This effort serves both to connect the urban space to the Indigenous communities and to suggest that Indigenous languages can be removed from their traditional, localized contexts of use.

The politicization of the Indigenous languages, and the movement towards detaching them from ethnolinguistic identity, is exemplified in the fact that three Indigenous languages were chosen not merely for pragmatic purposes but also as "representatives" of the body of Indigenous languages as a whole. As noted above, FOIRN's stance regarding the impact of the initial legislation argues that it has served to valorize and destigmatize *all* Indigenous languages by recognizing these three. The only non-Indigenous speaker at the UEA event, Catarino, the town council representative, was the one who called attention to the potential negative implications of the official language legislation for languages other than the three that were declared official:

> Is it possible that the co-officialization of the languages didn't accelerate the process of extinction of the others? It is possible that the distinction of three languages won't accelerate the extinction of others that won't likewise be so, ah, valorized? It's not that we shouldn't valorize the three languages, in my view, we should valorize all the languages, all the *etnias*, all of the twenty-two *etnias*, because they are all important in the municipality.

By contrast, Edilson Melgueiro, who focused his concern on the possibility of language loss, continually emphasized that he was limiting his comments to consideration of what was happening with the three languages that had been declared official, and how several studies had demonstrated the limited knowledge of these languages among urban youth (Sarges 2013). Max Menezes mentioned the other languages to say that they, too, were actually included in this policy, for they were protected in their territories, and he worked to counter the discourse of diversity as a problem:

We have to start talking about the question of the languages, the three co-official languages – the school here, Colêgio São Gabriel, says – it's a problem. It's *a lot of languages*. This is only going to cause problems. I say, look people – this is a richness. This is not a problem, this is a richness. We have to have *pride* at living in a region that has twenty-three Indigenous peoples, each people with their languages, a language, with their customs, their tradition – and why not valorize it, right? [emphasis based on original speech]

Here, Max was emphasizing the total number of languages spoken and articulating this as a resource, but he was speaking only about the challenge of incorporating even the three official languages into the educational sector. Diversity is important, he was saying, but it can be represented symbolically through the three largest languages so as to be more economically and pragmatically realistic.

The ideological debate being raised in these statements is extremely contentious. Is it more important to work on those languages that are at greatest risk of disappearing? (Catarino drew attention in his speech to his experience in the Warekena community of Nazaré, where most residents now speak Nheengatú and only the eldest speak the severely endangered Warekena language.) Or would it be better to focus on those that are already strong in order to reinforce unity among Indigenous people? This disparity involves not just the question of what it means to protect and promote languages, but also a discussion about what form Indigenous identity should take in the contemporary Brazilian state, especially in urban areas. The official language legislation demonstrates a commitment to a pan-Indigenous identity – which is significant mainly as a political construction – over and above individualized ethnolinguistic identities that are associated with cultural practices, beliefs, and stories. That is not to say that this pan-Indigenous, urbanized Indigenous identity should be taken as "inauthentic," but rather to point out the terms of debate that are taking place in this contested territory. Language revitalization in particular draws out the conflict between these two ideological positions held by Indigenous actors, as the question of whether expressions of pan-Indigenous identity can appropriately meet the needs of the entire population comes to the fore in the multilingual Rio Negro. Advocates argue that the legal elevation of Tukano, Nheengatú, and Baniwa serves to valorize *all* of the languages of the region; yet some speakers of non-official Indigenous languages resent the establishment of a legalized symbolic hierarchy of linguistic codes.

To be sure, sociolinguistic power differences existed long before the law, both as a result of Indigenous social structures and language ideologies and due to the actions and ideological influence of colonizers and missionaries. But given the depth of linguistic diversity in the region, and the historical importance of the link between language and identity in the exogamous social system, the choice of these three cannot be seen as semiotically neutral. The co-officialization of these three languages, alongside the claim that this law represents all Indigenous peoples of the area, works to entextualize the ideological position that privileges pan-Indigenous identity rather than ethnolinguistic affiliation; in this way, it simultaneously erases the relevance of the distinct identities of speakers of non-official languages, including those from language families and cultural groups like the Yanomami and Nadahup, whose practices are radically different from those of the three politically dominant cultural groups (Baré, Tukanoan, and Arawakan).

The "Real" Language Policy

This chapter has introduced the ways in which the involvement of the state – in this case, at the municipal level – in the planning and governance of Indigenous languages is implicated in the politics of being Indigenous in the urban area of São Gabriel and in the attempt to construct an urban Indigenous space. Analysing the different ways in which the 2001 legislation granting official status to three Indigenous languages in the region is understood and employed by different actors reveals the ideological significance of these actions as well as the limitations of such legislation as a strategy for language revitalization. This legislation cannot be easily classified as either "top-down" or "bottom-up," since its origins and justifications, and the ongoing attempts to implement its tenets, are all being simultaneously engaged by the state and by grassroots actors. Furthermore, ideologies underlying both the legislation itself and the ways in which it has since been seen and taken up by various actors provide insight into how the meaning of Indigenous identity is transformed by being established within the urban area, as well as into the contested idea that it is possible not just to bring Indigenous practices into the city, but to create an Indigenous city. The debate about the city's identity is embedded in the debate about the language policy and the limited ways in which it has been implemented. Discussing the official language legislation as being an on-paper – in other words, unreal – phenomenon is a way of drawing a contrast not only between the ideal and the actual reality of political support for Indigenous languages, but also between the legislated world of the urban centre and the authentic, material reality of the rural territories. Indigenous languages are being used in productive ways by both state agents and grassroots Indigenous organizations to influence the formation and reformation of identities, communities, and the state itself.

The official language legislation is one of the few examples of direct efforts to engage with the role of Indigeneity in the urban area, and the limited nature of its implementation – even ten years after the fact, as was highlighted in the commemorative event that provides the backdrop for this analysis – points towards the depth of the challenge facing language revitalization advocates. This challenge is even more visible with respect to attempts to reform the context of education in the city so that it more effectively incorporates Indigenous languages and cultural practices within urban students' schooling. These efforts form the basis for the discussion in next two chapters.

4 Education in the City: Defining Urban Indigeneity

During Indigenous Peoples' Week, in April 2012, I made a point of spending most of my time observing special events and activities being prepared in a few of the city's schools. The photos provided in this book were taken at the Colêgio São Gabriel (CSG), the oldest and largest school in the city (see Table 4.1 for a list of the city's schools at each grade level). The events held during this annual week of recognition were the ones that most of the principals and pedagogical coordinators from each school pointed to in highlighting how Indigenous cultures featured in schooling. These events included classroom-based activities (such as inviting a knowledgeable elder to tell students about Indigenous cultural practices), student research projects, and evening fairs at which students performed dances and songs, made and sold Indigenous crafts and local foods, and displayed the results of their research for parents and community members. At CSG, the most elaborate of the events involved a recounting of the arrival of the anaconda-canoe from whose body the original Tukanoan ancestors emerged, acted out by several classes' worth of young students.

Returning to the anecdote presented at the beginning of this book, in which a small child was described as "playing Indian," I want to consider how these ideas about Indigenous performances, as well as the constitution of public spaces and the creation of future publics, are manifested in schools, a central site of social (re)production. The type of space that is created in schools for Indigenous practices – and this includes the form that Indigeneity takes within them – shows that for the most part, children are being socialized to focus on cultural practices as performance and play rather than as parts of the more serious

Table 4.1. List of schools in the City of São Gabriel

School name	Grade levels	Funding source
Thiago Montalvo	Pre-1 (junior Kindergarten) to grade 2k	Municipal
Turma da Monica	18 months–grade 2	Private
Escola Adventista	Elementary and middle school (grades 1–9)	Private
Colêgio São Gabriel	Elementary, middle, high school (grades 1–9, years 1–3)	State
Dom Miguel Alagna	Elementary and middle school (grade 3–9)	Municipal
Dom Bosco	Middle school (grades 5–9)	State
Dom João Marchesi	Middle school (grade 5–9), high school (years 1–3)	State
Irmã Ines Penha	High school (years 1–3)	State
Sagrada Família	High school (years 1–3)	State
Instituto Federal do Amazonas (IFAM)	High school (years 1–3), college level vocational/technical training	Federal

Figure 4.1. Students rehearsing their re-enactment of the "anaconda canoe" origin story during Indigenous Peoples' Week.

Figure 4.2. Students rehearsing a dance performance for Indigenous Peoples' Week.

business of academics. This is visible not only in the limited allotment of curricular time for such information but also in the nature of the events (fairs and performances) and in the attitude of the students towards what they are doing and learning. For example, one young Baré man used the dyes provided to paint the English expression "Red Hot" on his torso. When I asked him what he had been taught about the meaning of body painting when he did this, he simply said, "I don't know, really – just that it's something that Indians do."

This performative ideology informs the background against which Indigenous language classes are discussed and, in limited cases, provided by the city's schools. In most of the schools there is no Indigenous language component at all: Indigenous languages appear only in the context of special projects, such as performances for Indigenous Peoples' Week or for visiting guests; or the teachers support the learning of Indigenous songs in music classes; or homemade "welcome" signs like the ones discussed in the previous chapter are hung on walls (pictured below, inside the main entrance of CSG). The only exception is that in the two municipally funded elementary schools, Nheengatú is taught as a second language until the fifth grade (5ª série). In each of these schools, two teachers work as Nheengatú language instructors (one in the morning and one in the afternoon) and rotate through the classrooms and grade levels. Each class receives one hour per week of instruction in Nheengatú. After the fifth grade, and in all of the other institutions (be they private, state, or federally funded), English or Spanish classes fulfil students' second-language learning requirements. Students are assigned to elementary schools based primarily on neighbourhood of residence; if a school becomes full, students submit their names to the municipal and state departments of education, which work to find a vacancy for them in another school. Parents cannot, then, seek to send their children to the municipal schools because they are interested in the opportunity to learn Nheengatú (or, alternatively, send them elsewhere in search of other types of educational programming). The limited numbers of students who take these classes do so essentially by luck of the draw.

This chapter examines language-in-education policies and practices to help readers understand both the language policy and the overall trajectory of revitalization work in São Gabriel. From both a symbolic perspective and a pragmatic one, the schools are central to language policy and planning efforts, including revitalization (McCarty 2011; Hornberger 2008). This significance remains even though language learning experts have long recognized that, with the exception of immersion models, especially for the youngest children, the classroom is far from an ideal site for language learning. Education is undeniably a powerful tool for shaping relationships among social groups, in both discriminatory and liberating ways, and language and linguistically defined identities are centrally involved in these processes. In discussions about the co-officialization policy (see the previous chapter), residents of São Gabriel almost always pointed out that incorporating the official languages into schools was one of the most important means of making this policy matter in reality. Broadly speaking, the significance of schools for language revitalization efforts is not simply a matter of their role in teaching the languages themselves. Rather, schools are quintessential public institutions: they not only shape the population and set the terms of appropriate adult membership in the community

Figure 4.3. Handmade welcome sign posted immediately inside the entrance of the Colêgio São Gabriel, the largest school in the city.

but also embody and represent the identity of the space in which they are embedded.

As I discussed in the introduction to this book, Indigenous people in the Rio Negro have come to view education as a liberatory force; they recognize the role it has played in their subordination as well as the need to control it in order to combat oppression (Luciano 2012). "Differentiated education," then, is seen as necessary if Indigenous peoples are to transmit their own forms of knowledge to their children and ensure that they have access to the kinds of opportunities associated with formal education. Over the past decade, several such schools have been established throughout the rural territories in the municipality of São Gabriel (Cabalzar 2012). In the urban area, however, schools rely almost exclusively on the mainstream Brazilian curriculum to define their pedagogical goals. Literacy in Portuguese remains the most important language-related goal of these schools.

There is little illusion among educators or parents that the very small amount of language instruction (where it is present at all) is sufficient for language learning, but producing competent speakers of the language is far from the only, or even the primary, purpose of these classes. Their meaning, as I discuss in greater detail below, relates primarily to the symbolic importance of schools as a public site where a future public community is being produced. The role of schools in the urban area, furthermore, is not simply to educate students – it is also to represent "the most Indigenous city in Brazil" to internal and external observers. Educational professionals – including teachers, administrators, and policy-makers – express multiple overlapping goals that draw, at different times and in different ways, on both micro- and macro-level social practices, on intentions that are situated within both local and supra-local (national, regional, global) processes.

A look at the current state of Indigenous language teaching and use in the city's classrooms, and at discourses about the ideal role these languages should play in urban education, makes apparent several different conflicts. Debates about Indigenous languages and about municipal language policy in classroom settings are rooted in much more profound differences in visions for the future of the city of São Gabriel, especially that of its Indigenous population. These practices and discourses arise at the intersection between state policies of multiculturalism, language revitalization projects, and the aspirations of individual Indigenous students. The predominance of Indigenous people in the schools, both as students and as teachers and administrators,

along with the general awareness of the political significance of education, means that symbols of Indigeneity, including languages, are being
deployed in intentional and productive ways that extend beyond their
curricular function.

Both political activism and academic analyses of Indigenous peoples'
education in Brazil have focused mainly on the creation of differentiated or alternative models of schooling (Weigel 2003; Cabalzar 2012;
Akkari 2012) rather than on the ways in which Indigenous students and
teachers experience "mainstream" Brazilian educational institutions, in
which many of them continue to study, teach, and act as administrators. A key component of today's governmental paradigm has been
the establishment of formal educational systems as the primary if not
exclusive means for attaining social mobility; anthropologists of education point to the degree to which this assumption characterizes both
analytical and lay perspectives about the value of school-based education (Wortham 2008; Froerer and Portisch 2012). In São Gabriel, this
assumption, while occasionally contested, strongly informs the use of
Indigenous languages and the construction of Indigeneity within the
classroom, and extends to views not only on how to create mobility for
students but also on how to develop the city. In other words, education
is being used to raise both students and the Indigenous identity of the
people and of the city into a higher social position. Symbols of Indigeneity – and this includes the three Indigenous languages now officially
recognized in São Gabriel – are drawn into formal educational environments in ways that demonstrate the modernity and "civilization" of the
cultures they represent. Rendering languages literate and developing
ways of using them in schools are processes that serve to "domesticate"
these otherwise uncontrolled and challenging languages (Perley 2011).
These policies and practices shape what it means for individuals to be
Indigenous in an urban context as well as what it means for São Gabriel
to be an "Indigenous city." The co-officialization law works, in some
ways, to create an Indigenous public space; in particular, the work to
bring Indigeneity into schools helps illustrate transformations in the
category of Indigeneity as a public identity.

Two themes serve as the starting points for analysing these processes –
the actual use of Indigenous languages within the classroom, and the
trajectory of hoped-for reforms to existing policy. Within these, I consider the limited overall presence that Indigenous languages and cultures have in the city's schools, the motivations for and implications of
choosing Nheengatú for this inclusion, and the pedagogical practices

surrounding its teaching. Taken together, these elements reveal underlying ideological challenges that must be addressed if language revitalization efforts in the city are to move forward.

Education in São Gabriel: Overview and
Political/Ideological Context

Structured education, regardless of the form it has taken and the specific
assimilationist practices that have been employed within it, constitutes
one of the most significant lifestyle changes imposed on Indigenous
peoples since the arrival of Europeans in the region. Even more than
experiences of language prohibition, the individuals I interviewed
talked about their early reactions to schooling in terms of the trauma of
suddenly having to follow a rigidly defined schedule, in contrast to the
freedom they had previously enjoyed. Education, and the introduction
of formal structures, were often contrasted with freedom. Although a
necessity within the capitalist economic system that now defines Indigenous as much as non-Indigenous Brazilians, education is accompanied by a compromise – one that Indigenous people who remember
the alternatives continue to lament, emotionally if not pragmatically.
The reorienting power of education comes not just from the content
of the lessons but also from the establishment of a new relationship to
time and place, a new way of defining transitional points in life (from
childhood to adulthood), and a new understanding of family, authority,
and nature.

The differentiated schools of the rural territories incorporate cultural
distinctiveness and Indigenous languages into these formal structures.
In the rural territories, Indigenous people continue to push back against
and even reject programs like Bolsa Família, which is designed to keep
low-income children throughout the country in school longer, when
they would otherwise be required to contribute to household income.
Nonetheless, Indigenous parents regularly pull their children out of
school during hunting or fishing cycles, not necessarily because of economic need but because these practices are, to them, vital to raising an
Indigenous child to adulthood. The impact that education has had on
cultural practices like these – including the imposition of government-
based rather than seasonal calendars, and the insistence on buildings
and classrooms as places of learning – is immeasurable. But at the same
time, the Indigenous people of the Rio Negro have shown a willingness
to make enormous sacrifices in pursuit of education, recognizing that

any possibility of retaining autonomy and self-sufficiency within the neoliberal state will depend upon it. The rural exodus has continued not only because of forces pushing people out of their communities but also – and perhaps primarily – because of the pull of educational opportunities in the city.

Educational professionals in the urban area face some unique challenges. The municipal and state departments of education (respectively, the Secretaria Municipal de Educação e Cultura, or SEMEC, and the Secretaria de Estado de Educação, or SEDUC), which are situated in the city itself, are responsible for the operations not only of the several schools within the urban area, but also of those in the rural interior, where the concerns and demands are extremely basic. Buildings are inadequately maintained, appropriately qualified teachers are difficult to find, and delivery of pedagogical materials and nutritional meals (the *merenda escolar* funded by the National School Nutrition Program) to the remote areas is expensive and time-consuming. Because the number of students in each of these schools is extremely small – sometimes only four or five children in total, across multiple grade levels – the state and federal governments question whether it is worth the expense of keeping them open. The challenges of operating community-based, differentiated schools consume a significant proportion of the time and budget of educational administrators. Such concerns are not as present in urban schools, and to the extent to which the administrative and political focus is on rural areas, the issues these urban schools face are not given as much attention. As with many other aspects of life in São Gabriel, a primary challenge these schools face is their association with loss of knowledge about Indigenous languages and cultures.

The desire for differentiated educational opportunities for children in rural communities emerges from several aspirations, including the desire to maintain residence on traditional lands and to preserve cultural practices. However challenging formalized programs like Bolsa Família make it to have it both ways in terms of obtaining an education and engaging in Indigenous subsistence practices, the idea that Indigenous languages and cultures are undoubtedly stronger in the rural territories than in the city further motivates the desire to establish these rural schools. The promise that is held in schools relates to equalization – that Indigenous children and communities will be able to access to the same kinds of economic privileges that are enjoyed by non-Indigenous Brazilians. Luciano (2012), himself an Indigenous scholar from São Gabriel, points out that in the eyes of the Indigenous people of the

Upper Rio Negro, the primary value of differentiated education lies in its ability to strengthen the access they have to the benefits afforded by white society without necessarily requiring them to sacrifice those that come from their own cultures. In other words, the desire to participate fully in a capitalist economy, in the Brazilian state, and even in the global community, is not seen as separate from the desire to retain cultural practices.

Before the relatively recent establishment of a network of Indigenous schools throughout the region, São Gabriel was the final destination along a path of migration that many Indigenous people followed in order to pursue educational opportunities for themselves and their children (a smaller proportion of individuals have continued to Manaus or other parts of Brazil in search of still more opportunity). Within the urban area there are two municipally funded schools (one at the pre-school and one at the primary level) and five state-funded schools (at the middle school and secondary levels), as well as one federally funded school (the Instituto Federal de Amazonas [IFAM], which offers both secondary programs and post-secondary training). The only private educational institutions are the Seventh-day Adventist school, which is attended mainly by non-Indigenous members of that church, and the "Turma da Monica" pre-school for children aged one to six years.

As the grade levels go up, from elementary to middle to high school, there are more students and more schools serving them, because these higher levels of education are still largely unavailable in the interior. While the type of curriculum and the extent of Indigenous differentiation vary among the schools in different districts of the municipality, the strengthening of the education system has also meant that larger centres – especially Iauaratê – are able to offer all of these levels of education and thereby reduce the degree of displacement that families experience. Informal conversations with residents of the rural territories who were visiting family members or attending training courses suggested that the presence of a school is a central determinant of the likelihood that people will remain in a particular community. Among the upriver Kotiria, for example, the community of Caruru-cachoeira, which is home to the main Kotiria school, is thriving, and other communities that house poles of this school (such as Jutica) remain relatively strong, while Arara, the island of Japú, and Taína now have only a few houses remaining (Rocha 2012).

Except for IFAM and the two small private schools, all schools in the city were founded by the Catholic Church and reflect this in various ways: the physical infrastructure mirrors non-Indigenous architectural styles; many schools are named after former Church leaders; and Catholic iconography is prominent. The relatively poor funding, especially for municipal schools, is apparent in the infrastructure of many of them, but beyond that, the physical environment is much like that of schools in other parts of Brazil. Students and teachers wear T-shirts bearing the name of their school as uniforms, and upper-level classrooms are decorated with images of Brazilian authors such as Machado de Assis or Graciliano Ramos, while the classrooms for younger students display Portuguese literacy tools (the alphabet and pictures of words associated with each letter). In contrast to the rural schools, where the small population of students means that all grade levels are collapsed into one or two classrooms and taught jointly, the urban schools are large enough that each grade has at least one class, and usually more than one. These classes are relatively large, with thirty to fifty students each.

That is the physical, economic, and ideological background into which Indigenous languages and Indigeneity are being inserted. The following ethnographic discussion of language teaching – in terms of the pedagogical practices for teaching Nheengatú and in terms of the justifications for teaching that language, and how intensively – sheds additional light on the central questions of language revitalization and urban Indigeneity.

Language Use in the Schools

The specific details of how languages (in this case, Nheengatú) are being taught helps illustrate educators' understandings of how they relate to the mobility and social identity of the students. My observations included sitting in on several Nheengatú-language classes at the two schools in which they are offered, as well as informal conversations and formal interviews with several current and former teachers of the language.

The Escola Infantil Thiago Montalvo provides education to the youngest group of students in São Gabriel, from kindergarten (pre-1 and pre-2) up to grade 2. The school is located immediately behind the military hospital, and facilities are small and poor, even compared to the city's other schools. There is no outdoor play equipment for the children, most of the classroom air-conditioners are broken, and class sizes are quite large, with around forty small children in each one. The director reported that all of the students at this school are Indigenous, since any non-Indigenous children in this age group attend the private Turma da Monica pre-school. On the second day of classes among the oldest students in the school (ages six and seven), the Nheengatú language teacher started working on literacy skills with the children. She wrote a few words in Nheengatú – *kãwéra* (bone) and *igara* (canoe) – on the blackboard and handed out pictures that had been hand-drawn by a former language teacher and photocopied several times, such that the lines were faded and the images unclear. All interactions took place in Portuguese, and this pattern continued throughout the school year. As the students completed their work, they approached the teacher to show her, and she offered corrections – many of them had forgotten the diacritic markings – and returned to fix their work. The teacher emphasized to me that literacy should be the central concern of their language education. She was new to teaching the Nheengatú language and had been asked at the last minute to take on this subject after the previous teacher had been moved to a school in the rural interior of the municipality. Before that year, she had taught Portuguese, and she had received no special training in second-language pedagogy. She was not particularly interested in Indigenous language revitalization or Indigenous politics and was teaching the class only because she had been asked to do so. Although both she and her husband were speakers of Nheengatú, none of their three children (ages seven, ten, and fourteen) could speak the language, and only the oldest, who had spent time with his paternal grandmother before her death, could understand it.

The younger students in the school, at the pre-1 and pre-2 (junior and senior kindergarten) levels, did not begin their Nheengatú classes until the second week, after they had spent several days adjusting to the routine of being in the classroom. This group was taught by a more experienced teacher who was a passionate advocate for Indigenous language education and who had been active in the Indigenous movement. From the beginning, the energy level in her classroom was palpably higher. Even in the early days of their classes, the students had learned a few phrases in Nheengatú (e.g., "good afternoon," "what is your name," "my name is ..."). The teacher used these phrases repeatedly, translated them into Portuguese only when the students did not respond after several iterations in Nheengatú, and encouraged the children, and me, to use these Nheengatú phrases. She also incorporated a physical-action greeting song each day. Two or three students (out of several dozen) were clearly much more comfortable than the others, and the teacher explained to me after one of the first classes that she knew their parents to be good speakers of Nheengatú who probably used the language in the home. The main focus of the first lesson I observed, however, was on words with the vowel "a" – she would list words containing this vowel, write them on the board, and ask the students to repeat them after her. Although this teacher's methodology incorporated more oral language use, then, this strategy demonstrated a continued emphasis on creating literacy, especially among the youngest students.

These starting points for Indigenous-language classes among the youngest students were different in some ways but also remarkably similar. Neither of the teachers had received any kind of pedagogical training in second-language education; neither had curricular materials to work with; and both had been chosen to teach this particular class simply because of they spoke Nheengatú, not because they had either aptitude for or interest in teaching it. Indeed, speaking ability was not consistently required when hiring teachers for these classes – one former language teacher identified herself as having only passive knowledge of the language, and acknowledged that she had been given the position by a friend during a time of financial hardship. This teacher was committed to her work as an educator and had put in extensive hours of extra time to bring her own language skills up to the quality she felt was needed, but this had not been required or asked of her before she began teaching the class.

A more experienced and involved Nheengatú-language teacher, Paula, showed me the notebooks she had accumulated over the years and the lesson plans she had developed. These consisted largely of vocabulary lists as well as stories, texts, and songs. All of the material was handwritten in a spiral-bound notebook or photocopied from another teacher's lessons and glued into the notebook. Paula had developed and gathered these materials and guarded the notebook carefully, since it was the only place in which her hard work was stored. Teachers who cared about their classes, both as part of their work and as a way of supporting their languages and cultures, put in many extra hours of preparation and received very little support to do so. Paula and I discussed the importance of creating materials that could more easily be given to each new teacher, and also of making them look more professional. She was very aware that the poorly drawn handouts – at one point, I even saw a set of exercises that had been copied with a mimeograph machine used by a grade 5 class – were in sharp contrast to the colourful hardcover textbooks that students used in all their other subjects.

I talked to several teachers about the possibility of deeper changes to the way the Nheengatú classes were being approached. If immersion classes were not yet an option, models of second-language pedagogy that encouraged greater student participation and that focused on oral conversation skills rather than on literacy might improve outcomes. Denivaldo Cruz da Silva, former director of FOIRN's education department and a native speaker of Nheengatú, suggested that these teachers needed a grounding in Indigenous pedagogy and that they should therefore be drawn from those educated in the Magistério Indígena program, especially since these language classes were the only "Indigenous" component of the curriculum in the city. The teachers were generally less interested in having these conversations, since the idea of building in more training and more work to change their approach to teaching was not viable within their already packed schedules. Creating pedagogical materials was seen as a means of improving the quality of the classes and cutting back on the teachers' workloads.

The above combination of factors – overworked and poorly trained language teachers, inconsistent materials, and uncommitted administrators – has had a predictable impact on language learning in the schools. Older students, who had been taking Nheengatú classes for several years, told me they were unable to remember anything they had learned in these classes – in most cases, the only Nheengatú phrases they could recall were "good morning" and "good afternoon." Experienced teachers confirmed that they felt they were starting from scratch every year, regardless of how long their students had been studying the language. The language was being given some space within the curriculum, then, but not sufficient time to allow it to grow to occupy additional spaces, with additional new speakers.

Informal Language Use and Indigenizing Pedagogical Space

There are other ways besides formal teaching in which Indigenous languages become relevant in schools. The choice of language of communication among students, teachers, and administrators points to the role that Indigenous languages play in these spaces. The curricular use of an Indigenous language relates to the establishment of a sanctioned public presence for Indigeneity; more informal patterns of use based on interpersonal choices form part of the public sphere. As I discussed in the previous chapter, the use of Indigenous languages for conversation reflects a greater acceptance of "Indigeneity in public spaces" but not necessarily the idea of an "Indigenous public space." Schools, which are powerful sites for transforming young social actors, demonstrate this same pattern.

School-age students had been raised in a world shaped by the presence of a reasonably powerful Indigenous social movement, so especially for those in their mid- to late teens, their primary attitude towards their Indigenous status was one of pride rather than the shame articulated and experienced by their parents. My conversations and focus group interviews with young people, and the sociolinguistic survey implemented in high schools by Kristine Stenzel and Flora Cabalzar (unpublished), indicated that the ability to speak an Indigenous language was a particular manifestation of this pride; indeed, among those who had never learned, their sense of shame related to their poor linguistic abilities. But this self-declared pride did not necessarily translate into using the language in peer interactions. During my observations in schools, only a few times did I hear Indigenous languages being used as a medium of conversation between students – most often this was among the IFAM students who had recently arrived from rural communities and who were housed at the on-campus dormitories with other rural students. These choices made sense and seemed purely pragmatic, given that even if one's peers spoke an Indigenous language, it might not be the same one. At the same time, however, interviews and conversations revealed that in most cases, even when they were aware that a colleague spoke the same language, students tended to default to Portuguese. As an exception, when they wanted to talk about something without teachers or classmates understanding them, they used their shared Indigenous language, which then served as a private code, inaccessible to the general public. Using it in this way allowed for privacy in public spaces. It did not change the public space from non-Indigenous to Indigenous; rather, it changed the social context from public to private.

Among teachers, whose grasp of the politics of language use was generally higher than that of their students (because of their age and social position), informal use of Indigenous languages was somewhat more common. Portuguese was the default language of communication among larger groups of teachers and between students and teachers, but in the staff rooms of the city's various schools, I often heard smaller groups conversing in Tukano or Nheengatú. As with encounters at the market and in other public spaces, teachers saw these rooms as spaces for reinforcing the kinship connections afforded through language – they would speak their language, they said, with other teachers who were relatives (which, in the social system of the Rio Negro, simply meant they belonged to the same language group). Many teachers were speakers of at least one Indigenous language, and especially among those who had been educated in the Magistério Indígena program, were highly aware of the political significance of their languages. One teacher I interviewed, a Baré woman who spoke both Tukano and Nheengatú, indicated that she switched easily between these languages with various colleagues and suggested that this gave her an advantage in her work because she was able to form stronger relationships with speakers of both.

The biggest challenge to using the language among colleagues came from non-speakers (including speakers of other Indigenous languages, not just those who were Portuguese monolinguals), who expressed that they felt threatened because they could not understand what was being said. This was often framed as a joke, as for example when a Nheengatú-speaking principal laughingly told me that when she heard teachers speaking Tukano among themselves, she made sure to let them know she could understand the swear words and pick out her own name, so she would know if they were saying bad things about her. Claims of ignorance and threat are significant ways of policing the use of Indigenous languages in public spaces; this situates Portuguese as a neutral, intelligible code and emphasizes the alterity of the Indigenous. Such workplace interactions were not limited to schools; they encompassed many different types of workplaces where relations among Indigenous employees became opportunities to form private bonds by using a shared language in public. Seeing this dynamic at work within schools, where the professionals in question were highly aware of the politics of Indigenous language use and suppression, points to the pervasive limitations on the development of an Indigenous public sphere.

These limitations manifested themselves even more strongly when Indigenous language interactions between students and teachers were restricted. Only those teachers who were otherwise involved in the Indigenous political movement (as leaders or former leaders of organizations, for example) indicated that they would use Indigenous languages with students whom they knew to be speakers. When I asked these teachers about the ways they used Indigenous languages in their public lives, their responses indicated a different attitude towards students than towards peers and colleagues. The use of Indigenous languages with the latter was not seen as requiring justification or explanation – it was simply a natural extension of the ways one greeted familiar people (in particular, relatives), albeit with a slightly greater note of caution in terms of accommodating non-speakers owing to the workplace's social dynamics. With regard to students, however, Indigenous-language interactions were politicized in two ways. Among students from the urban area whom they knew to have at least passive familiarity with an Indigenous language they themselves could speak, they would use it to encourage the student to do so as well. Generally, however, they indicated that the students preferred to respond in Portuguese. Among rural students who were struggling to learn Portuguese, both the politically active teachers and some others indicated that they felt it was best to provide them with support using their native language (often Tukano). Such actions, however, were politicized in at least some cases, in that some school principals viewed it as potentially detrimental to the students' learning of Portuguese, and as requiring too much of the teachers' time that could be better spent supporting a larger group of students. Thus, depending on the degree of resistance and scrutiny they faced, some teachers were uncomfortable making this effort. Teacher/student interactions, which are in some ways pedagogical even if they occur outside the classroom, exemplify, much more than peer interactions within either group, the idea that speaking an Indigenous language is a political choice.

Language-in-Education Policy: Implementation and Justification

One question I often asked of various leaders and educators in São Gabriel was how it had come to pass that, of the three official Indigenous languages in the municipality, Nheengatú had been the only one chosen for use in the city's schools. I continued to ask this question of many different parties because it quickly became clear to me that when they recounted the background to that decision, there was no uniform recollection of the political and institutional logic that had informed it. Each person represented his or her explanation as authoritative and factual, yet there were substantial differences not only in points of focus but also in recollections of events. Furthermore, the interpretations involved, and the policy that operates in practice, do not necessarily align with the written records (such as the language policy documents themselves). These interpretations therefore become sources of insight into how language and Indigeneity are conceptualized in this context and how these perspectives may come to govern the implementatiu of policy even when they are not actually present in the legal texts.

The decision to offer classes in only one of the three official Indigenous languages came about primarily as a result of limited funding. In and of itself, this has been controversial. Some Indigenous people feel that it manifests a clear inequality among the languages – even the official ones – and (again emphasizing valorization rather than language learning as the primary goal of these classes) suggest that they would prefer to reduce the number of hours of each language to offer classes in all three. As noted earlier, the time spent on Nheengatú is already minimal (one hour per week per class), and clearly insufficient for language learning. For at least some advocates of language classes, however, the purpose of these classes is not primarily to increase the number of speakers of the language. While some Indigenous leaders believe it is extremely important for students to learn to speak their Indigenous languages, and feel that it is the responsibility of schools to teach them something in these languages, others either implicitly or explicitly suggest that the value of Indigenous-language classes in schools has nothing to do with teaching the language. For them, what matters is valorization. The teaching of an Indigenous language in the schools symbolically demonstrates to students and parents that these languages have a place in formal education and in public.

Currently, school administrators in São Gabriel lean heavily towards this latter perspective. For them, assessing the success of the classes is not simply a matter of inquiring whether students are learning to speak the language. So classes may be offered in only one of the region's many languages, but what really matters is the performative element – the valorization and promotion of Indigenous identities. But this approach has a categorizing effect: Indigenous students find themselves generalized, homogenized, and contrasted against non-Indigenous Brazilians, and this elides important distinctions among the many Indigenous cultures of the region. The language-in-education policy, then, goes even further than the official-language legislation in invoking a "representational" Indigenous identity and lending weight to the idea that politicized, rather than individualized, identity is most significant.

The idea that this representative language should be Nheengatú has been closely scrutinized. Tukano parents are particularly emphatic in contesting this choice: several of them have objected to their children learning Nheengatú rather than "their own" Indigenous language. Members of other Tukanoan language groups are less inclined to make this argument, for the implementation of Tukano as a *lingua franca* has meant that many of them have come to accept (sometimes wholeheartedly, other times grudgingly) the use of Tukano in lieu of their own languages. Within this shift, however, there is an awareness of the Tukanoan ideology that language does not simply mark one's identity; it *constructs* that identity, as discourses about language shift towards other Indigenous languages emphasize the identity-based implications of these changing uses. One teacher I spoke to, for example, was Tariana, but indicated that she spoke "as though I were Tukano." Among a group of Kotiria and Dessana from the mixed community of Jutica, many of the Dessana had adopted the use of Kotiria more regularly, which their in-laws teased meant they were "becoming Wanano (Kotiria)." Insofar as to speak a language is to be a member of that group, Tukano parents were uncomfortable with the choice of Nheengatú. But while they often used the terminology of ethnolinguistic identity in critiquing the Nheengatú classes, they did not extend this point to indicate that greater support for non-official minority languages was also needed. The appeal to ethnolinguistic identity only went so far in these discussions – while it was important for Tukano children to learn Tukano rather than Nheengatú, both financial considerations and the pre-existing decision to make the three languages co-official could be used to justify teaching Tuyuka, Kotiria, and other Tukanoan children the Tukano language.

The choice of Nheengatú was not semiotically or ideologically neutral. That language occupies a complex social position in the Rio Negro region: it is contested with regard to its relationship to Indigenous identity as well as to the particular vision it presents about Indigeneity in the city. As I discussed in chapter 2, the "romanticization" of Nheengatú into an Indigenous language and the de-emphasis of its role as a colonial *lingua franca* has intensified as the political stakes involved in recognizing Indigeneity have been raised. Although the Baré have made an effort to stake a claim to the language as their own, using the ideological positioning of language/identity connections (which are common among neighbouring groups) to articulate this relationship, Nheengatú remains less strongly associated with a specific group than any of the other languages. The fact that the Baré language is no longer spoken at all (Maia 2009), and the particular need the Baré therefore have for a language that can help authenticate them as Indigenous, is shifting the language away from its role as a *lingua franca* towards that of an ethnolinguistic identity marker (a performance that has complex consequences for non-Baré native speakers of Nheengatú).

This reconceptualization of Nheengatú – from colonial to Indigenous, as well as from communicative to identity-marking – is ongoing and contested, however. This sheds light on additional debates about its use in Indigenous-language educational programming. As a *lingua franca* among Indigenous people (one that, it should be noted, is no longer spoken by colonizing settlers), it may be used to mark Indigeneity in a more general way, without focusing on the complex interrelationship of difference that characterizes the multilingual social context of the Northwest Amazon. To some extent, a level of neutrality is available to Nheengatú that is not available to Tukano, which is part of a system in which marking and articulating the differences between groups is central to social relationships. It is in the Baré effort to reconfigure their relationship to this language – an effort that is taking place primarily within another field of relationships, one in which they have to situate themselves in relation to the state rather than in relation to other Indigenous groups – that the ability of Nheengatú to serve this role is being weakened. As it becomes a marker of a particular ethnic identity, it has entered into the power dynamics of competition over which language(s) should be valorized in which ways, when as an Indigenized *lingua franca*, it had remained outside of such competition.

At the same time, the historical effort of both colonizers and the Baré themselves to use this language as a marker of greater proximity to "civilization" means that the valorizing function of Nheengatú has its limitations. Despite the efforts among politically powerful and active Baré leaders to change the meaning of the language, it remains the Indigenous language most strongly associated with non-Indigeneity. This is especially true in the urban area and among older people who have lived in the city for decades, having moved there at a time when being Indigenous was a source of intense shame. These people may have embraced the Indigenous movement's goal of improving the lives of the region's people, but they have also internalized a vision of the dichotomy between civilized and uncivilized, and they manifest their pride by emphasizing their ability to behave in a civilized manner.

Two women who are involved in Nheengatú language education, one a principal and the other a former teacher, provide examples of how these ideologies work in relation to this language. Both of these women are over sixty, and both have lived in the city since their teenage years. In my interviews with each of these women, both emphasized in their vision for the future of the city that it should become a cleaner, more developed, more organized place, and both associated the problems the city was facing with an inability among some Indigenous people (including then-mayor Pedro García) to understand how to behave in society. In discussing the importance of Nheengatú language classes, both of these women emphasized the teaching of a standardized form, with a heavy focus on literacy. In an interview (March 2011), the principal said that she "supports the teaching of Indigenous languages in the school, but [her] priority is that the students come out more educated." The Portuguese language polysemy around the word *educado*, which can mean both "educated" and "polite," signals one of the underlying themes she expressed during this interview – Indigeneity can be included and expressed only insofar as it can be manifested in a "civilized" manner. In her view, the main thing that the city needed in order to improve itself was a greater emphasis on cleanliness, order, and organization – demonstrable markers to outsiders that "this is not a city full of dirty Indians." For some, then, the choice of Nheengatú as the representational Indigenous language for use in schools – the most visible site to non-Indigenous outsiders, as well as the most high-status location of Indigenous language use in active functioning – was a way not of contesting, but of *continuing*, its historical role as a colonial marker of the transition from savage to civilized.

The formally offered explanations for the choice to use Nheengatú among the diverse group of urban students do not, of course, refer directly to these ideological positions. Rather, they draw on two main arguments – a geographic position based in the official language legislation, and a claim to demographic dominance – that are themselves indicative of the effect of ideological filters on interpretations of reality.

The geographic argument references the co-officialization law as saying that the implementation of that law's articles should be regionally determined (emphasizing the use of Tukano along the Uaupés and its tributaries, Baniwa on the Içana, and Nheengatú on the Rio Negro). The argument is that because the city of São Gabriel is on the Rio Negro, it falls within the space that the law defines as Nheengatú-using. Yet the law itself makes only a brief reference to these territorial distinctions, and this is with regard to the use of radiophone communications (see

Appendix, Article 2-I). In additional documents submitted in support of the policy's development, the regional distribution is mentioned, but in a descriptive rather than a prescriptive manner. That is to say, in noting that each of Nheengatú, Tukano, and Baniwa serves as a *lingua franca* for one of the major river systems in the municipality, the legislative commission that authored the documents made the case that the selection of these three was sufficient to serve the needs of the diverse Indigenous inhabitants of the region. These texts do not, in fact, prescribe a differentiated application of the co-officialization law, nor do they describe the actual situation in the urban area, where permanent and temporary migrants from all of these linguistic territories cohabit and interact. These understandings, which have emerged within discussions of the law in the educational sector, have served as one justification for the selection of Nheengatú. The pre-existing ideologies about linguistic territoriality inform the ways in which one policy (the co-officialization law) is used to structure the terms of another policy (the language-in-education curriculum) and may even supersede the text of the original policy.

The second popular explanation, the demographic one, also draws on assumptions and perceptions that may not be entirely rooted in the actual state of affairs in São Gabriel. Educators suggest that Nheengatú is the most widely spoken Indigenous language in the city, and therefore best-suited to meet the needs of the population. The problem with this explanation is that the decision was made in the absence of supporting survey data confirming that Nheengatú is, in fact, the most widely spoken Indigenous language in the city. In 2011 a sociolinguistic survey of the city was initiated by Flora Cabalzar and Kristine Stenzel, working in consultation with the Instituto Socioambiental (ISA), to help gain a better perspective on this complex multilingual situation. The results indicated that while the largest proportion (35 per cent) of students claimed Baré as their ethnic identity (compared to 15 per cent Tukano, the second-largest group), the Indigenous language most likely to be spoken by high school students was actually Tukano (14 per cent said that they speak Tukano well, compared to only 10 per cent for Nheengatú). Baniwa, the third official language, was farther down the list on both of these counts (6 per cent of the population, with 5 per cent of students saying they could speak the language well).[1] It may be that the large proportion of students claiming Baré ethnicity indicates that most parents who speak an Indigenous language are speakers of Nheengatú, but it is also likely that perceptions of its dominance are

being influenced by ideological factors – including its stronger association with urbanized, "civilized" Indigeneity.

An additional component of this ideological influence can be seen
in expressions about the difficulty associated with each of the three
official languages. Many people expressed the perception that Nheengatú is the "easiest" of the three official languages to speak and understand, while Baniwa is the most difficult and Tukano is somewhere in
the middle. These people rarely clarified what they meant by "easier,"
but the relatively simple phonology and morphosyntax, along with
high proportion of Portuguese borrowings, may in fact make Nheengatú easier for students to pick up in a classroom environment. A
few people did suggest that actually, Tukano was easier – these were
mainly adults who had been raised by Tukano-speaking parents and
who had been exposed to the language though they claimed no knowledge of it themselves. That said, several educators told me that efforts
to introduce Tukano language classes had faced resistance from non-
Tukanoan parents, who were concerned that it would be too challenging for their children. Tukano has never been offered as a curricular
material in any of the city's schools, though the Catholic diocese has
sometimes supported extra-curricular courses for adults and youth,
which were attended by both Indigenous and non-Indigenous residents of the city. People who had participated in these classes in the
past expressed appreciation for them but rarely claimed any practical
knowledge of the Tukano language, lamenting the lack of continuity
that would have facilitated their language learning. These discourses
about the relative "difficulty" of each of the languages highlight an
additional ideological point regarding the role these languages should
play in children's education – they should not require too much energy
or effort on the part of students, lest this detract from other, more valuable subjects.

The contested status of the Nheengatú language as Indigenous, and
the perception that it is not only a language of wider communication
(rather than a primary identity marker), but also a language that helps
tame and civilize a form of "difficult" Indigeneity, mean that its use in
the school curriculum is contested not only by those who oppose the
use of Indigenous languages in schools but also by those who feel that
it is an inadequate representation of Indigenous presence. The inclusion of this specific language, then, as the curricular one, constitutes
an incorporation of Indigeneity into a high-status, formal educational
context, in such a way as to minimize its threat to non-Indigenous

dominance. The limited way it is included, and the attitudes towards pedagogy, further strengthen this ideological position.

No one disputes that the Indigenous component of the educational curriculum in the city is weak. Some, of course, believe that this limited presence is not a problem, as other pedagogical concerns are much more pressing. Those who do believe that Indigenous languages should be strengthened within the classroom take on, as an additional component of their already high workloads, frequent efforts to press for reform. This group of language activists is remarkably unified with respect to their view of the first step in this process – the inclusion of Indigenous-language classes in *each* of the three official Indigenous languages in *all* of the city's schools. In 2012, one of the state-funded secondary schools (Irmã Ines Penha) was working on a project that would allow them to offer such classes, giving students the opportunity to choose which of the three languages they would study to meet the curriculum requirements. The principal and several of the teachers at the school were strong advocates for Indigenous education and political reform; they had attempted unsuccessfully to implement this program for the 2012 school year, but continued to work throughout the year to secure funding for future years (as of this writing, in mid-2016, such funding had not been established, and in the face of opposition from the 2012–16 mayor's office, the group's efforts have waned). This group contends that selecting one of the three official languages undermines the legal equality of these languages, but also acknowledges that the ability to choose among them would be an important factor to allow people to learn the language that best represents their identity. Many of the people involved in this struggle see the establishment of classes in the three languages as merely a first stage in the development of a strong Indigenous component for education in São Gabriel, not as a sufficient end point for implementing the policy or for valorizing Indigenous cultures.

Overall, however, this view of improvement continues to prioritize the symbolic presence of the languages, rather than improvement of students' linguistic abilities. The idea of changing the framework for language teaching in one or more of the Indigenous languages – for example, by introducing an immersion, partial immersion, or bilingual/bicultural education model – is not mentioned within these discussions of how to modify the existing city schools, even though these frameworks have been shown to be much more effective methods of teaching and maintaining minority languages (Hornberger 2008). The emphasis on fairness invokes the local ideology of equality among the languages, but without, it is worth noting, attempting to bring the official Indigenous languages into balance with Portuguese. Again, the underlying binary between Indigenous and non-Indigenous persists in such a way that it dilutes the value associated with each individual Indigenous language, and any inclusion of additional Indigenous languages places them in competition with Nheengatú rather than with Portuguese. The pressure these activists are bringing forward, then, focuses on the type of Indigenous identity that is allowed a presence within schools, but without constructing a serious challenge to the hegemonic role of Portuguese. The debate over the identity of urban schools themselves – as either "Indigenous" or not – further illustrates the overall sense that the role of Indigeneity is tangential, rather than central, to institutional identities in the city.

Categorizing "Indigenous" Schools

Within the city's schools, non-Indigenous ways of being – including clothing, food, building structures, daily routines, classroom materials, and language use – are so ubiquitous and firmly entrenched that the very minimal presence of Indigenous symbols and practices becomes significant. Although language is only one of the cultural practices that receive some degree of symbolic inclusion (along with regional foods, clothing, and musical and dance performances), it presents a particularly rich way of analysing ideological contestation, because it is the only element that has been selected for inclusion as a curricular subject. Courses on "Indigenous arts" have been discussed and proposed but do not currently exist in any of the city's schools. Other cultural practices – for example, dances – are used as performative symbols during special events. Students are taught only the steps involved in these dances, not the spiritual and social meaning behind them. The physical and political structures of the educational institutions, and the practices and discourses of educators and administrators, work to transform these Indigenous symbols into representations of Brazilian diversity and multiculturalism. Discussions about the presence of Indigenous languages or other aspects of Indigenous culture take place in a political and social-educational context that emphasizes not only Brazilian national identity but also students' preparation for participation in the mainstream capitalist economy.

Taken together, these conditions establish the Indigenous as "other," as the marked category against a non-Indigenous Brazilian norm, even when most or all students, teachers, and administrators in a given classroom or school are themselves Indigenous. This perspective has been contested by people working in educational administration, such as Donato Miguel Vargas, the director of SEMEC's Department of Indigenous Education from 2008 to 2012. The department had a permanent staff of four people, sharing a small office with one desk (for Donato) and one large table that the other three staff members used. During an interview (19 June 2012), Donato recounted a conversation he had had a few years earlier with the education secretary at the time, during which he suggested a complete overhaul of the structure of SEMEC in São Gabriel. The restructuring would create a Secretary of *Indigenous* Education, such that the administration of the system of differentiated schools focusing on Indigenous identity – including at least one new school, to be established in the urban area – would be the default in the municipality, and a smaller subunit within it, the Department of Non-Indigenous Education, would take responsibility for one or two mainstream institutions located in the city. Basically, he was saying that in a municipality in which Indigeneity is the norm, the existence of a department such as his made little sense, and that non-Indigeneity should be treated as the marked exception in need of separate oversight. Although he remembered this proposal as being well-received, the idea was never brought to the town council or formally discussed outside of SEMEC itself.

The very minimal amount of Indigenous language teaching in urban schools, then, is part of an ideological construction whereby formal education is based on non-Indigenous norms and Indigeneity is a marked or differentiated category. What constitutes an "Indigenous school," and what it would mean for city schools to be labelled as such, becomes a significant debate in this framework. However dominant Indigenous people are within the city (numerically, if not politically), the structures they encounter there, including not only the schools but the bodies that administer and oversee them, are based on non-Indigenous frameworks. This means, for example, that while the mayor and the deputy mayor from 2008 to 2012 were both Indigenous people, their offices were not based on Indigenous understandings of governance and social organization. There is no clear structure of Indigenous leadership to provide a counterbalance to these non-Indigenous structures of the state and other institutions. So even where Indigenous individuals are in positions of authority within schools, this does not translate into Indigenous control over education or to the founding of "Indigenous schools."

"Indigeneity" is not simply an anthropological category; it is also a legal one, and just as Indigenous people living in urban spaces occupy a grey area in that regard, so too do the institutions in which they operate. Strong controversy exists regarding whether the city's schools can or should be formally classified as "Indigenous." With the 2001 National Education Plan, the federal government established the category "Indigenous school" and attached to it a different set of criteria for the curriculum and student assessment, along with regulations about funding for certain types of differences. Any funding for Indigenous language classes, for example, or for the incorporation of other locally relevant cultural practices and knowledge, depends upon this categorization. Educational administrators have had to consider this all-or-nothing framework of Indigeneity for the schools and assess how well the label allows them to meet their pedagogical goals. Initially, the high proportion of Indigenous students led to uniform acceptance of the idea that the city's schools should be considered Indigenous. In 2009, however, as schools were preparing to take the Prova Brasil – a standardized test for assessing school performance throughout the country – local officials at SEDUC argued that Indigenous schools were ineligible for participation in these tests. In 2012 the federal government clarified the policy so as to indicate that such schools could choose to participate but were not obligated to do so (Rede Globo 2012). Because of the perceived benefits of these standardized tests and their relevance to success in the mainstream Brazilian context, the administrators of schools funded by the state of Amazonas (which includes most of the schools in the city; see Table 4.1) elected to change the status of the schools so as to be able to offer these tests.

The decision to participate in this test, based on the desire to ensure that students were receiving a quality of education on par with that of the rest of the country, came at the cost of the ability to offer Indigenous language classes within the state-funded schools. The two schools funded by the municipality – Thiago Montalvo, which goes from pre-school to grade 2, and Dom Miguel Alagna, a grade 3–8 primary school – retained the Indigenous label and thus continued to receive a small amount of funding for teaching Indigenous languages within the curriculum. In these two schools, as noted above, the (already minimal) Nheengatú language instruction ceases after grade 5, when students begin to learn English or Spanish. These foreign languages are seen as much more necessary as students reach these more serious levels of their education and begin to think about the trajectory of their lives beyond primary school. In this regard, then, education is an especially potent example of how the trajectory of social mobility is construed as going from rural Indigeneity (or even "Indianness") towards mainstream, urban Brazilian society.

Most parents, teachers, and administrators define their priorities for Indigenous students in terms of providing them with opportunities for geographic mobility outside of São Gabriel. Maria Luisa, who taught Nheengatú classes at Dom Miguel for two years, expressed little concern that her children (ages eighteen and twenty-five) were unable to speak Nheengatú, but she proudly referenced her daughter's success at university in the Northeast and expressed hope that her son (a less serious student) would score highly on the *vestibular* (Brazil's standardized test for university entrance) and enter a good school outside of the region. Given the lack of economic opportunities available in São Gabriel, she worried that her son would fall into destructive patterns, including alcohol and drug use, and she saw schooling outside of the region as a means of escape. Though a Nheengatú-language teacher herself, Maria Luisa had not been motivated by a desire to contribute to language revitalization; she had simply accepted the assignment given to her as a qualified teacher who also happened to be a speaker of that language.

The value of learning Indigenous languages is linked mainly to the possibility that learners will return to Indigenous territories. When urban youth who do not speak any Indigenous languages express a desire to learn them, these hopes are connected to the goal of improving communication with older, rural Indigenous people. For parents, literacy in Portuguese was seen as most important – indeed, it is indispensable for any wage employment – and their secondary wish was for their children to learn English or Spanish. In an anonymous interview, one teacher and language advocate told me she used the students' desire to learn these international languages to motivate them to value their Indigenous languages. She had been educated about language acquisition research, and she drew on this awareness to suggest to them that becoming bilingual at a young age would help them learn additional languages later in life. Some political leaders, including FOIRN representatives, emphasized the importance of English, knowledge of which would allow youth to make valuable contributions to the lives of local people, for access to specialized educational programs over-seas and connections with the global Indigenous movement would depend on their ability to speak English. For both individuals and the region, strengthening the presence of English would provide a path for "moving forward" – towards globality, and towards increased outward connections. Overall, positive social mobility was associated with geo-graphic mobility away from the rural territories – and away from the use of Indigenous languages.

The debate over whether the schools should be classified as "Indig-enous" is, in many ways, a debate over whether Indigeneity is a desir-able thing to teach and to aspire to. The current framework suggests that for many it is not. The significance of these practices is too limited and too localized, and the economic challenges the people of the region face are too big. Both in the city and in the rural territories, now that the idea of Indigenous schools has become a reality, a discussion is emerg-ing about what graduates of these schools should hope to become. As a result of improved access to formal credentials as well as a stronger knowledge base in the curricular materials, these students are emerg-ing with a view to labour market opportunities. Within the communi-ties themselves, there is really only one option – to work as a teacher in an Indigenous school. Young people are also receiving support for training in health care positions, but these are not jobs that allow them to remain in one place and serve the needs of a single community. Instead, these Indigenous people – most of them health agents, along with some nursing technicians and a few nurses – travel with teams of nurses and doctors and provide services through periodic visits to the communities along the river systems. While these are desirable posi-tions, they are more so for young, unmarried Indigenous men than they are for those who are caring for a family, and especially for women during their childbearing years. They do not, in other words, allow one to remain in one's own community while applying the structured edu-cation gained during schooling to provide something of value to that community.

While it is less prominent in the city, the question of what education is preparing these students *for* is a pervasive one. As Maria Luisa's visions and fears attest, answering this question depends on recognizing the paucity of opportunities available for students to make use of the cre-dentials they acquire. Indigenous people have come to understand that education can transform their lives, but they have also observed the gaps in its ability to do so given the economic conditions in São Gabriel.

Some raise questions, then, about what "quality of life" means and whether a capitalist definition is too limiting, while others accept that both Indigenous cultural practices and life in the rural, remote communities is a thing of the past and that the future may only be found beyond this region. For this latter group, the idea that São Gabriel is a space of transformation from Indigeneity into modernity (rather than a way of either modernizing Indigeneity or Indigenizing modernity),[2] and from the ways of the past into those of the future, manifests itself not only in the aspirations they express for their children but also in their vision of what the school should offer them.

Orienting to the Outside

The attitudes and linguistic practices described above fit within a pattern whereby educators, parents, and students alike are orienting themselves away from the rural, Indigenous territories and ways of life and redefining their expectations. The visions and aspirations that parents like Maria Luisa express for their children involve pushing them to move "forward" and find opportunities in places outside the Upper Rio Negro. In addition, however, the emphasis on Indigenous language use as an act of "valorization" and a performance of generalized Indigeneity means there is an external audience towards whom this performance is directed. Furthermore, the language of "valorization" commodifies Indigenous difference – and in the minds of at least some educators, one way that young Indigenous people can gain access to something of "value" is by developing the ability to perform this difference (see also Virtanen 2012). To borrow Bourdieu's metaphorical framework of social and political capital, the value of Indigenous languages here is being defined by the terms of the dominant marketplace, rather than through the creation of an alternative marketplace defined by Indigenous or other local interests (Patrick 2003).

Even those who support Indigenous language classes and presence in schools have tended to orientate themselves towards the perceptions of outsiders – including those who are temporarily living in São Gabriel – in their justifications and advocacy efforts. One teacher who had attended university in the Northeast told me:

> I talk a lot with the students about the valorization of identity – of the identity that we have, that we shouldn't be ashamed of what we are, because there, outside, you are only valued if you are Indigenous and

speak an Indigenous language. *If you say that you're Indigenous, but don't speak any Indigenous languages, you have no value at all.* This is what I saw living out there ... They ask – what languages do you speak? *And if you say none, what kind of Indian are you, really?* So there's a – a – these studies made me see this reality, how – *how our language really is valorized out there.* [anonymous interview, 9 July 2012, emphasis mine]

From this teacher's perspective, the relevance of language to identity was not based on Indigenous ideologies, but on how non-Indigenous Brazilians understood what it means to be Indigenous. While she herself said she did not feel that the inability to speak an Indigenous language should be cause to question a person's authenticity (especially in cases where a young person was making an effort to understand his or her culture), she felt that she hadn't fully understood the importance of language until she realized how it was seen by outsiders.

This type of commentary assumes that students in São Gabriel will migrate, either temporarily or permanently, to other parts of Brazil, and invokes the perspectives of those outside the region, prioritizing them as the audience for these types of performances. This external orientation is further emphasized in the way that non-Indigenous Brazilians in the city of São Gabriel are discussed. The non-Indigenous students in the city's schools – and specifically, the high-status children of military members – play an important symbolic role in defining how most residents want the city to be seen. Because these students are usually present in the region temporarily (for two years), and because many of them complain about this posting in a remote, inaccessible place without the entertainment options to which they are accustomed, the local people are acutely conscious of the image they will be taking with them when they leave and of the message they will be carrying to the rest of Brazil about Amazonas and its people. Indigenous people often express their desire to counter the stereotype of the backward, savage Indian that they believe many people still have about them – pointing out, for example, the "normality" of their clothing choices and houses, or emphasizing achievements within the mainstream market in which they take pride, including the count of Indigenous students who have obtained undergraduate and graduate degrees.

Non-Indigenous students' educational needs are discussed differently from those of the majority Indigenous population. The former are a small minority of the schools' student bodies, yet they are prominent in discussions about pedagogical quality. Denivaldo Cruz da Silva remembered an occasion when he was working in FOIRN's education department and had gone to talk to the principal at Dom João Marchesi middle school – a Baré woman who had been a childhood classmate of his – about strengthening the Indigenous component of the curriculum. He described her as practically throwing him out of her office, telling him that she was under far too much pressure from members of the military to ensure that their children would not be held back by spending a couple of years in São Gabriel. The disproportionate focus that non-Indigenous students receive reflects both their higher social status and differences in their presumed career goals and opportunities. The nature of their fathers' positions does mean, of course, that by definition they are likely to leave the region, and in terms of their education, this is associated with the need to receive repeated assurances that their ability to attend university will not be diminished by a poor-quality education.

The unspoken correlate here is that Indigenous students are not entitled to the same expectation, at least not to the same extent as these military youth. This principal from Dom João Marchesi was among those who harshly criticized teachers who used Indigenous languages to facilitate the transition of recently migrated students from the rural territories. While emphasizing the importance of supporting students who were likely to attend university in the future, she also said it was the responsibility of these Indigenous students to improve their Portuguese-language skills so that they would be able to complete even preliminary levels of education. Her presumption was that if these students were likely to return to a horticulturalist way of life anyway, their educational needs were not an important priority. Indigenous cultural practices and knowledge, for parents and educators who think this way, may be quaint and amusing for the purposes of school events but should not be allowed to distract from classroom material. An Indigenous leader will sometimes push back against this perspective, suggesting that the city is Indigenous space and that non-Indigenous students should therefore adapt themselves to the local language in the same way that they would if they were attending school overseas. But that stance amounts to a thought experiment rather than an actual proposal for reform; it is taken to emphasize the ongoing marginalization of Indigeneity even in a majority Indigenous environment. Non-Indigenous Brazilian students are few in number, but even so, their presence in the city's schools overrides the possibility of creating and enacting a strong policy of Indigenous-focused education. As the principal in this

example shows, these positions that place the non-Indigenous population at the centre of discussions about education are not emerging
exclusively from non-Indigenous actors.

Indeed, this centralization extends to the discourses of those who promote and support Indigenous-language classes. They proudly observe
that non-Indigenous students are often the ones who are most interested
and most excited to learn about the local culture. This positioning uses
the perspectives of this high-status outsider group to highlight how the
city of São Gabriel and its Indigenous character can be reconfigured as
a positive feature, but it still relies on a performative identity and on
the approval of spectators. Within the urban space, then, and especially
within the complex and multipurpose public institutional context of
schools, people orient themselves towards an external spectator when
demonstrating their identity. In doing so, they are exploiting a well-
understood pattern in Brazilian Indigenous politics of self-conscious
cultural displays (Conklin 1997; Oakdale 2004; Fleming 2010). This suggests the degree to which awareness of the relevance of identity performance for Indigenous political recognition has become part of the daily
lives of Indigenous people at a more subconscious level. Yet at the same
time, devaluation of Indigenous people continues even in the ways in
which Indigenous languages and practices are being used.

The frequent mentions of the non-Indigenous population by educators in the city give the impression that, even in contexts where the
majority is Indigenous – and in most of the schools in São Gabriel, non-
Indigenous people are a very small minority – the presence of *any* non-
Indigenous people renders the space non-Indigenous and requires the
use of the default, hegemonic language and culture of the colonizers. The
facility with which most Indigenous people can switch to Portuguese
combines with the ideological devaluation of their "home" languages
and the ignorance of non-Indigenous peoples to solidify the ongoing
prominence of Portuguese as the language of public use in São Gabriel.
Analysis of schools' use of Indigenous languages and other salient
symbols of Indigenous identity (clothing, dances, musical instruments,
food, etc.) demonstrates the ways in which non-Indigenous hegemony
has imposed a particular structure on Indigeneity in São Gabriel. Even
in "the most Indigenous city in Brazil," then, Indigeneity is always seen
as marking "difference," and its incorporation into schools occurs at the
level of tolerance vis-à-vis the broader norm of whiteness. Even though
most students and teachers are Indigenous, the schools in which they
study and work pay little attention to their cultures, languages, and

practices, and furthermore, confine them to marked categories ("Indigenous schools," special events like Indigenous Peoples' Week, etc.). In addition, many of my observations make clear that simply being an Indigenous person does not necessarily mean that someone will take a pro-Indigenous position. The emphasis on the educational needs and goals of non-Indigenous students not only reinforces these values but also serves to maintain a hierarchy among the students themselves. On the one hand, then, the Indigeneity of the city is repeatedly highlighted, but only in such a way as to recognize and maintain its "difference"; on the other, students are reminded of the lower status of this difference through the centralization of the educational priorities of non-Indigenous students within a non-Indigenous system.

Educational Transformations and Indigenous Politics

Land, health, and education are often cited as the three main poles of Indigenous political activism. With the demarcation of the Indigenous Territories of the Rio Negro secured, Indigenous people are heatedly debating whether to allow mining companies access to their territories. Meanwhile, improving the health of this impoverished and marginalized population[3] remains a long-term struggle on many fronts. But at this point in time, education is perhaps the most easily identifiable shared goal for the Indigenous movement; the strengthening of Indigenous schools is seen as the next major step in achieving some form of cultural and political autonomy. As discussed in the introduction, however, the political framework within which this discussion takes place – both at the national level, in the form of the constitution, and at the local level, with the rural schools understood as the primary locus of cultural preservation – makes it difficult to identify the path to educational reform in the city of São Gabriel.

The idea of educational reform has been circulating in the city for a little over a decade, mainly as a result of the widespread participation of at least a few teachers based in the urban area in the Magistério Indígena (MI) and subsequent degree-granting accreditation programs. These programs – the former led by the municipal department of education, and the latter offered by the Universidade Federal de Amazonas (UFAM) and the Universidade do Estado de Amazonas (UEA) – were developed after consultations among Indigenous advocates, government representatives, and academic supporters, with the primary aim of helping Indigenous teachers meet new federal credential requirements as part of their goal of improving the quality of public education throughout Brazil. While these programs are targeted mainly at those teachers in remote rural regions who began in the profession after obtaining only a primary-level education in Salesian schools, many people who are now teaching in schools in the urban area or in immediate surrounding communities have also attended these programs, especially the university ones. Because these programs are so deeply enmeshed in the political implications of education for Indigenous people, as well as Indigenous education as a concept, experiences within them are often highlighted as transformative in individuals' understandings of the significance of schooling. The MI program in particular is explicitly oriented toward Indigenous pedagogy; it focuses on clarifying constitutionally defined Indigenous rights and on ensuring that teachers are specially trained to offer "differentiated" rather than mainstream education. These sites, then, have been central to the development of a particular activist vision of how Indigenous knowledge should be included in schools, in the city of São Gabriel as much as in rural communities. People trained in these programs now occupy teaching as well as administrative positions in the municipal department of education and in individual schools.

In the city, however, the types of projects these actors have imagined have been almost completely without practical implementation. The most detailed plan for creating differentiated education in the city emerged from SEMEC's Department of Indigenous Education during the 2004–8 administration, at the same time that the secretariat was discussing the proposal that Donato Vargas – himself a graduate of the MI and UFAM's Indigenous training program – had submitted for a complete departmental overhaul. At that time, a detailed model of a multilingual, multicultural differentiated school was created, supported by the municipal government, and approved for federal funding. In this model, each cultural group present in the city would be housed in its own small *maloka* and taught using its own language, origin stories, and unique cultural practices, similar to what is found in the differentiated schools in outlying communities. These small groups would join together for larger events and learning activities to discuss and learn about the other cultures, and to reflect the connections among them in the urban area. Mismanagement of funds by the municipal government – a problem that plagues many projects in São Gabriel – led to this project's failure. Since the idea had been carefully developed and well received, I asked both the original proposers and other supporters of urban Indigenous education whether this proposal could be revived. The responses were tepid – most of those who had submitted the original project felt burned out after watching all their hard work fall apart at the last minute; others who might have taken it up on their behalf suggested that they preferred an incremental rather than a radical approach to change, since it might result in *something* being accomplished rather than nothing at all. The idea of reforming the city's schools to better incorporate Indigenous languages and cultural practices, then, was brought forward mainly by a group of people whose vision had been shaped by the same forces that had led to the founding of differentiated rural schools. While the focal points were different, including recognition of the need for a multilingual and multicultural model,– the motivation for creating this type of school was the same – to support and strengthen Indigenous identities and cultural practices.

But the number of people expressing concern about urban schools, and who have the time, energy, and political power to contribute to that debate, is far fewer than the number devoted to discussing how to improve rural schools. FOIRN-organized educational assemblies, for example, are held in the city itself, but attendees from rural schools far outnumber those representing the urban area. At a May 2012 assembly, for example, the urban group Tawa (from the Nheengatú word for "settlement") comprised six people, while each of the five rural districts sent at least twenty. Also, while all of those who are concerned about Indigenous education in the city are deeply frustrated about the absence of Indigenous languages or ways of being in the schools, they do not necessarily agree on how the situation could be improved. As the different ideological positions regarding the meaning of Indigeneity and its role in São Gabriel suggest, the residents of the city have differing perceptions of their community's identity.

When I asked policy-makers, Indigenous activists, and members of the general public about São Gabriel's official language policy and its implementation, all of them expressed their disappointments and their hopes for reform almost exclusively with reference to education. Although there is limited potential to revitalize and strengthen endangered languages through schooling (especially through non-immersion models of classroom instruction), this discursive emphasis strengthens the status of education when it comes to considering how, when, and why particular languages are taught (or not taught) in formal contexts. Indigeneity has been marginalized as a consequence of its limited and marked incorporation in schools, and it is difficult at best to contest a non-Indigenous framework. Ideologies that emphasize the symbolic valorization of Indigeneity dominate the pedagogical approach, even among supporters of the Indigenous movement and language education. The revitalization of languages (and cultural practices), and the creation of new ways to use (and express) them among the urban population, remain distant goals with little political or ideological support.

Current practices as well as efforts to reform them incrementally reflect an underlying view of Indigeneity in São Gabriel – that it is both marginal (next to non-Indigenous ways of being) and diluted (next to rural Indigeneity). That Indigeneity is represented linguistically by Nheengatú – a contact language whose status as "Indigenous" is contested, besides being the Indigenous language spoken by those who have most closely accommodated themselves to non-Indigenous ways of being – has helped make expressions of difference within the urban area more acceptable to a perceived or actual non-Indigenous public. Ideologies about Indigenous identity – in particular, the indexical binaries between urban/rural and Indigenous/non-Indigenous – manifest themselves in schools that shape Indigenous students for participation in non-Indigenous life; they also help reveal that these are not merely conceptual binaries, but rather manifestations of extreme differences of power and status. Both on paper and in practice, municipal educational policy has restricted the expressions of Indigenous identity by urban students; it is preparing them for a life that prioritizes participation and success in the Brazilian mainstream. The identity being created for the city is "Indigenous" in a way that is designed to be non-threatening – that focuses on symbolic performances of Indigeneity and on ensuring that Indigenous people remain outsiders rather than on centralizing the Indigenous values and experiences of urban São Gabriel. Even more than the official language policy, schools are demonstrating that while there may be space available to bring Indigeneity into the public sphere, that space is small and restricted in shape.

5 Making an Indigenous Public: A Perspective from the Non-Official Languages

As the previous chapters have shown, within most of the public sphere in São Gabriel, constructing an Indigenous city has focused on using a small number of languages as a means to carve out and mark space for Indigeneity in general. These languages are seen, by at least some Indigenous leaders, as sufficient to meet the needs of the diverse Indigenous population, from both a communicative and a representational perspective. In terms of what it means to bring Indigeneity into the city, or to create an Indigenous public space in the urban area, the debate concerns what Indigeneity *is*. One aspect of this debate – briefly mentioned in the discussion of the official language policy in chapter 3 – has been the conflict between those Indigenous people who focus on elevating a pan-Indigenous identity vis-à-vis an equally generalized non-Indigenous Brazil, and those who are most concerned about particular ethnolinguistic identities. Those who prioritize the latter view of identity have felt excluded from the decisions about whose ways of being will dominate within the pan-Indigenous model, and interpret this opposing position as based on self-interested political goals rather than on "authentic" Indigenous traditions. These positions are, of course, never static, and different individuals may emphasize different identity categories at different times of their lives or in different social contexts.

In terms of creating policy and constructing an Indigenous urban space, those who advocate for pan-Indigeneity have undoubtedly been more successful, and that is the framework that has emerged as the dominant approach to working for Indigenous recognition. The official language legislation, with its selection of three representative *linguas francas*, and the language-in-education policy, which singles out

Nheengatú as the only language for curricular use, embody this vision of how to Indigenize the city of São Gabriel through representative valorization. On the other side of this debate are speakers of the many non-official languages of the region, who are faced with "minority" status.[1] The urban-dwelling speakers of these languages are marginalized on two counts – they belong to language groups or speak languages that are not dominant enough be legally recognized as "official," and they are at least partly excluded from their home communities and cut off from other speakers of these same languages as a result of their residence in the urban area.

The consequences of this conversation differ depending on which language group is being discussed. For some members of language groups with very few or no speakers remaining, it is enough to document or gain knowledge of *any* aspect of their own language and to fight for broader political recognition of their rights as Indigenous peoples. For others, such as the Arawakan Kurripako, the question of whether their language should be recognized as distinct or subsumed as a dialect of Baniwa (or indeed, of how many dialectal boundaries exist among the various languages of this family spoken in the region) is the most relevant status-related question. These diverse issues were beyond the scope of my research, and beyond what I can cover in this book, but deeper exploration of any of them would undoubtedly lead to interesting insights about experiences of Indigeneity from this position of double-marginalization.

Few of these groups, however, are taking steps to challenge the dominance of the pan-Indigenous model. To examine this type of advocacy more thoroughly, I involved myself with a group of speakers of Kotiria (Wanano). The Kotiria are among the groups most committed to the contrasting vision of diverse, particular Indigineities and to the preservation of their own ethnolinguistic identity. They are one of the Tukanoan language groups and participate in the exogamous cultural system, and the Kotiria language is spoken mainly in some of the most remote and difficult-to-access parts of the municipality, along the Upper Uaupés on both sides of the Colombian border. During my fieldwork, I helped establish a formal organization for the promotion of Kotiria language, identity, and culture now known as AIPOK (Associação Indígena do Povo Kotiria; Indigenous Association of the Kotiria People). This organization represents all of the Kotiria, including those who live along the Upper Uaupés; but all of the people on the executive, as well as most of the active, contributing members of the association, live and work in the urban area.

Most of these people are employed as teachers in the municipal or state school system, and many of their discussions have focused on their long-term goal of establishing a Kotiria school in the urban area. This school would allow their children to be educated in their language and about their culture. It was with regard to this specifically urban project that I became most strongly affiliated with this group, and I have continued to advise and support them since leaving São Gabriel in September 2012.

A census conducted by the Instituto Socioambiental (ISA) in 2003 determined the total Kotiria population to be 1,560, one-third of whom live on the Brazilian side of the border (Stenzel 2004: 23). An informal survey conducted by AIPOK members suggests that around thirty-five families (defined by the patrilineal head of the household) make their permanent homes in the city of São Gabriel; the total number of individuals within these families is unknown, as is the number of Kotiria women who have married and raised families that are non-Kotiria. This latter role is an interesting one, as some of the most vocal and active participants in AIPOK, including the president, Franssinete Ferraz Henrique, are married women whose children are not counted as

Figure 5.1. Miguel Cabral presenting the Kotiria of the city with the AIPOK registration documents, August 2012.

Kotiria. Most of these families have lived in the city for at least a decade and have come to consider it their home. There is no particular area of the city in which the Kotiria are concentrated; rather, they are dispersed throughout the city; and since they rely almost exclusively on walking as their means of transportation, they often have little contact with one another. Several of them work as teachers and within the municipal administration; others make their living selling the products of their gardens and other foods at the municipal market or as street vendors.

Although the Kotiria language remains strong within the rural communities (Chernela 2013), migration into the city is viewed as a threat to the language and as a cause for significant concern. Stenzel (2013) predicts that Kotiria children raised in São Gabriel will become monolingual Portuguese speakers within two generations. My own observations of Kotiria people born in the city (including adults up to thirty-five years old) support this prediction – many of the first generation of urban-born adults already do not speak Kotiria and claim, at most, passive knowledge of another Indigenous language (usually Tukano). I encountered only a few very young children who were second-generation urban Kotiria, and the language of communication around them was indeed exclusively Portuguese. Based on my observations and interviews with AIPOK members and other urban-dwelling Kotiria, I estimate the number of speakers of the Kotiria language living in the city to be about sixty.

The Kotiria cultural advocates who comprised the executive of AIPOK upon its registration in August 2012 had already been working together informally for more than a decade. Securing status as a legal organization was an important step for them, for it would allow them to set up a bank account and to receive profits from projects,[2] as well as to apply for governmental and non-governmental support. The organization's official documents specify that they are to act as a voice of authority on behalf of the Kotiria people, both in São Gabriel and in the rural area, and that their goals are to collect information for the purpose of preserving and transmitting the Kotiria language and culture to future generations. Throughout its history, AIPOK's central goal has been to found a Kotiria school in the urban area, and a significant proportion of their efforts has been directed towards that end. While the participation of various members has waxed and waned, with some losing interest and others coming on board later, the process of formalizing themselves as an association and consulting with past academic allies (most notably, Janet Chernela, who helped develop the statute we used in the registration process) has led to the development of both habits of practical advocacy and a consciously crafted set of goals that they have identified as most important for the group.

The experiences of AIPOK as an organization, and of its individual urban-dwelling members, serve as useful portals for examining the often unrecognized challenges facing urban language revitalization. By focusing specifically on language ideologies underlying the discourses and statements made by members of this group, I came to see that, in addition to the difficulties this group shares with any language revitalization effort (absence of funding, lack of support or outright hostility from the state, lack of interest or engagement among community members, etc.) a pervasive set of conflicts underlies discourses and actions that are, on the surface, not only similar, but also would suggest support. That is to say, the barriers to the preservation of the Kotiria language in the urban area emerge not simply from those who explicitly oppose language revitalization, but also from other Indigenous political advocates, and indeed, from within the group itself. Furthermore, the challenges they faced revealed disputes regarding what it means to be Indigenous in the city, in that they reflected strong dissatisfaction with the diminished focus on individual languages.

The Origins of AIPOK: Motivations and Expectations

How AIPOK members joined together to work on preserving Kotiria tells us much about their current activist practices and political commitments. The idea for the school took shape during the 1999 sessions of the Magistério Indígena (MI). Several Kotiria teachers who participated in this program highlight it as their moment of awakening (*conscientização*) – the point when they became aware of their rights as Indigenous people and of the gravity of the threat of language loss. A few of the Kotiria MI graduates, led by Domingos Cabral, began talking about creating a school that would allow their children to be educated in the Kotiria language and in the Kotiria culture. This group involved itself in the effort to establish a Kotiria school in Caruru-cachoeira, and many of the members have been important contacts and participants in an ongoing language documentation project led by Kristine Stenzel, which is also generating pedagogical materials. The Kotiria Khumuno Wʉ'ʉ differentiated school began its life with a series of linguistic/pedagogical workshops in 2002–4, in which the urban population actively participated; it began functioning through a central site in Caruru-cachoeira and several "extension classrooms" in the smaller surrounding Kotiria communities. In 2008 another successful expansion brought the level of education offered by the Kotiria school up to the middle-school level (grade 8).

As they observed these successes in the rural territories, the urban Kotiria began to feel disconnected from that progress and to express frustration regarding when they might see similar efforts directed towards their own needs. It troubled them that despite their own contributions of time and energy, their children might be unable to access the benefits accruing to the rural Kotiria; they feared that the next generation would lose its connection to the Kotiria identity. The growth of the rural school and the publication of pedagogical materials for use there have been paralleled by punctuated, but short-lived, moments of success among the urban Kotiria, as they work to gain recognition from representatives of the municipal government, the state department of education, and organizations like FOIRN. Occasionally, the group's hopes have been raised by government agencies' expressions of solidarity with their goals, but these have rarely been followed up with material support, and the group is well aware that the rate of language shift is continuing unabated. Despite this, AIPOK's leaders remain committed to their vision for a future in which the Kotiria language, culture, and identity will be recognized and thriving within the urban area as well as in the rural territories.

This narrative, which emerges from transcripts of recorded interviews and meetings among AIPOK members, highlights the key events that were identified as important by the various members of the group who were authorized to speak on behalf of the others and the association as a whole – Franssinete Ferraz Henrique, the current association president, Miguel Cabral, the founding president of the (unofficial) organization, Efraim Brazão, one of the most passionate advocates for the school, and Domingos Cabral, the individual most strongly associated with the genesis of the idea. This simplified, sanctioned narrative, however, elides some of the conflicts, contestations, and contradictions that emerge among the group members. Furthermore, the discursive emphasis on certain priorities and principles reveals that group members are constructing ideological positions that are making it more difficult for them to achieve their goals. Because language ideologies generally remain below the surface of political and social action, exposing and clarifying these (Dauenhauer and Dauenhauer 1998; Kroskrity 2009) is a necessary step towards implementing effective projects. In the absence of this clarification, members of AIPOK are invoking arguments and engaging in actions that are not necessarily working in concert with one another, and that are being heard (by policy-makers and other Indigenous advocates whose support they have sought) in ways that the proponents have not intended. As with many of the other language revitalization themes discussed in this book, these conflicts often relate to a vision of what form Indigeneity can and should take in the city; in this context, they also raise specific questions of both *why* and *how* the city can be Indigenized.

The Urban Kotiria and Discourses of Endangerment

The narrative presented by AIPOK representatives situates their interests within a particular set of goals related to the endangerment and potential loss of the Kotiria language. These goals have not emerged in a cultural vacuum, but rather in connection to a global discourse of language endangerment – a discourse that, as many anthropologists have pointed out over the past decade, frames and shapes the experience of language shift and the possibilities for combating it in ways that may undermine the local autonomy its proponents work to promote (Hill 2002; Heller and Duchêne 2007; Dobrin, Austin, and Nathan 2007). As Jane Hill asks so powerfully in the title of her 2002 text, when it comes to advocacy for endangered languages, "Who is listening, and what do they hear?" Hill's article focuses on what can happen when outside actors engage with language revitalization in ways that may not always serve the needs of the minority communities that speak (or have historically spoken) those languages. Similarly, the story of the urban Kotiria reveals that the community's own relationship to these globalized discourses may result in the adoption and absorption of conflicting ideologies that ultimately undermine a group's stated goals.

First and foremost among these ideologically laden ideas is the concept of "endangerment" or threatened "extinction" itself, which is invoked uncritically as one of the main reasons for AIPOK's existence and for the founding of an urban school. Although the metaphor of "extinction" has been criticized by some language activists (Leonard 2012; Leonard and Haynes 2010), the seriousness of this threat has been one of the motivating forces among members of AIPOK. The pattern of multilingualism rooted in language-based exogamy has meant, among at least some Tukanoan people, that the possibility of language shift has become less visible. So much of their culture depends on linguistic difference that even though they see shift happening around them, and even though some languages have in fact ceased to be spoken, they cannot really imagine a world in which their language no longer matters. In several interviews (one with a Dessana man and one with a Kotiria man), I heard the observation that even though the interviewees' own children did not speak the language, they were certain that the language could not disappear, because others would continue to speak it. The importance of the language to the group is such that it is almost impossible for them to think of it not being used somewhere – generally, as the presumption has it, in its traditional homeland. The awakening experienced by Domingos and the other MI participants came about as a direct result of their questioning this presumption of safety and continuity, as the broader picture pattern of language shift became clear. Members of AIPOK, then, in their common discussions and formal proposal documents, often cite academic assessments of the language and the risk of its disappearance in their efforts to generate support for their endeavours.

At the same time, the AIPOK leaders often expressed that their principal concern was not that the Kotiria language might cease to be spoken, but that their own children might be unable to speak it, for this would disconnect them from their culture and identity. When I asked why this mattered to them – what, in their view, was being lost when someone could not speak his or her own language – all of the answers were a variation on the simple point that someone who could not speak Kotiria could not really be Kotiria. Any sense of pride of identity they had as individuals – especially among the men, who were traditionally expected to transmit their patrilect – was visibly diminished when they discussed their children's language abilities and identities. Although this group of people was committed to language work in general and demonstrated support for projects directed at the language as a whole, they emphasized that they perceived the language as strong and vibrant on the Upper Uaupés and that it was in São Gabriel that it was being lost. These advocates, in other words, drew on the same perceptions of security and visions of linguistic continuity existing *elsewhere* that I heard from others who dismissed the possibility of language loss despite the shift happening within their own families.

For the urban Kotiria, the meaning of language loss was not felt most significantly in relation to the possibility that their language might be removed from the global picture of linguistic diversity, but much more immediately, in the observation that their children were unable to be fully Kotiria because they had not learned the language. Their frustration with the ways in which they felt personally excluded from the benefits of language documentation and educational differentiation projects related to this aspect of their underling reasons for creating the group. Efraim Brazão recounted during my initial meeting with the group that "our thinking was to sponsor the school up there, right, those of us who are residents here. But unfortunately it didn't work out ... because nobody sponsored us like that, directly." He emphasized what he perceived as a lack of reciprocity in terms of the support the urban Kotiria had given to the rural school relative to that which they have received in their own pursuits. The urban group was aware that the school in Caruru-cachoeira was a major step towards increasing the viability of the Kotiria language and cultural practices beyond the current generation, but they still felt that something was missing in relation to their own personal experiences and to those practices. Indeed, they feared that the founding of this school would ultimately be used as an argument against the urban school they were advocating, since the case for its necessity would be less compelling in terms of its role in cultural maintenance.

As a whole, the discourse of language loss and extinction invokes the idea that Jane Hill (2002) refers to as "universal valorization," not the loss as it is experienced and felt by particular individuals. AIPOK members use the concepts of language and cultural survival and the risk of language extinction to frame their arguments, but these structures do not necessarily help them address their "principal concern," which is that the language will be unavailable to a particular group of people (their children). Efraim continues:

> So we started to think, with groups that – the ones that are here, you know, because there are also some that are not here with us right now ... so the **most – biggest of our concerns was for our children who are losing our culture.** Because the truth is that, *there*, **they have it. There, they have** *dance*, *talk*, **and here we don't**, most of the talk is in Portuguese, right, I have my children who only speak Portuguese, today. [bold emphasis added, italics reflect emphasis in original speech]

Urban group left out of lang. revitalization efforts

The worry articulated by Efraim relates less to language endangerment than to the identity of his (and his colleagues') children. This is not merely a matter of focus; rather, it reflects the difference between an individualized and a collective need or interest. Within the Tukanoan system, children who are unable to speak the language face a fundamental loss of identity. Language, in Tukanoan cosmology, is a "badge of identity" in the sense that it labels and highlights that identity in a performative manner, but also in the sense that, in wearing that label, the speaker comes to embody that identity (Jackson 1989). Language constitutes, forms, and creates Kotiria identity. When I asked in an interview why it mattered for his children to be able to speak the Kotiria language, Miguel Cabral paused and thought carefully before saying:

> Because I – I was, I am Wanano, and I speak my language. **If I say that I am Wanano, and I don't speak my language, I'm only, I'm – I have this – this name, but, I'm not speaking.** I think that this isn't right. No – no – **he can say, so you aren't Wanano.**

Among global language revitalization activists, the intimate relationship between language and identity is often mentioned as a reason to work so hard to preserve Indigenous languages.[3] Yet the experiences of the urban Kotiria demonstrate that claims to value this language/identity relationship are not necessarily backed up with actions that are attuned to the idea that language loss is deeply personal and directly experienced. Many linguists and global revitalization activists view language as a "group right," not an individual one, and its preservation *somewhere* is sufficient for the recognition of this right, even if it cannot be preserved for all of the group members.

The reference to "group rights" – which includes the complex idea of language rights or language as a right – draws attention to another discourse that has been adopted by AIPOK. Conceptually as well as pragmatically (in the form of references to legal documents), the discourse of rights is prominent in the arguments AIPOK members make regarding why there should be a Kotiria school. The question of rights emerges immediately when members explain why they formed their group, with teachers highlighting the role the MI program played in raising their awareness of their rights under various national and international agreements. They describe the MI as a transformational experience during which participants came to recognize that outside documents afforded them the right to continue to speak their language and to be supported in their efforts to preserve it. In this regard, AIPOK's efforts are situated not only within an activist movement for increasing attention to languages or culture in a general way, but also a social justice and restitution-based framework that looks to hold the

Brazilian government accountable for the commitments they have made to Indigenous people.

The arguments AIPOK puts forward in seeking recognition and implementation of means to provide these rights form the crux of the discussion here. The 2009 formal proposal submitted to the Municipal Department of Education referenced no fewer than five distinct laws and constitutionally defined rights, providing specific citations and arguments about how each of these mandated support for the proposal the urban Kotiria were presenting. These references to legally enshrined rights served as a way both to sustain hope and to emphasize the moral authority of the claims AIPOK was making, even in light of the ongoing political difficulties they were facing in terms of seeing their aims implemented in practice. AIPOK members express strong confidence that, if they can secure a property and construct a building in which to house the school, the prefecture will have no choice but to provide the ongoing funding to sustain it. The moral and legal responsibility associated with rights has generated an expectation that supersedes awareness of and disappointment with the municipal government's limited willingness to take practical steps towards implementing programs that would provide real and concrete benefits to the Indigenous population.

But at the same time, the rights-based framework of educational policy has had a complex and under-studied impact on the actual experiences of individuals. Language rights have usually been conceptualized as belonging to groups rather than to individuals (May 2003; Kymlicka and Patten 2003; Patten 2009). On the one hand, this makes sense, for language does not exist within individuals, but only in its social use, and from a legal protectionist framework, it cannot be said to belong to any one person. The urban context, however, immediately requires us to a redefine what the group *is*, and *where* it is – a question that scholars of language policy have cast this way: Does language, as a right, attach to persons or to places (García 2012)? The view of language as a right also raises the question of what responsibilities individual group members have to work for the realization of these rights on behalf of the group, especially in relation to their other rights and responsibilities as individuals.

To understand this rights-based orientation, then, we must examine the additional rights that this group of people has yet to see recognized and genuinely met, including the right to a basic level of economic security and access to health care. Unemployment, the inability to provide for the basic needs of children or elderly family members, and the health-related hardships of living in a remote place with little medical attention combine to create an overarching sense of despair that characterizes Indigenous lives in São Gabriel. Economically speaking, as climate change renders traditional agricultural and fishing practices increasingly untenable, wage employment opportunities for Indigenous people are limited to three areas – the military, the health care sector, and the educational sector. Indeed, as access to education has improved, especially in the communities themselves, the concern has turned to the question of what the graduating students will do with the knowledge they have received, and how they will be able to find paid employment that allows them to stay in the community and contribute to its growth and improvement. In many cases, the only obvious way for students to apply the knowledge they have acquired in school is to become teachers and pass that knowledge on to future students.

Creating the school would raise the status of the Kotiria language and its speakers, and also meet the needs of Kotiria individuals by securing stable employment for current and future teachers. This latter aspect has had an unacknowledged impact on conversations among AIPOK members and on the group's ability to achieve its goals overall. Because the Brazilian constitution's recognition of language rights amounts to a commitment that each Indigenous community will have a teacher who speaks its own language, a problem emerges: there are not enough vacancies to employ all of the existing Kotiria teachers in the small, remote Kotiria communities. As a consequence, many of the teachers involved with AIPOK have been displaced from their positions in other (non-Kotiria) rural communities as teachers who can speak the local language become available. Because of the size of the municipality and the paucity of available positions, this has meant that many have had to relocate their families far away, or leave their families behind in one part of the municipality while obtaining work along another of the river systems. The ideological importance of one's primary language matters here as well. Kotiria teachers would never put themselves forward for consideration for positions in Tukano-speaking schools or communities, for example, even though many are fluent Tukano speakers, and despite the fact that its status as the *lingua franca* of the Uaupés, including in large centres such as Iauaratê and Taracuá, means that a larger number of positions are available for this language. Because they are unable to claim the Tukano language as their own, they are ineligible for consideration based on local ideologies.

Although the teachers who belong to AIPOK express support for these language rights in a general way, they are obviously concerned that those rights are being implemented at the expense of their ability to meet their own basic needs. But at the same time, this rights-based language provides them with a framework for articulating their claim that a Kotiria urban school would provide their children with an appropriate education, and them with a level of security – something they see as part of this set of rights. This goal is understandable, given the high rates of poverty, insecurity, and extreme human suffering they see around them. But this motivation does not necessarily translate into a commitment to the kind of hard, thankless, unpaid work that is required during the early stages of a language revitalization project; efforts to get such projects off the ground and to find sustainable funding rarely generate income for the participants.

Financially *and* ideologically, then, the members are not all operating from the same position with respect to their efforts to create this school. AIPOK presents itself as unified in its goals. Even though each member of the group is motivated more strongly by one or the other of the two "principal objectives" (the desire to ensure the transmission of their language, and the assurance of secure employment), these objectives are represented as jointly held by all group members. While founding a Kotiria school would, in fact, overcome both these challenges, they are not inherently compatible at all stages of the process. Those members who are more concerned about job security than about cultural revitalization do not display the same level of commitment to activities or meetings that are designed to consider interim activities, and they express a greater willingness to give up the struggle and seek other alternatives as funding opportunities are rejected. Particularly at this early stage, this ideological distinction is worth clarifying, acknowledging, and examining for possible solutions to collaborative challenges.

The Displacement of Indigenous Identity

The vision expressed by AIPOK members is of a space within the urban area – a school – that would be fully Kotiria. They are calling, in other words, for a rejection of two things: the pan-Indigenous vision of identity captured by the co-officialization law and the language-in-education policy; and the current acceptance of carving out space for Indigeneity within public space instead of creating, from the ground up, an Indigenous public space. The challenges they face, however, involve not just questions of how this should be done, but also the question of whether doing it is desirable or possible. In other words, can Indigenous cultures, which so often invoke connections to place and territory, be transplanted out of those territories? And by extension, what are the practices that define the Indigenous cultures that are being preserved? Such practices include subsistence horticulture, communal living arrangements, and relationships to the land and the seasons that are, undeniably, difficult to incorporate into an urban lifestyle. Some Indigenous activists consider it impossible to maintain Indigenous culture in the city.[4]

Efforts to engage in language revitalization in the urban area run directly counter to these discourses of authenticity, in which "original," apparently unchanged cultural practices – especially those that are performative, such as language, storytelling, dances, and the food and drink consumed during ceremonies – must be valorized, while all of the versions that can be found in the urban area are understood as corrupted. To illustrate, while I was filming a *dabucuri*[5] in February 2012, three different people approached me to explain that I was not seeing the "true culture" but rather something that was "all mixed up." In another conversation, a Tuyuka leader who was observing the FOIRN-organized Indigenous Women's Conference (Encontro das Mulheres Indígenas), asked me what the focus of my research was. When I told him I was examining urban Indigenous identity, he provided me with a few names of individuals I should talk to, emphasizing that they were some of the only people living in the city who were still aware of the "original" culture. When I asked him whether he believed it was possible to live in the city and continue to practise the culture, he declared unequivocally that it was not – the community *is* the culture. Barbra Meek (2011) discusses a similar dynamic: in Yukon, the valorization of elders' ways of speaking risks rendering language inaccessible to learners and young people. In São Gabriel, the urban/rural divide overrides the age-based one. In these examples, Indigenous culture is idealized as static across both time and space – it should be unchanging moving into the future, and for the sake of that, it must stay in its traditional location.

Given these existing ideologies about the relationships among Indigeneity, cultural practices, and place, AIPOK's desire to create a differentiated school in the urban area is significant in and of itself. For various reasons, thirty-five Kotiria families have made their permanent homes in the city of São Gabriel, and they feel that, having established their families and livelihoods there, they cannot return to life in the upriver communities. From their perspective, residing in the urban area does not mean that they and their families should be deprived of the benefits of differentiated education and cultural revitalization. Their efforts to implement such programs, however, face opposition from influential people within both the municipal government and Indigenous political organizations, who rely on these ideologies of place-based authenticity and who are responsible for distributing the scarce resources available for these types of programs.

At the same time, AIPOK members themselves continue to affiliate in some ways with these ideological foundations that complicate their ability to achieve their self-defined goals. Ideologies, it must be said, are always like this – complex and contradictory, as well as rarely consistent with what we say we want to achieve (Gal 1998). The challenge for those who are passionately concerned about language – including those who are engaged in revitalization activism – is to bring those contradictions to a level of awareness that would allow for recognition of the real challenges they face in accomplishing their stated goals.

In AIPOK's case, a reliance on the urban/rural dichotomy, including a somewhat hyperbolic invocation of a complete and total disconnect between the urban people and their Indigenous cultures, emerges in the funding proposals they put forward. For example, in the 2009 proposal for the urban Kotiria school that they submitted to the municipal prefecture, the Kotiria teachers who would ultimately come to lead AIPOK noted that "in the communities ... culture, language, and customs remain intact, without any destructive interference. In the urban area, the lifestyle is *completely different*" (emphasis mine). Their adoption of this binary opposition between community and city situates AIPOK as partly accepting this discourse of rural authenticity even as they contest the idea that a complete loss of culture is inevitable upon moving to the city. This connection between rurality and Indigeneity is buttressed by the significance of place in the formation of identity, particularly for patrilocal Tukanoan cultures like the Kotiria. Because outsider women move to their husbands' communities following exogamous marriages, the emphasis on the use of the patrilect in public spaces works to constitute the identity of that community. As Janet Chernela (2004; 2013) has observed, this pattern is strengthened by language socialization practices that discourage and shame children for using their mother's language as they reach the age of greater involvement in public life.

These are the ideological conceptualizations that make using Portuguese in public in the urban area something more than an act of convenience. Intentionally or not, doing so becomes an act of place-claiming. As with many aspects of Tukanoan identity and cultural concepts, connections among language, place, and identity are circular rather than linear. That is to say, while language makes the place, and language makes the identity, place also makes the identity, in a series of recursive and reciprocal semiotic processes. Place of origin is vital to a person's identity – a sense of rootedness is strongly associated with the place where one was born, and Tukanoan naming ceremonies involve the shamanic transportation of the ancestral spirit of the name-holder from its spiritual origin in the "Milk River" through a description of the physical geographic space until it arrives at the place of the child's birth. The possibility of returning to that place of birth will always be open to that person and provide him or her with a site of grounding in the world. Just as the public use of Portuguese in the city works to stake a claim to the space in potentially unintended ways, these ideologies result in perceived differences between Indigenous people based on place of birth. Urban-born Indigenous people belong, inherently, to Portuguese space, and this makes it difficult for some Indigenous activists to see the importance of their learning to speak their own languages.

For those who believe that a language must be maintained in its authentic form based on its role in rural communities, these beliefs make it impossible both to experience an Indigenous lifestyle in the city and to become fully rooted in an Indigenous identity after being born in the urban area. From this perspective, efforts to preserve languages and cultural practices in that space are mistaken at best and destructive at worst (since they divert resources from programs in the rural areas). The regionalized structure of most local Indigenous organizations, including FOIRN, magnifies the impact of these voices and attitudes within the local political economy. The city itself has no formal representatives to act on behalf of urban Indigenous people. FOIRN's main office is in the city, but its political authority comes almost entirely from residents of the surrounding rural areas. Urban residents may make a claim to the FOIRN director or to the organization that represents the region of their personal or familial origin, but their interests as urban Indigenous people are not treated as a political priority. AIPOK, then, can expect little support from other Indigenous organizations; indeed, it has to somehow counter the perception that it is undermining the hard work that has gone into creating differentiated schools on the Upper Uaupés by trying to draw away resources and by further reducing the limited incentives for students to stay in their communities of origin.

The Role of Language Learners

In situating its goals in connection to language revitalization, and in expressing the goal of constructing a school, AIPOK has also drawn attention (albeit not necessarily deliberately) to the role that potential language learners play in establishing and shaping urban Kotiria identity. Just as the city and Indigenous people born in it have a precarious claim to an authentically Indigenous identity, so too are learners of local Indigenous languages subject to ideological questioning. Ironically, that questioning applies less to people who are trying to learn a language other than their patrilect, because the depth of the association between patrilect and identity is such that there is simply no way of talking about or conceptualizing how it would work for someone to have to learn this language. The Kotiria have two distinct ways of describing their linguistic abilities – on the one hand, the verb *dubu'e* describes the process by which a child acquires the patrilect and conveys the sense that it is a natural process, while on the other, the verb *bu'ero* (to learn) highlights the conscious effort involved in developing the ability to speak the language of others. This latter term is generally associated with the concept of mimicry, as in the phrase *khayo bu'ero* ("learn to speak the way he does") (Chernela 2013). My efforts to probe the question of how one might describe a person learning to speak his or her patrilect later in life were met, in general, with bafflement. Neither *bu'ero* nor *dubu'e* quite seemed to fit respondents' conceptualizations of what was happening.

In this way, too, the case of the urban Kotiria presents some big-picture questions that must be asked by advocates and scholars of endangered language communities and language revitalization, as increasing attention is also going to the question of how revitalization complicates academic understandings of what it means to be a speaker and who is able to claim access to the related identities (Shulist 2016a). In the case of the Kotiria, the inability to describe the process by which an adult might learn to speak his or her patrilect implies that at least some Kotiria people see a barrier to becoming fully Kotiria during adulthood. Because these people are working to construct a school in which their children can be educated in the Kotiria language, the distinction between *bu'ero* and *dabu'e* (in English, perhaps between acquiring and knowing, and learning and imitating) is based not on process or method, but rather on identity and, to some extent, age.

These questions further tie in to the complicated and contentious issue of authenticity within Indigenous politics. Where language is fundamental to Indigenous identity and activists emphasize this in order to generate support for the often nebulous concept of revitalizing a language, the flip side of this position is that those Indigenous people who have never learned their language, for whatever reason, are excluded from full access to that identity. Various actors influence the policing of Indigenous authenticity, including government agents, NGOs, and other Indigenous people. With urbanity already generating questions about the legitimacy of certain Indigenous identities, members of AIPOK often push back against these ways of contesting the authenticity of their claims about the importance of language and culture to them and their children. This contestation, however, does not necessarily dispute the idea of authenticity in itself; rather, it refocuses the criteria for determining Indigeneity from place to language. The foundational reason for the involvement of AIPOK's urban members, after all, is their concern for the identity of those who cannot speak Kotiria. These urban Kotiria dispute the idea that living in the city constitutes a barrier to legitimating their identity; but in emphasizing that their children need to know the language to truly be Kotiria (and not just to understand Kotiria culture), they reinforce the notion that linguistic ability is an appropriate measure of an individual's authenticity.

Although some of AIPOK's leaders are aware that to engage effectively with language revitalization, they will need to recruit potential language learners, the position these potential learners find themselves in is fraught at best. The experiences of Adilson, one of the oldest Kotiria people to have lived most of his life in São Gabriel, capture these challenges well. Adilson was born in Iauaratê in 1976 and arrived with his parents (a Tariana mother and Kotiria father) in the city when he was four years old. He considers himself a passive speaker of Kotiria and a somewhat stronger speaker of Tukano, which his parents often use to communicate with each other in the home, and which was the language of broader communication during his early childhood in Iauaratê. He is now married to an urban-raised, monolingual Portuguese-speaking Baré woman, and his two young children (at the time of my fieldwork, ages two and four) were exposed to Indigenous languages only because they lived with Adilson's parents, who continued to speak Tukano to each other. He consistently expressed a desire to be more connected to

Kotiria cultural practices, but he felt excluded from Indigenous organizations, including AIPOK, in which he participated sporadically and tentatively. He described to me several occasions on which his self-identification as Kotiria and the validity of his opinions about Indigenous political issues were called into question – by rural Kotiria, by other members of AIPOK, and most potently for him, by FOIRN leaders – as a direct result of his inability to speak the language. These experiences have left him reluctant to become involved with AIPOK or to engage more actively in language learning efforts. His first-hand knowledge of what it means to grow up as an urban Indigenous person and his direct experience with exactly the type of loss that AIPOK members express concern about are, paradoxically, the very points that make it difficult for him to engage with the organization's goals. This paradox is an important area to address if the Kotiria are to make a significant impact on the state of the language in the city.

Adilson's story is illustrative not simply because of the challenges he has faced, but also because he is alone among urban-raised non-speakers in the amount of effort he has exerted to engage in revitalization movements. Other youth and young adults, including his three younger sisters, are passionate about helping their community and improving the lives of Indigenous people, but they invest their time in activities that are not as strongly focused on language and culture (e.g., on strengthening their involvement in national and international youth networks, and on using activities such as hip hop, theatre, and radio programming to support young people in their efforts to stay away from or get off of drugs and alcohol by providing a supportive and positive environment). These are not the apathetic, disaffected, or troubled youth sometimes invoked by language activists in São Gabriel and elsewhere as the ones who are difficult to reach. Rather, they are knowledgeable and politically engaged young people who spoke to me repeatedly about their wish to learn the language and understand the culture, but who did not really seem to have a sense of where to begin. In the absence of an invitation from Kotiria-speaking relatives, or of Indigenous language advocates coming to speak to them about how they could use language within their existing efforts, there was little room in their busy lives to find these opportunities. Seeking out and attending to non-speakers like Adilson and other young Kotiria adults in São Gabriel could be an important pragmatic step for AIPOK's urban language revitalization efforts, but ideologies are hindering that group's willingness to branch out in this way.

Ideologies of Education and Learning: Proposing the Kotiria Bu'eri Wʉ'ʉ

Given the ambiguous status of potential language learners, it is worth further evaluating the ideological basis for AIPOK's proposal for an urban Kotiria school (to be known as the São Gabriel Kotiria Bu'eri Wʉ'ʉ, or Kotiria House of Learning), and its centrality to their vision of supporting Kotiria language and culture in the city. This importance is partly explained by the general value associated with education both for language and for Indigenous politics as a whole (see chapter 4). As residents of the urban area, the children of AIPOK members have easy access to stable, high-quality education, at least relative to the inhabitants of the upriver territories. The question at hand is how these schools can help maintain and promote their languages and cultures.

The arguments AIPOK members make for how the school could help accomplish this goal reveal two competing discourses about what the role of that school should be. Each draws on different ideologies expressed among academics about the relationship between minority languages and educational settings. Bilingual intercultural education programs are viewed as a necessary part of the struggle to maintain Indigenous cultures and languages, and of efforts to ensure the autonomy of Indigenous communities (Henze and Davis 1999; López and Sichra 2008; Hornberger 2008). At the same time, advocates for these forms of schooling often point to the benefits of "mother tongue" education in improving the educational outcomes experienced by Indigenous children (Crawford 1989; McCarty 2003). This latter position proceeds from the commonsense view that attempting to teach a child literacy skills in a language other than his or her primary language creates major challenges, and that providing education – especially at the earliest levels – in the child's primary language is extremely important for the reduction of systematic inequalities.

The urban AIPOK, ultimately, cannot benefit from the latter discourse. But they do make use of it, in part because they have seen how this argument contributed to the success of the Kotiria Khumunu-wʉ'ʉ in Caruru-cachoeira. There, however, the children arrive in school with Kotiria as their dominant language. The argument hurts the urban Kotiria, since the idea of using bilingualism to ensure equality for those who have difficulty with the dominant national language leaves no place for the use of Indigenous languages in a city in which all of the children not only are proficient in Portuguese but also have little or no knowledge of the heritage Indigenous language. Although the proposals AIPOK members have developed (in consultation with me and with other academic partners) articulate their goals in terms of language revitalization and ensuring that their children are able to learn their language, everyday conversations with group members revealed the ongoing assumption that they should be able to mirror the structures and methodologies (including curricula and pedagogical materials) created for their relatives on the Upper Uaupés. Pedagogically, however, these children require second-language acquisition material, or immersion schooling models, rather than transitional literacy models.

With the Kotiria in particular, the emphasis on a school as a site for language preservation and transmission was a frustrating thing for me to confront as an academic ally, for I am all too aware of the limitations of this domain for increasing the use of minority languages. Based on this knowledge and on my assessment of the current level of endangerment facing the Kotiria language in the city of São Gabriel, I began my involvement with AIPOK by encouraging them to consider other strategies for language revitalization (for example, consciousness-raising about in-home language use, the use of community centres for cultural activities and socializing among Kotiria who live in different parts of the city, and the development of a master/apprentice model), either instead of or concomitantly with their efforts to establish a school. The rapid rate of shift away from the use of the Kotiria language, the extent to which the teachers' commitment to the cause of its revitalization has not translated into transmission in their homes, and the seemingly insurmountable political and financial barriers hindering the establishment of the school led me to believe that, since a school was likely at least a few years away, strengthening the language in the meantime was of paramount importance. There is a quite common belief (globally widespread) that schools are the places of language learning; I treated this position as a misconception (Hornberger 2008). My suggestions for alternative projects were acknowledged politely but with little enthusiasm and no follow-up effort. As I became more deeply involved with the organization and got to know more of its members, I came to understand that my arguments were not in any way changing their sense of the relative value of schools compared to other potential sites for language revitalization. I came to realize that treating this belief as a misconception, or something that could be overcome with training and discussion, did not account for all of the reasons why the idea of a school held such a powerful sway over the minds of my collaborative partners.

Here, a conflict emerged between academic and local ideologies about the process and meaning of learning a language and acquiring linguistic knowledge. The AIPOK members often told me that they "did not have time" to "teach" their children the language. Academic research into psycholinguistics and child language acquisition has emphasized that the belief that children need to be consciously *taught* a language is simply incorrect, and I drew on my knowledge of this research and my position as an authority about language to "correct" this assumption. As I patiently explained psycholinguistic theories to various individuals, they asked questions, nodded, and interjected "Oh, really?," then lamented their children's inability and told me at later meetings again that they wished they had time to teach them. Franssinete, the president of AIPOK, was one of my closest friends in São Gabriel, and someone with whom I had spoken about this process several times, since her four children ranged in age from two to thirteen during my 2012 fieldwork period. She and her husband, Wilson, do not share any common Indigenous languages (he is a native speaker of Nheengatú); however, their children are cared for by a Kotiria-speaking relative of Franssinete's, and their maternal grandfather and other relatives were staying in their home during the prolonged illness of their grandmother (Franssinete's mother, who eventually died). The older two children would occasionally demonstrate some understanding of Nheengatú, but for the most part, conversations in Indigenous languages took place only among adults, and children were addressed exclusively in Portuguese.

Part of the ideological challenge involved here relates to visions about the point at which someone is entitled to use a language, and to the general discouragement of the types of language errors common among learners. I saw the implications of this process, along with other elements of Kotiria ideologies of acquisition, in the challenges I faced in my own efforts to learn the language. Because my family situation precluded the option of immersing myself in a Kotiria-speaking environment, I hired Miguel Cabral to provide daily lessons for several months. The implications of what Miguel, Franssinete, and others were saying about their lack of time became clear in these lessons, as the time-consuming process of teaching me to write took a central place in these lessons. Although my academic training in linguistics made it relatively easy for me to pick up on the conventions of written Kotiria, my ability to form sentences and remember vocabulary remained extremely poor. Despite this, Miguel and others often praised my ability; one individual even suggested that my knowledge was equal to his own, because he could speak but not write, while I could write (when I heard it being spoken) but not speak.

The emphasis on writing, and the importance of being able to write in order to claim full knowledge of the language, ties back to a fear of working with the language among those who lack this "complete" linguistic paradigm. In some cases, perhaps because of its relative rarity, writing may even have come to supersede speaking as the central element of linguistic knowledge. Several group members, including Miguel, emphasized their strong desire for their children to learn to read and write their language, but de-emphasized the need for them to learn to speak it – that part would be nice, if possible, but what they wanted most to see was their children writing, reading, and understanding their Kotiria tongue. As Fleming (2009: 41) points out, among the people of the Rio Negro "literacy is seen as an end in itself, and talk about literacy is the manner in which education comes to be understood as having a self-evident value." The need for complete knowledge, including literacy, combines with an emphasis on textuality (Hugh-Jones 2010) and a puristic ideology that discourages imperfect use (Aikhenvald 2003b). My own attempts to use the few Kotiria words and phrases that I knew, and to apply language-learning techniques I had used in other contexts – that is, to stumble about without much regard for the errors I was making in my efforts to make myself understood, and to build upon those errors as part of the learning process – were met with some polite recognition before the listeners immediately switched to Portuguese and changed the subject.

It was in this context – which emphasizes complete linguistic knowledge, including literacy – that the teachers were correct to claim that they did not have time to teach their children. The school thus became an absolutely vital component of their language revitalization activities, since only a school could provide them with the structure necessary to ensure the transmission of all of these aspects of linguistic knowledge while providing them with an income and maintaining the child's progress through the educational system. This particular ideological conflict was a powerful one, because it concerned the relationship between academic allies (myself included) and the local Indigenous people themselves, in addition to informing the type of help, guidance, and suggestions that I had come equipped to provide. Understanding the Kotiria view of acquisition and language teaching – something that this picture touches on only very briefly – is necessary if a pedagogical method is to be developed that is fully based on local understandings of what it means to learn a language and how it is that the language should be learned. Imagining a school that works more fully with this view of language, despite an audience of students who have essentially no Kotiria knowledge upon arrival in school, would be a radical departure from current models of bilingual education.

Identifying the Barriers to Kotiria in São Gabriel

The above discussion has taken into account how language ideological conflict emerges, in various ways, to create different visions of how to solve the problem facing the urban Kotiria. Another area of disagreement emerges when we take another step back from these ideas to consider how AIPOK members explain and understand the challenges they face. In other words, what do they identify as the aspects of urban life that cause or exacerbate the attrition of Kotiria language use in the city, and how do these interpretations match up with social scientific observations? Because the Kotiria describe the city as "fundamentally different" from the rural territories, and because this difference is understood as a threat to Indigenous cultural practices, it is worth examining further what, specifically, has created this difference in their perceptions.

AIPOK documents and discussions highlight particular points of concern that they see as the causes of cultural erosion. These diagnostics provide useful insights into how the people involved view and engage with the idea of urban Indigeneity. In this regard, three prominent themes are apparent: the amount of linguistic diversity and the need to use Portuguese as a language of communication; the ubiquity of technology and media that connect Indigenous youth most strongly with the non-Indigenous public of the world "outside" of the region; and the greater tendency towards a disjointed, capitalist lifestyle rather than the collectivist one encountered in rural communities. Two questions emerge regarding these visions of why the city is such a challenging environment for Indigenous practice. First, are they an accurate reflection of the differences between city and community? And second, what does it mean to centre them in discussions about visions for the future of Indigeneity in the city? How are they being addressed strategically, and what is being missed when we focus on these elements?

The most complex of these points is the idea that cultural diversity is more significant in this space than in rural areas. In some ways, this idea is based in an obvious truth – that the greater population makes it more likely to find a larger number of cultural groups in contact with one another – but that truth elides the degree to which a very high degree of diversity within communities defines the experience of exogamous cultural groups. Interestingly, AIPOK's 2009 school proposal document drew particular attention to intermarriage as a threat:

> Intermarriage with other ethnic groups has had a major impact on social interaction, and principally on language and culture. We would like to clarify this point for further reflection; the speaker from the Wanano language group who marries a speaker of another language comes to interact in the home using only Portuguese because they don't understand one another in everyday conversation in the mother tongue, and the children are born speaking only Portuguese, ending up unable to understand or express themselves in their parents' languages, and still less to read or write in their language. This causes the parents to worry, since they observe day after day of their peoples' languages being completely forgotten, along with the traditional knowledge transmitted within them. [emphases mine]

This claim about the challenge of intermarriage and the need to use Portuguese to communicate was repeated more than once, with reference to each individual who was present, during my first meeting with the teachers' group. As I was introduced to each person, they identified themselves as Kotiria, usually referencing the community in which they were born, then identified the group membership of their spouse, and closed with a phrase like "so unfortunately, I am unable to speak my language with him/her."

But intermarriage, like linguistic diversity and multilingualism, is not something that is new to the Kotiria people as a result of urbanization – indeed, as I have mentioned throughout this book, linguists and anthropologists have cited the traditional ideologies of linguistic exogamy as protective of, rather than threatening to, the region's remarkable linguistic diversity (Sorensen 1967; Jackson 1983; Stenzel 2005). Claims that intermarriage is a threat, then, do not fully capture what has changed or is changing in the urban area. In some ways, this claim that intermarriage is a threat may be seen as an absorption of outside discourses about language endangerment that emphasize "commonsense" notions about language shift. At a generalized, global level, organizations with which many Indigenous people have become familiar, such as UNESCO, cite bilingualism and intermarriage as predictive of shift. That said, it would be naive to dismiss the fact that there is a qualitative difference in the type of multilingualism found in the urban area and the type that has characterized Tukanoan society for generations. A central part of this difference relates to how, unlike the traditionally egalitarian structure among linguistic codes within the exogamous social structures, colonialism has created a hierarchical set of relationships among codes, with Portuguese undeniably occupying the top position. In focusing on exogamy and diversity, AIPOK misdiagnoses the problem, eliding the importance of this power differential as well as the spatialized socialization practices (through which the public defaulting to Portuguese is, as discussed above, more than mere convenience) that reinscribe indexical relationships between urbanity and non-Indigeneity.

The second identified problem also has an immediate surface-level truth to it, and here, the implications are less a matter of misdiagnosis and more a matter of focusing on technology as an inevitable problem (or at least, a sword that can be turned double-edged) (Eisenlohr 2004). Young people in São Gabriel do, in fact, spend much of their free time watching Portuguese television, surfing the Internet, and playing online games. Their parents' concerns that they are developing aspirational goals that are based on what they see in this "outside" world are borne out by fashion and media choices and by expressions of admiration for television personalities. Efforts to draw young people away from these forms of entertainment and towards a revaluation of Indigenous ways of being have relied primarily on an either/or argumentation that echoes the puristic ideologies of "tradition." Focusing, for example, on Indigenous language texts recounting origin stories, rituals, and myths (Fleming 2009; Andrello 2010; Hugh-Jones 2010), rather than on new domains and genres for their use, generates a perception among young people that they have to renounce all communication technologies in order to be accepted as authentically committed to their cultures and identities. A few exceptions to this pattern of thinking emerged not in relation to technology specifically, but in theatre workshops I participated in at the Catholic Youth Centre, where local narratives were discussed as possible sources for presentation material and compared positively and with enthusiasm to the plots of telenovelas or popular movies. In other words, it was when urban Indigenous youth were able to see these myths in terms of the stories around which they were orienting their lives, and able to imagine their relevance to things they already liked and related to, that they became engaged with the idea of embracing their Indigenous cultural practices.

While the local Indigenous movement has been increasing its use of the Internet and social media to raise awareness of the political concerns facing Indigenous people, both an ideological and a pragmatic barrier are hindering efforts to convert the "cultural nerve gas" of media technologies into "electronic smoke signals" (Zellen 1998: 25) that would benefit Indigenous languages. The pragmatic barrier is that in the remote communities where many of the speakers of the languages still live, electricity is often unreliable, irregular, or non-existent, and access to the Internet is obviously impossible. Social media have benefited the Indigenous movement by enabling it to send its message *outside* of the Rio Negro region, to other parts of Brazil and to the international community of Indigenous activism; but revitalizing the language will require ways to connect and communicate *within* the region, many of whose parts are difficult to access (both physically and electronically), and the costs associated with such efforts may not worth the limited benefits. Interestingly, the primary exceptions to this pattern have tended to be speakers of Baniwa, several of whom have taken to using that language on social media such as Facebook and Twitter – another public space in which they are doing more to assert the presence of Indigeneity than they are to communicate ideas. In lamenting technology and outsider popular culture as threats, then, the older generation of Kotiria leaders may *creating* a barrier between urban youth and language revitalization activism.

The last problem listed, that of individualism and disunity, is also pertinent, though as the discussion of language rights earlier in this chapter attests, the premise that Indigenous people are inherently more inclined towards collective interests is far from unquestionable, given that the desire for individual identity is an important component of urban Kotiria activism. At the same time, in terms of quotidian social practices, an important barrier is created by the geography of the urban area, where the distances between groups of relatives and speakers of the same language are much more significant than in smaller communities. The city of São Gabriel is small, but even so, those who lack resources for transportation, who often work multiple jobs besides raising their families, and who may have health conditions for which they receive inadequate medical attention, lack the time and energy to walk to the houses of their relatives, or to community centres and other points that can act as meeting places. This constitutes a major barrier to their continued connections to one another. Pockets of patrilocal patterns emerge around the city as people build houses on pieces of land owned by their fathers or other relatives, but these remain limited by the amount of space available on most urban plots. AIPOK's very existence is part of the effort to combat the unfocused and individualistic dynamic of the urban area; that organization is working to establish itself as the locus of a unified Kotiria perspective, one that mirrors the idea of a coherent "community" of the kind found in rural contexts. This is not to say that either AIPOK or the rural communities are homogenous or uncomplicated bodies; the point, rather, is that they allow for some degree of discussion to take place among community members that can be presented as reflecting the group's interests. In this way, the diagnosis of a need to create and strengthen a Kotiria place and site in the city is both powerful and far-reaching as a way of understanding what it means to re-envision an Indigenous city.

Imagining the Future of Kotiria in São Gabriel

This account of AIPOK illustrates the challenges of engaging in language revitalization in an urban area in part because the discourses that its members have seen work for others are not working for them. In addition, the specific visions they express regarding the ways in which their language and culture could be preserved in the urban context reveal important ideological factors that are influencing the outcomes of their efforts. The Kotiria example is relevant for understanding differences in opinions not only about why language matters in the urban area, but also about how it should be learned and what it means to be a speaker. These questions, and the multifaceted ideologies connected to them, have a significant but also surprisingly tangled role to play in the future of the Kotiria language and culture in the city.

The example of the Kotiria helps us better understand the complex impact of state policies as they relate to Indigenous peoples and Indigenous education from the perspective of a group that is marginalized and poorly represented within existing policy at all levels of government. Indigenous political activism and federal recognition of Indigenous peoples' cultural rights both focus primarily on programs and policies implemented in rural areas and officially demarcated territories. Because educational policies supporting the maintenance of traditional practices and languages are geographically determined, Indigenous people living in urban areas face significant challenges when they try to secure support for promoting and protecting their languages and cultures. At the same time, the municipal language policy within São Gabriel has created a framework that makes it more difficult for speakers of non-official languages to obtain broader support for their projects outside their traditional communities (where the policy establishes that the dominant local language should be considered "official"). In attempting to navigate the complex political, legal, and social situation in which they find themselves, the urban Kotiria have sought ways to make the laws and policies work to their favour. Insofar as Northwest Amazonian Indigenous peoples are multilingual and linguistically egalitarian, the emphasis among the Kotiria on creating space for their own language constitutes a strategy not just for revitalizing their own language, but for embodying Tukanoan Indigeneity among an urban public.

In drawing attention to the challenges, contradictions, and ideological conflicts that have hindered AIPOK, this case study has revealed the need for much more significant discussion about the barriers to urban language revitalization and the role that academics can play in it. AIPOK and the urban Kotiria are engaging in a courageous and creative endeavour to introduce a new kind of education for a population (urban Indigenous youth) that is as misunderstood as it is marginalized, and in doing so, they are encountering complex intersections among ideologies at multiple levels. At least some of the ideological positions discussed here – in particular, questions of literacy and the importance of the home as the primary site for language revitalization – have been identified as potential challenges for AIPOK. In my own conversations, my position as an academic outsider situated me as the "expert" on the "truth" about how language should be learned, and drew on scholarly work that has treated beliefs like the Kotiria's as misconceptions. This approach turned out to be unimaginative, ineffective, and, ultimately, ontologically inaccurate. As with past work situating academic understandings of language in terms of their ideological frames (Collins 1998), my experiences call into question what it is that we, as allies, are actually *doing* when we advocate for the preservation of language in specific ways, with particular conceptualizations of what language is, of what kinds of linguistic knowledge should be prioritized, and of what it means to "know" a language. Treating the Kotiria positions as rooted in meaningful and relevant ideologies rather than as misconceptions and misunderstandings, and inviting the Kotiria to help develop pedagogical models and revitalization programs, could do a great deal to formulate more effective strategies and to deepen the academic understanding of language and its uses.

6 Revising Expectations: Reflections on the Research Process

As noted in the introduction to this book, I began this research with the goal of establishing a collaborative research relationship with one or more groups of Indigenous people living and working in the urban area. The preceding chapters have made clear that the realities in São Gabriel clashed with this idealized goal in many ways. Ultimately, however, these spaces of tension became relevant points of consideration in and of themselves. That is to say, the challenges I faced allowed me to analyse disjunctures between several models and ideologies of "collaboration" – between my own (academic, Western) view and those of my Indigenous interlocutors, between an idealized version and one rooted in decades of past collaborations and projects, and between the two disciplines within which language revitalization movements are most commonly studied (linguistics and anthropology). These ideologies, and the collaboration processes that have emerged in relation to language in the Upper Rio Negro, became, in and of themselves, topics of analysis that help illustrate the challenges to language revitalization in this urban environment.

Theorizing Collaboration

Over the past few decades, linguistics and anthropology have both undergone radical shifts in their understandings of the roles they play in the communities where they work, and of the responsibilities they have to support efforts to improve the conditions faced by those often marginalized populations. Especially with regard to language revitalization – an issue that inherently involves an overlap between technical linguistics and social and political concerns that are more in the wheelhouse of anthropologists – it is perhaps surprising how little interaction there has been between these closely related disciplines. Within linguistics, the concern for language loss and its impact on both minority-language speakers and global cultural diversity has expanded since the "call to arms" issued by Hale and colleagues (1992), in which the authors brought to a widespread audience of language scholars the idea that linguistic work should move away from salvage efforts designed solely to create a record of the languages and consider working to save these languages. The Hale article was one among several that brought attention to what was by then a widespread problem (see also Fishman 1991; Crawford 1995). Anthropologists, for their part, have been forced by the communities they work with to recognize the role that their discipline has played in enabling and exacerbating colonial domination; this conversation has been occurring on a large scale for a few decades longer; the 1960s and 1970s decolonization movements contributed to radical shifts in anthropological theory and methodology (Biolsi and Zimmerman 1997). That researchers must be aware of the political and social implications of their analyses and publications, and contribute something of value to the communities in which they work, is now central to ethical anthropological research.

Language loss became a concern among linguists largely as a result of recognition from within the academy itself, as scholars working in widely disparate geographical and social contexts began to understand how widespread the phenomenon was and consider how they could collectively address it. At the same time, Indigenous and minority communities engaging in decolonization efforts have themselves brought language and cultural practices to the forefront of struggles for autonomy, and anthropologists have responded by demonstrating the wide range of roles they can play in these struggles (from cultural brokers to project facilitators and advisers). This latter shift has been felt more forcefully and deeply than the former, as calls to thoroughly rethink both the methodological and theoretical approaches to knowledge at the most fundamental levels (Smith 1999; Scheper-Hughes 2000; Fluehr-Lobban 2008). In Latin America in particular, where this period of upheaval in the discipline of anthropology coincided with broader political struggles against military dictatorships, an engaged and politicized approach to ethnography has become dominant. Scholars at Latin American institutions have seen the struggles of the marginalized members of their societies as part and parcel of their own struggles against oppressive regimes. These perspectives, as well as widespread awareness among the studied populations themselves, have made a politicized anthropology the norm rather than the exception in this region (Albert and Ramos 1989; Rappaport 2007; Ramos 2000).

The two disciplines are related and address similar themes regarding the implications of language shift and cultural change. That said, they have different trajectories that have resulted in the development of contrasting theories and practices of collaboration with respect to revitalization (Shulist 2013). As a generalization, the approach taken by documentary linguists has resulted in a concrete – if somewhat uniform – set of practical ways of working with communities to address language endangerment and support their revitalization goals, whereas anthropologists working on collaborative ethnographic projects have tended to expose the various conflicts and contradictions that complicate these movements as well as discourses about them.[1] In many ways, I deeply admire the pragmatic approach that linguists take and recognize the tendency of anthropologists to examine details and resist oversimplifications of that sort that are often necessary for any kind of action to be taken. (The vernacular term for this is "paralysis by analysis.") But at the same time, I believe that language documentation work would benefit from a sharper focus, both theoretical and practical, on the role of power in the research process and its outcomes. This aligns with the observations of other linguistic anthropologists and sociocultural linguists who have examined the impact that ideologies and practices within the discipline of linguistics have had on the social lives of people within the endangered-language communities in which they implement their projects (Collins 1998; Hill 2002; Ahlers 2009). My own efforts to establish a collaborative research project related to language revitalization in the urban area of São Gabriel revealed that this idea is far from simple; furthermore, many of the complexities and challenges have resulted directly from the ideological perspectives and practical actions of others who have engaged in collaborative language work in the region.

Increasing attention is being paid to the ethics of linguistic fieldwork, and scholars of linguistics have broadened their focus to include more about the methodology of documentation and revitalization (Rice 2006; Czaykowska-Higgins 2009; Dorian 2010). But for the most part, linguists have not concerned themselves with the question of *power* in relation to their efforts. Awareness of the need to support Indigenous and minority communities that have been marginalized by state and corporate actors has not led to a deep questioning of what power is, what it means, and how it is perpetuated or distributed. Assumptions persist regarding what constitutes a "community's needs," as well as what role linguists can play in helping meet those needs. Academic linguistic interests are still seen as often clashing with the urgent needs of community members, and with few exceptions, the discussion focuses on ensuring that these diverging interests can be balanced, rather than on radically rethinking what it means to talk about language as an object of study (see, for example, Hinton and Hale [2001] and Gippert, Himmelmann, and Mosel [2006], and, for exceptions to this pattern, Rice [2009] and Leonard and Haynes [2010]). This pattern has emerged as a result of practices that focus on teaching aspiring documentary linguists to address a specific set of questions that revolve mainly around the analysis of linguistic structures; and even insofar as they have moved to incorporate language-in-use in addition to more traditional elicitation, language-in-use is generally treated as a tool for better understanding these structures rather than as an element of interest in its own right. Goals for fieldwork are usually defined by the linguist and advisers before the fieldwork starts, in contrast to – as has been common within anthropology since the advent of participant observation – allowing questions to be informed by conditions in the field (Ahlers 2009).

The end result within linguistics has been a set of formalized mechanisms for incorporating local needs into language documentation projects, which themselves commodify linguistic information and knowledge, transforming the language that is being preserved into something captured in books, on recordings, and in digital archives. Advocates for reforms to documentary linguistic work (e.g. Ahlers 2009; J.H. Hill 2006) have paid significant attention to the powerful possibilities afforded by ethnographic methodologies, which bring to the surface ideologies, local linguistic cultures, and how language constitutes and creates identity, culture, and spirituality in different ways depending on the context. For documentary linguistics, the central problem is that language may sometimes not be detachable from the cultural context in which it functions, and may not be analysable as an object outside of its uses, meanings, and purposes (Debenport 2015).

As a scholar with training in both anthropology and linguistics, I am aware of the contributions that each of these disciplines can make to meeting the needs of community members. In some ways, my idealized vision of a collaborative research project broke down because it was somewhat naive and unrealistic to hope that the type of trusting relationships this would require could be built in such a short period, given that I had no pre-existing contacts or in-depth understanding of a complicated social and linguistic situation before my arrival. But this does not fully account for the change that is taking place with regard to language, culture, and Indigenous identity among the diasporic urban Indigenous population of São Gabriel. My efforts to engage with language revitalization in terms of what language is and can be in the local context – especially in a diverse, rapidly shifting urban context – crashed against the barrier of how my collaborators had come to understand documentation and revitalization projects, and the role that I was expected to play within them.

Ensuring that academic projects are conducted with the interests of community members in mind is a central part of working in São Gabriel, and I assumed that this meant my approach would be well-received. But I did not understand the degree to which past research encounters had shaped not only what it meant to work "collaboratively" but also what it meant to talk about language and cultural revitalization, and the extent to which my focus on the urban area did not fit within that pre-existing model. Before my first visit to São Gabriel, the high degree of multilingualism, the proportion of Indigenous people in the urban area, and the existence of the municipal-level language policy suggested to me that the situation would be of great anthropological interest. Because of the social and political importance of language in the region, I expected to find active efforts towards which I would be able to contribute expertise based in my academic training. Those expectations were subverted almost immediately by the actual local situation, in that most language revitalization work in São Gabriel was focused on the rural territories surrounding the city. Those projects that have concerned themselves specifically with urban people – notably the co-officialization law and the Sunday morning gatherings that support cultural activities as well as the sale of horticultural products – have been developed in consultation with non-linguists (with the exception of the political linguist Gilvan Müller de Oliveira, whose work focuses more on policy than on language itself).

In the Northwest Amazon, several linguists have been involved in long-term collaborations both independently and through ISA. ISA has been a major force in scholarship about Indigenous peoples and in Indigenous advocacy in the region. Its headquarters are in Sao Paulo, but it also has offices in several other Brazilian cities and sites of research interest, including in São Gabriel, where the ISA office is a hub of activity: it hosts ISA-affiliated researchers in its rooms and attached housing units, as well as organized consultations, workshops, and meetings between local Indigenous leaders and academic researchers regarding joint projects or advocacy efforts. The building itself is in a beautiful location overlooking the beach and was built by Indigenous experts using local and traditional materials. One of its most notable features is its thatched roof, which absorbs the sound of torrential Amazonian downpours in ways that contrast sharply with the tin roofs that non-Indigenous outside builders chose to use on many of the other buildings in town. In the main area, which is open to the public most weekdays from 9 a.m. to 6 p.m., a half-dozen computers provide free access to the Internet; also available is a library that, while small overall, is rich in information about the local area and its peoples. By providing housing and in other ways, ISA has helped support a significant proportion of the anthropological and linguistic research in the Upper Rio Negro, and is explicitly engaged in political advocacy on behalf of the region's people, working in close consultation with FOIRN, as well as local governing bodies, to make decisions about how to meet this population's needs. ISA has been involved in supporting and informing the demarcation of the Rio Negro Indigenous Territories, as well as in the establishment and ongoing operation of the system of differentiated schools (see earlier chapters). Researchers affiliated with ISA are still involved in consulting on the process of language standardization, in the development of university programs related to Indigenous governance, and in efforts to recognize and incorporate Indigenous medicinal knowledge and practices into health care systems. ISA's NGO structure means that researchers engaging in collaborative research in the Rio Negro have access to a network of knowledge and that Indigenous people and organizations have a standard body to approach for assistance and consultation. The disadvantage of this framework, of course, is that the organization acts as something of a gatekeeper with regard to what kinds of projects are likely to benefit both researchers and local communities. Researchers (such as myself) who are unconnected to ISA are more difficult to incorporate into existing structures of consultation.

ISA researchers have been directly involved in language revitalization work in several ways, including, most prominently, in documentation and differentiated schooling implementation, as well as in the publication (jointly with FOIRN) of a series of monographs documenting the narratives and myths of several of the peoples of the region.

Their efforts have been vital to the development of writing systems, pedagogical materials, and training programs for Indigenous teachers. Documentary and descriptive linguistic work has focused mainly on traditional communities, where the most knowledgeable speakers live and the widest range of uses can be observed; the only anthropological research focusing on the urban area and emerging from this primary collaborative body is that of Cristiane Lasmar (2005; 2009). Preliminary sociolinguistic work evaluating the situation in the city was initiated in 2011 by Kristine Stenzel and Flora Cabral, as well as by a few master's-level research projects (Melgueiro 2012; Sarges 2013); these represent a major step towards implementing language planning initiatives in the urban area. But until this point, the fact that linguistic work has remained centred in the rural territories and focused on documentation efforts, channelled through the organizational support structure of ISA, has helped define a specific type of collaborative relationship that does not fit with the urban area. My decision to focus on the urban area therefore made it difficult for potential collaborators to imagine what role I might play in these projects, to the point that FOIRN was unsure about how to proceed with my application for institutional research ethics approval, since there was no community of reference whose leadership they could contact. Thinking through the types of collaborative efforts that have informed these two main ways of engaging with language revitalization in the area – (rurally focused) documentation for pedagogy, and (symbolically focused) language policy, I came to understand the influence of academic ideologies on what it means to be urban, Indigenous, and concerned with language.

Policy as a Collaborative Product

The impact of the municipal-level official language policy in São Gabriel has been, as I discussed in chapter 3, much more complex than it may first appear. Examining the development of the policy as an idea, the arguments for or against it, the role played by academics in its establishment, and the focal points of its implementation is also worthwhile, to gain a more complete understanding of why it has not been as effective as many advocates had hoped in improving the viability of Indigenous languages in the city.

As I described earlier, the idea of co-officialization grew out of a spontaneous discussion among a class of Indigenous leaders and educators in the Magistério Indígena (MI) program, along with consultation from Gilvan Müller de Oliveira, a political linguist. Müller presented the proposal for the legislation to the Indigenous representatives who attended the annual FOIRN assembly in 2001. This group responded approvingly to the idea, but the format of this assembly did not provide much room for thoughtful consideration of its full implications or for debate about its specific terms. Each year, during this assembly, between fifty and one hundred representatives of Indigenous organizations, outside agencies (such as FUNAI, ISA, and the municipal government), and interested parties present reports about conditions and ongoing activities and consider ideas for projects and advocacy efforts. Because of the difficulty and expense involved in transporting people from remote parts of the region into São Gabriel for meetings such as these, many ideas and issues are discussed during these visits, and each day's work often runs for twelve to fourteen hours to address all topics and hear the various voices. While questions and debates emerge at these meetings about topics that are especially controversial, the notion that languages should be supported was not questioned in 2001, and there was little debate about whether the policy being suggested was an ideal way to go about it. In general, then, after the initial consultation between Müller and the MI students, the terms of the policy were not considered or evaluated by a body comprised of many differently positioned Indigenous people. Rather, with the approval of Indigenous leaders and after consultation with a few close Indigenous colleagues, Müller was entrusted with the task of defining and submitting the terms of the policy, which was presented to the council a few months later. This policy was developed so quickly that little attention was paid to the deep connections between language, identity, political status, and power relationships, or to understanding the social and ideological challenges that might emerge during efforts to implement the law. So, although a "lack of political will" was the most frequent response when I asked people why they thought the policy had never, as they put it, come off of the paper, a deeper explanation for the lacklustre commitment to implementation can be found in the ideologies that informed its establishment.

One element of these ideologies relates to the question of standardization. Official status is generally accompanied by a sharp increase in the written use of a language; indeed, this expectation is built into the terms of the policy as passed in São Gabriel (see Appendix). Each of the three newly official languages has *some* writing available but a very shallow tradition of literacy, and only Baniwa has a degree of accepted standardization (based mainly on the orthographies used by Bible translators). When the policy was being developed, the question of standardizing the three official languages was ignored or downplayed, though during my conversations with educators, government officials, FOIRN representatives, and the general Gabrielense public, the need for standardization was almost always mentioned. Individual orthographic choices were a topic of frequent commentary; pedagogical materials were critiqued by those who disagreed with the written forms chosen; the production of official government information or announcements was considered impossible without a standard to turn to; and uncertainty and insecurity about individuals' ability to write "correctly" kept them from writing at all. For Nheengatú in particular, this is coupled with an ideology of linguistic purism whereby some varieties are viewed as inferior because they incorporate Portuguese borrowings, to the extent that speakers criticize the use of Portuguese borrowings even when no one can think of an alternative lexical item with a Tupi origin. With respect to written forms, Nheengatú speakers tend to have strong views about the "correctness" of one form or another, even though they may disagree as to which is the correct one. For example, I have seen at least four variant ways of writing the very common phrase meaning "welcome" in Nheengatú – *poranga pesika, puranga pessika, puranga pesica,* and *porãga pesika.* Although the meaning of variation differs among each of the three Indigenous languages (in Tukano, for example, it marks both region and clan status), the people of São Gabriel share an ideological valuation of standardization, and contend that public, official languages should and must have a standard form.

On the surface, this is a discussion about seemingly minor details such as diacritics and whether to represent the high back unrounded vowel common in Tukanoan languages with [ɨ] or [ʉ]; but in reality, it is a question about what urban Indigeneity looks like. Central to this, and related to the ideology of standardization, is the idea that Indigeneity in its modern, urban, "civilized" form is literate and consistent. When a text is created in an Indigenous language, the form is often contested; at the very least, it becomes the subject of commentary, as even in the case of short, simple phrases, political, ethnic, regional, and historical attachments are associated with particular orthographic choices. For example, in July 2012, while making plans to celebrate my son's first birthday in São Gabriel, I asked for help creating a multilingual "Happy Birthday" sign (see Figure 6.1). Several people suggested this task was impossible, since "no one knows" how to write in their languages (a problem that was heightened by the fact that the concept of "happy birthday" is not one that is expressed in the local Indigenous cultures). I finally found three speakers of Tukano[2] who could help me construct and write an equivalent phrase (*Ãyu Mʉ'ʉ Ya'anama* – "happiness on your day"). While we agreed to settle on the form as presented here primarily because of space restrictions, the speakers who helped me made sure to tell me that the choice indexed a particular region (Paricachoeira), and one of them expressed frustration that it was the "simplified" version because it didn't conform to the orthography developed by French linguist Henri Ramirez (1997).[3] All of the Tukano speakers who attended the party (including many from other Tukanoan groups who knew the language instead of or in addition to their own) were able to read it, and furthermore, most were able to explain the differences indexed in the orthographic choices. Many of these speakers described themselves as unable to write or, at best, insecure in their ability, despite their clear awareness of several aspects of the debates about Tukano orthography. These interactions reiterated to me that the semiotic significance of writing was very salient to these speakers and that written texts played a powerful role in the valorization they sought for their Indigenous languages.

Most Tukano speakers do not see the social factors marked in the orthographic variants as centrally important; for them, the main goal is to agree upon forms and to consider how much, if at all, the orthography can or should be simplified to facilitate learning. While Tukano speakers may comment on choices of different variants as regionalized markers and indicate that they would have made different orthographic choices (most frequently with respect to ʉ versus i), they rarely make any claim to the "correctness" of one of these choices over another. Instead, they appeal to the differences as indicative of the pressing need to create a unified standard with which speakers, teachers, and learners can be comfortable. Nheengatú speakers, by contrast, often suggest that certain orthographic choices prove that the writer was unaware of the correct form, and probably not a very good speaker. One Nheengatú-speaking teacher, who has been extremely active in implementing differentiated Indigenous schools and teacher training programs, is particularly emphatic about the use of nasalized vowels rather than an "n" in words like "porãga" and in the name of the language itself (preferring the form "Yegatu" to the more frequently seen form I have adopted throughout this book), and laments the poor quality of

Nheengatú represented on the few signs that are available. Another former teacher of the Nheengatú language in the city's municipal schools has complained about this form, saying that her students find it much more intuitive to use the forms with the "n" included, instead of the marked nasal vowel.

So, the question of standardization has not been resolved even though these languages have been official ones in the municipality for more than a decade, during which the production of written materials has been mandated by law. But this is not because academic actors have shown no interest in the process. Rather, standardization has been pursued only recently for Tukano and Nheengatú because of the approach to collaboration taken during the development of the law. Many Indigenous leaders communicated that it was Müller who told them that a written standard was unnecessary and that the idea of a single "correct" way of writing was a Eurocentric concept that they did not need to apply. Each person should therefore be able to write in the official languages using the orthographic conventions that he or she found most comfortable. In the Rio Negro, however, this approach – admirably based on a goal of promoting greater egalitarianism among varieties – has proven ineffective. The fear of writing "incorrectly," even though lack of standardization means there is no such thing as "correct," presents a major barrier to individual and collective efforts to use the languages in an official capacity. In schools especially, even those who teach the languages often express uncertainty about their linguistic abilities in general, primarily because they do not trust that they will be able to teach students to write "correctly." FOIRN has recently broken away from this model of thinking promoted by the original legislation; since 2013, after decades of contradictory and often frustrating advice from linguists, it has been leading workshops to discuss standardization for each of the languages.

The failure to address – or even to examine – people's feelings about written language before developing an official language policy that would depend heavily on this form was a significant miscalculation, for it failed to acknowledge the importance of social, rather than purely linguistic, factors relating to language and its uses. It also demonstrated the type of power relationship that defined the outcomes of this collaborative effort, in that Indigenous leaders and speakers of Indigenous languages deferred to Müller as their teacher and as the expert on linguistic issues. The failure of this approach to written language in the local context has contributed to a stronger sense, on the part of FOIRN and other Indigenous activists, that to improve the quality of research

Figure 6.1. Multilingual "Happy Birthday" sign – the decorative sign that a friend made for my son William's first birthday party in July 2012, including text in Portuguese, English, and Tukano.

about their peoples, local, Indigenous linguists and anthropologists must be trained and recognized.

Furthermore (see chapter 3), choosing only three of the many languages still spoken in the region has connected proponents of this policy to the ideology of pan-Indigeneity rather than to individualized ethnolinguistic identity. Indigenous leaders, represented mainly by FOIRN, are clearly interested in reducing the stigma associated with Indigenous identity and cultural practices, and in advancing Indigenous autonomy and control over material and immaterial resources (such as education and health care), and cultural revival and language revitalization play a distinct role in these efforts. Yet at the same time, the actions and discourses of these actors, while paying lip service to the "diversity" advocated by academic outsiders, often focus on strengthening the larger Indigenous languages (specifically the three co-official languages) rather than investing in the preservation of *all* languages. Speakers of some of the now minority (non-official) Indigenous languages – including those members of AIPOK with whom I was closely involved – express frustration with FOIRN's actions in this regard, noting that they exacerbate power imbalances between speakers. Because the policy was created without extensive consultation among the various interested parties and representatives of diverse interests, these considerations remain inadequately addressed. Given that proponents of the policy explicitly reference the idea that the targets of their efforts are in the urban area, it is particularly interesting that the main arena for consultation and discussion was a FOIRN assembly attended by representatives of the rural area. Ideological conflict has been a major barrier to the implementation of this policy, and this consideration of the history of its development further suggests that anthropological insights and types of questioning could have been particularly useful in developing a language policy to meet the needs of this community.

Urbanity and Language Documentation

Language policy as a means to support Indigenous languages has been held back by various academic influences on the collaborative project and by the failure to fully address certain issues when considering how such a policy might work. A much deeper and more pervasive set of complications characterizes work relating to the documentation of languages and cultural practices. Both linguists and anthropologists have been extensively involved in these efforts in the Northwest Amazon, especially through the production of pedagogical materials for use in the differentiated schools (as well as in consultations about establishing those schools) and through the publication of a series of texts (jointly published by ISA and FOIRN) called "Indigenous Narrators of the Rio Negro" (*Narradores Indígenas do Rio Negro*, or NIRN). The former projects have been discussed extensively throughout this book; the latter require further clarification and explanation. Each of the NIRN texts has been co-authored by two Indigenous people – one elder member of the language group, who is considered an authority on the myths and stories being represented, and one younger member of the community (usually a family member of the elder), who is more literate in Portuguese and who translates and transcribes the narrative. The production of each book is overseen by one of several anthropologists who have conducted research with the language groups in question for many years. The series began in 1995 with the republication of the 1980 volume of Tukano narratives, *Antes o Mundo Não Existia* (Before, the

World Did Not Exist) (Umúsin and Tolamãn 1995). Since then, seven further volumes have been published documenting the traditional origin stories and important myths of the Dessana, Kotiria, Baniwa, Tariana, Tuyuka, and Tukano groups.

The documentation of these myths and stories – even if written primarily in Portuguese rather than in the relevant Indigenous language – has been viewed as important to cultural valorization in the Rio Negro region, much more so than among other Amazonian Indigenous groups. Stephen Hugh-Jones (2010) has examined why the textual representations in these books have taken hold among the Tukanoans, when, by contrast, the Xavante (for example) have been more inclined to embrace visual representations of Indigenous identity. He attributes this pattern to pre-existing ideologies and social practices whereby transacting such materials informed the establishment of kinship ties (exogamous marriages) and alliances and forcibly claiming them was a part of aggressive conquests. In this region, the idea of culture as a material good and as something that could be rendered concrete for use in political and economic exchanges transferred well to similar uses in relation to claims against the state. At the same time, choices as to what is to be documented in these politically powerful texts are not to be viewed as simple or neutral. Just as with the co-official languages, each of these examples has come to stand as a representation of Indigeneity, and the form this Indigeneity takes is presumed to be in the best interests of *all* Indigenous people of the region, though of course that is not always the case.

Education (and differentiated schooling in particular) functions in much the same way as the documentary series – as a tool that the Indigenous inhabitants of this region have chosen as a focal point for their claims against the state. Language documentation efforts have in many ways been easy to connect to these existing goals and activities. Documentary linguistic work has come to occupy a specific place within the discipline of linguistics, evolving from what was once seen as merely a means of data gathering for descriptive and theoretical analysis into a respected subfield in its own right – one that requires a unique and valuable set of skills for conducting fieldwork and presenting a grammar. These grammars are often directed mainly at the academic community but are usually accompanied by materials prepared for the community's use, or are written in such a way that the more metalinguistically aware members of the community are able to use them to develop such materials. Field methods focus on gathering as much information as possible about the language, its structures, and its variations. This includes recording, transcribing, and analysing materials drawn from elicitation sessions, narratives, and naturally occurring speech from a variety of speakers and, ideally, representing a range of positions and identities (based on age, gender, and social rank, for example). But in these cases, too, although the outcomes of the projects are seen as representing and serving the interests of Indigenous people as a whole, they are produced in power-laden contexts that are not often acknowledged by academic linguists when they are making their choices.

This solutions-oriented approach to documentation and revitalization has costs. Academic linguists tend to arrive at field sites with a set of predetermined goals and outcomes and a definition of community interests that assumes that producing linguistic material is the best way to meet local needs. As a result, it is nearly inevitable that linguists conducting this type of research align themselves with members of the community that express similar concerns, often dismissing the voices of those who may doubt the importance of language revitalization or who view it as inherently wrong or misguided. Similarly, the project of language documentation requires working to find, record, and gather information mainly from the most fluent speakers of the language, where possible in the context of everyday conversation – though in the Northwest Amazon, the focus on recording myths and traditional knowledge limits the degree to which these naturalistic data become the subject of published work (Fleming 2009). As a consequence of these goals, linguists naturally spend their time with a particular group of people and become most powerfully invested in the interests expressed among that group.

The social realities of the Northwest Amazon are such that, for both of these documentary projects, these interests have been best served in alliances and collaborations with rural populations. At the same time, ideologically, the indexical linking of rurality to Indigenous languages, perpetuated through these activities, has meant that "preserving the culture" and "documenting the language" have involved consultation with rural peoples and support for their efforts to reduce the rate of migration towards São Gabriel. The goals of linguistic field research having been pre-defined, the linguist necessarily seeks out a community of speakers of one language to document all forms of the language used by people in different social positions in different types of interactions (Gippert, Himmelmann, and Mosel 2006). Given the nature of multilingualism and linguistic territoriality in the Upper Rio Negro, this means working within the interior communities where most native speakers of these languages live, and where some of these languages continue to be used as the language of daily activities. Differentiated Indigenous schools serve two purposes in this effort: they support the transmission of Indigenous languages and cultural knowledge while also reducing the need to move to the city to pursue educational opportunities. Despite the high proportion of Indigenous people living in São Gabriel, that city is seen primarily as a threat to Indigeneity and Indigenous lifestyles. As discussed in previous chapters, especially with respect to the urban members of AIPOK, FOIRN's regionally defined organizational structure does not include any representatives designated to serve the interests of urban people. The only option that residents of the urban area have is to look to the representatives of the home territory of their ethnic group, where they may never have lived and which they may never even have visited. Needless to say, their interests may not align neatly with the concerns and priorities of the communities whose interests the organizations were created to serve, and their status as full members of that community who deserve such representation is construed as suspect. This organization model informs relationships with non-Indigenous outsiders (including both researchers and the state). These structures further reinforce an ethnolinguistic conceptualization of Indigenous groups or communities of interest, inscribing a limited potential for developing collaborative relationships that would reflect the complexities of multilingualism, contact, and identity in the city of São Gabriel.

In São Gabriel, urban-dwelling Indigenous people are often strong speakers of their languages who contribute, through recordings, transcriptions, and elicitation sessions, to these efforts to document and develop materials. The results of this, however, do not pay attention to their own social circumstances: their living situations do not inform the development of field strategies, and the benefits they are understood to be receiving from the research relate less to their direct personal needs and more to their links to a distant and abstracted "community," even while the continuity of their language is being secured through their participation. When languages have very few speakers and essentially no intergenerational transmission is occurring, even in the rural region – as is the case with Tariana and Waikhana (Piratapuya), both of which are being overtaken by Tukano along the Uaupés and in the region of Iauaratê (Aikhenvald 2003b; Stenzel 2005) – any hope of language revitalization must focus on the context in which the only remaining speakers live. When a language has very few speakers, the

needs of linguists and the interests of a community may line up relatively neatly, at least in the initial stages. Languages with larger numbers of speakers, or with higher rates of intergenerational transmission
and stronger chances for survival within some part of the Upper Rio
Negro territory – such as, for example, Kotiria, or the three co-official-
ized languages of São Gabriel – raise a more complicated set of concerns when it comes to defining the interests, and even the boundaries,
of the speech community.

These observations about the situation in the Northwest Amazon
support the observations other anthropologists have made about the
ways in which academic ideologies intersect with local understandings
of language and structures of governance in ways that support certain
practices and that constrain others (Collins 1998; Hill 2002; Errington
2003). Given the influence that scholarly ideas about the value of language have had on the idea of language endangerment as a global phenomenon, revitalization is one of the most significant areas in which
these ideologies come into contact with one another. The case of the
Kotiria revealed a central challenge emerging from these relationships,
especially for the urban population. Urban areas, which are sites of
extensive contact and heterogeneity, have rarely drawn attention as
places perhaps worthy of anthropological attention; too often, their
particular communities and cultures have not been viewed as worth
describing. Social circumstances have steered linguists away from
examining urban speech and socialization practices towards gathering
linguistic data among fluent speakers in more remote areas. This pattern emerges, of course, not from hostility towards the urban population, but rather from linguists' desire to provide the best support they
possibly can for the future of the language.

A further disjuncture between the real and the prototypical occurs
when moving from documentation to revitalization. Here, the question
of terminology that I raised in the introduction comes of the fore again,
as different actors use different terms to describe their goals in relation to language. These terms are not in any way synonymous: "valorization," "preservation," "salvage" (*resgate*), and "revitalization" all
connote different priorities. In the Upper Rio Negro region, missionary, linguistic, and anthropological interests have combined with local
valuations of myth and systematic notions of cultural property to influence the production of a particular type of text and a particular relationship to the written word and to documentation as a linguistic practice
(Fleming 2009; Andrello 2010; Hugh-Jones 2010). Thus, the conventions

of documentary linguistics have been absorbed into a system of beliefs about "culture" by Indigenous residents of the region and have come to be seen as a necessary in order to define, secure, and protect cultural property for transmission to future generations.

In my own work, I have focused on the word "revitalization" largely because, in the context of the urban area, Indigenous cultural practices, including languages, are discussed as something that needs to be "brought back." My own observations suggest that this entails seeking new ways of being and living Indigeneity that can work and grow within this environment. The documentation of these texts is vital to ensuring that the cultural knowledge contained in them does not disappear, and connects to a holistic understanding of language as part of a cultural system. But that documentation is also related to an unchanged and unchanging cultural "authenticity" that is ultimately detrimental to this type of revitalization. Meek (2011) illustrates how the valorization of elders' ways of speaking in Yukon has contributed to an anxiety among young people and learners about their own linguistic ability, which ultimately discourages the increasing use of these languages. In the same way, anthropological efforts in the Upper Rio Negro to document, encourage, and destigmatize traditional Indigenous practices have discouraged the expansion of the language into new domains and genres in ways that would engage the interests, concerns, and social practices of urban Indigenous youth. Also, the local ideological understandings of linguistic competence tend to inhibit revitalization efforts by limiting the opportunities for semi-speakers to practise their abilities.

An additional aspect of academic, and particularly documentary linguistic, influence has been the degree to which education and pedagogy have been the sites of focus for implementing language-based activist efforts. Yet linguistic involvement in other sectors, especially those that provide essential services to Indigenous people, may offer significant benefits both for the population itself and for the prospects for language revitalization in the city. In the health and financial sectors, for example, Indigenous people who speak little Portuguese experience distrust and discrimination; for example, they are overcharged for banking and market services in cases where elderly people who have recently arrived from the communities are unable to communicate their complaints. Even the use of Portuguese inflected with Indigenous-language patterns (e.g., "Tukanized" Portuguese, for residents of the Uaupés basin) creates a sense of insecurity about communicating with

health care professionals and administrators; this is reinforced by a history of discrimination that was particularly potent at these sites. FOIRN
director Max Menezes highlighted the importance of using the official
Indigenous languages to strengthen the confidence of Indigenous people in these contexts, not only in terms of their ability to communicate
their needs and concerns more accurately, but also in creating a sense
of belonging and of relating to the person providing the services. This
would help overcome a pattern of anxiety that has characterized Indigenous interactions with the public sector. In discussing the contribution
of a translator, Max noted:

> And it would be diminished [the fear]. I see, geez, there's my relative,
> I'll go talk to him, he'll help me. And so I feel really strengthened in that
> moment. But if there are *only* the whites, if I'm only seeing all white faces,
> right away I get scared. To speak incorrectly. And of – after – when I
> speak incorrectly, this guy is going to laugh at me, you understand. This
> already makes me scared to talk. And *that* fear itself helps make me speak
> incorrectly, you understand. [interview, 30 July 2012)

Linguists' expertise could be just as useful in the training and selection of translators for these contexts, or in providing workshops for
existing personnel (both Indigenous and non-Indigenous) about the
importance of language in meeting the needs of the population, as it is
in developing curricular materials for differentiated schools.

On the surface, these are simple suggestions, but they entail a fundamental rethinking of the approach to language and collaboration
taken by the discipline of linguistics. Conversations about changing
these practices are now taking place, but meanwhile, linguistic research
methodologies continue to primarily reflect a specific set of academic
linguistic concerns that do not necessarily encompass the full range of
language-related needs that a diverse, multi-sited speech community
often has. The example of AIPOK illustrates that people have other
reasons for doing language revitalization work besides preventing a
language's disappearance. The speakers of Kotiria in São Gabriel do
not need to be convinced about the value of their language continuing into the future. Indeed, it is because they recognize the importance
of language to their culture as well as to their personal identities that
they are profoundly concerned about the implications of language shift
within their own families and they feel left out of the gains being made
by their rural relatives. Linguists' discourses emphasize the continued

survival of the language as a code and its documentation for both scientific analysis and community-based teaching. For many parents in São Gabriel, the loss their children experience as a result of not speaking the language of their own ethnic identity is harder to articulate and relates to an inability to understand themselves and their place in the world. My friend Patricia, for example, who speaks both Kotiria and her mother's language (Tukano), told me she believed that some of the powerful Indigenous political figures in the city were "lost," and that because they did not speak their *own* language (though they were speakers of other Indigenous languages), they were more susceptible to corruption. Preservationist linguists, while helpful to these people to the degree that their interests overlap, are not necessarily concerned about identity-based relationships, with what it means to be a speaker of the language, with who is allowed to claim ownership of the language, or with what language loss (and revitalization) might mean to these people.

Community, Conflict, and Contradiction

Although there are many differences among them, all of the political projects related to language and cultural preservation and revitalization in the Rio Negro region have multiple consequences, and all of them prioritize the needs and voices of some Indigenous people while marginalizing others. With regard to language policy, the already powerful Tukano, Baré, and Baniwa groups have been strengthened through the selection of three languages, while in documentation efforts, the voices of the growing urban population have been erased from the textual record of "culture" that is being produced. In community-based collaborations and research endeavours, these erasures have both a symbolic and a practical impact on the definition of Indigeneity, for the projects are understood to be taking place in the best interests of the Indigenous community as a whole.

Throughout this book I have occasionally used the term "community-based" as if it was a clear-cut and straightforward descriptor, when in fact these disjunctures reveal it is not. The question is not merely one of internal politics and of different positions and factions within a community; it also raises the question of how "community" is being defined in the first place. São Gabriel is a complex place, and to discuss language and collaborative linguistic research under the assumption that particular types of benefits extend to everyone in "the community" is both inaccurate and pernicious.

Another point I have left beneath the surface of my discussion throughout this book has been the degree to which my collaboration with two different groups – FOIRN, in my effort to better understand the barriers to implementing the language policy, and AIPOK, in their own attempts to form an urban school – put me in the position of trying to support two projects that, even though both were directed at improving the languages of the urban area, were in fact at odds with each other. This division did not become clear to me until I had been working for several months with both groups and had begun to understand the ideologies underlying their goals, and the disputes and debates that were (and are) ongoing. While such divisions are extremely common among the Indigenous people of São Gabriel (as one would expect in a city of this size, in which the large Indigenous population includes a multitude of positions and interests), they remain unstated within local politics. Debates and discussions focus on the power divide between Indigenous people as a coherent group and the non-Indigenous state in which they live. The cohesiveness of the former is established through an extensive and ongoing process of debate, inclusion, and exclusion for the purpose of developing goals, which are then articulated by the organizations (most notably FOIRN) that represent Indigeneity to outsiders.

The heterogeneity of São Gabriel brings to the surface the degree to which community is something that does not exist outside of these political and social processes. Thus, community-based researchers must make decisions about how to insert themselves into these activities. In linguistic work, and especially in endangered-language linguistics, discourses describe a uniform goal and set of solutions towards which communities of speakers must necessarily be working and in which linguists can invest themselves. These decisions, then, are often made without conscious consideration, and their outcomes therefore often include unexpected and unintended complexities. Community-based collaboration is a worthy goal; that said, disagreements over the fundamental basis for conducting a particular type of research project, and the terms according to which it should proceed, can be among the most powerful sources of insights about language ideologies, social and political decision-making, and communication (Field 1999). Language revitalization in the urban area of São Gabriel (and probably throughout the region) cannot be considered a uniform project, and a great deal of messy reality remains to be explored there.

A basic binary between urban and rural can also be seen in discourses about what can or should be done about Indigenous languages in each of those two environments. Documentation, the pedagogical materials generated by it, and the production of cultural texts all serve the needs of rural communities, while "valorization" functions for the urban comunity. As such, the rural territories are the ones that receive support for specific languages on an individual basis, emphasizing the value of continuing to speak these languages, both for the sake of the population of speakers and for the preservation of the language itself. Valorization, by contrast, accounts for Indigenous languages in generalized terms and draws attention to the idea of linguistic diversity as a singular source of "richness" for the city of São Gabriel. The hope is that reducing the stigma attached to Indigeneity and its symbols will help raise the status of Indigenous people, and by extension *all* of their languages and customs. This difference represents another reason for linguists' stronger involvement in rural territories; it also explains the extent to which documentation does in fact meet the needs of this portion of the Indigenous population even while leading to the erasure of the alternative position. The idea of "valorization" is prominent among groups that have political power in the urban centre, including in FOIRN; as a result, those urban residents – such as AIPOK members – who represent minority interests are less able to generate support for their efforts. Both factions apply some of the discourses of language revitalization. The region is sociolinguistically diverse, and it would be imprudent for Indigenous leaders *not* to pay attention to outsiders' interest in this fact; that said, the ways in which those leaders refer strategically to the role of language in Indigenous political practice reveal a more complex situation. The forms of community-based collaboration that have been used in the region have shaped not only models of research relationships but also visions of language and its relationship to politics and, even more importantly, of the boundaries of "community" itself. Acknowledging this messiness and clarifying the terms of this ideological debate (Blommaert 1999) is a necessary step towards expanding collaborative efforts to improve the prospects for the Indigenous languages of the Rio Negro region and for understanding the experiences of urban Indigenous residents.

Social Factors in Urban Language Revitalization

It is necessary to think in terms of power and marginalization in academic collaborations. My efforts to work on language revitalization in an urban context demonstrate not only how this population is excluded from most of these endeavours, but also how projects focusing on language and culture have paid only limited attention to some of the most serious outcomes of the widespread oppression experienced by Indigenous populations. These concerns – which include extremely high rates of alcoholism, drug use, and suicide, sexual and domestic violence, and the trafficking of young Indigenous women by wealthy business owners and members of the military – are often invoked in arguments supporting initiatives such as differentiated schooling that will help keep people in their communities. There, some feel, they are more likely to be safe, for they will be more strongly connected not only to their cultures and identities but also to their parents. Urbanity – with its disconnections and with its saturation by media images of material wealth that is unattainable for most Indigenous youth – constitutes a threat not only to intangible cultural practices but also to the physical survival and health of the people.

These issues have strengthened the resolve of rural populations to keep their children in their communities. Urban Indigenous people, for their part, have sought solutions by switching religions (in the hope that the strict prohibition of alcohol within Evangelical Protestantism will protect their children), strengthening their involvement with their churches, seeking government resources, and developing personal networks. Alcoholism has been described as a serious barrier to the implementation of educational programs (Rezende 2010), and many urban Indigenous people are so focused on meeting the immediate needs of their families that language and cultural revitalization work is not on their radar. Anthropologists studying health and psychology have examined the local meaning of alcohol use and how traditional medicine has been used in health care (Souza and Garnelo 2007; Garnelo and Buchillet 2006), and some medical training programs have been consulting with Indigenous groups to find culturally appropriate ways to communicate knowledge about the body, health, and care (Shankland and Athias 2007). Up to this point, however, conversations about language and cultural revitalization have been taking place separately from conversations about Indigenous health, except when it comes to promoting the ideal of recognizing Indigenous medicinal knowledge.

In fact, because cultural revival activities have often been associated with parties at which the ways of consuming alcohol have changed (see below), some leaders (including Justino Rezende, a Tuyuka leader, author on education, and Catholic priest) express suspicion about the idea of "revitalization" in general.

While these concerns may not be directly related to language loss, linguists working in São Gabriel, as in other endangered language communities, can hardly avoid noticing them. An ethnographic vignette from Meek's work with the Kaska people of Yukon expresses the emotional content of some of these aspects of linguistic fieldwork:

> As I wrote out the verb paradigms for Kaska, the radio news broadcast reported that another First Nations person was stabbed to death (by accidentally falling on a knife repeatedly), another guy froze to death on his way home from a friend's, and elders throughout the Yukon were being hospitalized for pneumonia. Suddenly my obsession with documenting and analyzing Kaska grammar seemed even more urgent and yet not urgent at all in the face of these tragedies. (Meek 2011: 13)

During my own fieldwork, this feeling of a disconnect in priorities was ever-present. I heard about the suicides of children as young as twelve, about the death of the twenty-year-old brother of one of my friends in a boating accident after a night of heavy partying, and about a murder, in a bar fight, that had been witnessed by another friend's thirteen-year-old son. The quotidian priorities of the people with whom I was speaking about the significance of language and cultural identity felt all-consuming when they came to the surface. One day, I went to schedule an interview with a former teacher and political leader, and as I waited on his porch, I was joined by two middle-aged women, sisters, who were waiting to procure his healing services, for he was also a respected healer. Both of the women were also teachers, and, interested in my work, they told me about their experiences in the classroom, where they had come from, and their own linguistic knowledge. Unthinkingly, I asked them about their current family situations – whether they were able to speak their language (Tukano) with their husbands and children in the home. When the healer arrived, I learned that the reason for the visit was that the younger of the two was being severely beaten by her frequently intoxicated husband and that she was concerned about the safety of her children, especially her teenage son, who was starting to threaten his father and attempt to intervene in their fights. I realized that everything they had told me about the linguistic components of their home life needed to be reinterpreted in light of the violence in that relationship. This conversation would not be the last one in which my research focus prevented me from recognizing the reality of the lives that people were telling me about, and I found myself feeling guilty for emphasizing the importance of language maintenance when their immediate concerns – for their physical survival, and that of their children – were so much more salient.

It has become clear to me that it is often futile to talk about language and cultural survival without accounting for the physical environment and whether it can sustain the population. Environmentalism and cultural protection are, for better or for worse, intimately linked in many remote areas of the world, perhaps most self-evidently in the Amazon (Dove 2006). Yet the urban environment is equally involved in the survival of cultures and languages, for Indigenous peoples' physical survival is threatened by the heightened ways in which they are affected by poverty, violence, and the drug trade. North American Indigenous people, in collaboration with anthropologists and linguists, have had some success in articulating their holistic vision for revitalization as a matter of psychological healing (Chandler and Lalonde 1998; Abadian 2006; Meek 2011). Imaginative collaborations of this kind are urgently needed in the Northwest Amazon. Many linguists and anthropologists are focused on cultural preservation and language documentation; fewer are interested in questions of health, psychology, and social issues; and as a result, the latter, urgent needs are being inadequately addressed even while they threaten to render the former work ineffective.

One cultural revitalization project implemented in the downtown core of São Gabriel stood as a salient example of the destructive impact that high levels of alcohol have on these efforts. A *maloka*[4] structure was built in one of the most high-traffic parts of the city – immediately behind the gymnasium and adjacent to the public football pitch – as a project envisioned by ISA-sponsored researcher Melissa Oliveira. In consultation with FOIRN, Oliveira organized the construction of this space as a means to valorize cultural practices through visible displays, to provide a source of income for people through the sale of traditional artisanal products and local foods, and to offer a gathering place where Indigenous identity, languages, and ways of being would be celebrated and encouraged. A FOIRN-affiliated organization that supported local agricultural producers (Associação dos Povos Indígenas de Produtos

Diretos da Roça, which roughly translates as the Indigenous Peoples' Association for Horticultural Producers) took responsibility for the space's ongoing maintenance and organized a weekly gathering, which was held every Sunday for several years. Members of the association would sell homegrown food and drink during these gatherings. In early 2014, this structure, along with the store where FOIRN sold Indigenous crafts and books, was destroyed by arsonists, and in the absence of a gathering space, the association has not continued its operations. Both the revenue generated for Indigenous horticulturalists and the visibility associated with a weekly event in the town centre have been, for the time being, lost.

These gatherings had had a negative side, however, with regard to perceptions they generated about Indigenous peoples and their cultures. Most of sales were of *caxiri* (manioc beer) and *cachaça*, and extreme drunkenness was very common at these events. I enjoyed attending most Sundays while I was there, but I usually left before noon, once it became difficult to carry on a conversation without being disrupted by someone who had been drinking heavily, and fights often broke out throughout the afternoon. Almost all of the non-Indigenous people I knew in São Gabriel, and many of my Indigenous friends, expressed surprise that I attended at all; their perception of these gatherings was strongly negative and almost entirely focused on the drunkenness, rather than on the positive elements that continued to have a presence. For example, people conversed with one another in various Indigenous languages while attending, and it was not uncommon to hear either Tukano or Nheengatú used on the microphone by representatives of the organization. The *dabucuri* was also used to mark special occasions, and smaller-scale music and dancing with instruments such as the *cariçu* periodically took place when enough dancers were available. These positive aspects, however, were confronted with negative public perceptions that discouraged many people – Indigenous as well as non-Indigenous – from attending or supporting this site of cultural revival. One Kotiria teacher described to me his perceptions about how the weekly gathering had changed:

> Right at the beginning when she [Oliveira] was here, it really did work out. It was a cultural encounter, people selling their – their typical food, their regional drinks. *Without* alcoholic beverages before. People danced the *dabucuri*, they danced these – these Indigenous dances, it was cool to see it. I would always go check it out. But after she left, I went over with someone,

and we didn't stay. There was no continuity ... So when you go there and see it, right ... it's just electronic music they play there. They don't have people playing the *cariçu*, playing the *mawa*, that they had before. There's alcoholic drinks. When people get there now, it hasn't always been like this. Right away they say it's wrong, right, ah, these Indians, they never stop drinking, these Indians. But right at the beginning, it was wonderful, it was cool. (interview, 15 August 2012)

This desire to participate in cultural valorization and revival, but not in contexts involving heavy drinking, was expressed by many Indigenous people that I knew, including people who were otherwise actively involved in Indigenous political organizations. Although this specific gathering was the most prominent example, the scepticism often extended to conversations about hypothetical "cultural revitalization" events.

As Gone (2008) points out, questions about mental health and substance abuse are often bound up with practices of colonization and cultural control, and discussions of how to address these concerns in contexts of discrimination and oppressive power relations must be approached cautiously and critically. In São Gabriel as in many parts of the world, the role that churches have played (and still play) in defining the moral value of sobriety *and* in suppressing a range of Indigenous cultural practices cannot be ignored. Indeed, many of the voices (both Indigenous and non-Indigenous) speaking out against these kinds of events are situated within the Catholic Church, especially now that the current bishop, Dom Edson Damian, has made the prevention and treatment of drug and alcohol abuse a major priority. Many social services in the Rio Negro region, including care for persons with disabilities, support for transition from incarceration, and alcohol and drug treatment facilities, depend entirely on the resources and willingness of churches, and the Catholic Church in particular has pushed steadily for a more culturally aware approach to those services.

At the same time, however, these actions cannot entirely mitigate the colonial nature of Christianity's presence in the region. The extent to which addressing the serious social issues facing the people of São Gabriel has become the responsibility of the churches rather than autonomous, Indigenous-led initiatives raises a further point about cultural affirmation. The kind of financial support necessary to engage in sustained efforts to combat any of these challenges always requires Indigenous organizations to look outward, replicating colonial power dynamics. At the same time, not all Indigenous leaders consider these social concerns to be problems at all. Denivaldo Cruz da Silva is uniquely situated to talk about these issues, having spent eight years working at FOIRN before moving, in late 2011, to a position administering a new alcohol and drug treatment facility on behalf of the local Catholic diocese. During an interview (21 July 2012), he observed that FOIRN did not acknowledge these social concerns as matters of importance for Indigenous people as a collectivity – insofar as they were problematic, it was at the individual level. Yet the use of alcohol (including by children) during parties is a matter of cultural importance. The conflict revolves, again, around what Indigeneity means and how it should be expressed. At least some Indigenous people point out that the nature of alcohol use, and the strength of the beverages consumed, has changed significantly (Souza and Garnelo 2007), and argue that the suggestion that this is simply "the way things are" for Indigenous people is offensive on its face. "Cultural revitalization," however, has become embedded in this debate in terms of whether people choose to attend or support certain types of events at which cultural practices are affirmed and performed. Many who feel uncomfortable with the degree of intoxication seen at these events simply refuse to participate in cultural revitalization efforts. These debates further demonstrate the need to imagine a movement for cultural (and linguistic) revival that will seriously address the complexity of the concerns around alcohol, drugs, parties, cultural autonomy, and the involvement of religious institutions.

Steps Forward

This combination of factors – the ways in which existing collaborative work has contributed to the power dynamics involved in language and cultural revitalization activities, and the fears and challenges that urban Indigenous people face that discourage them from summoning the time, energy, and resources to think about those activities – provides the backdrop for thinking about ways to move forward as academic allies in these efforts. The earlier discussion about "the community" as something that cannot be presumed to pre-exist in the urban area is, perhaps counterintuitively, actually a very hopeful place to begin thinking through the next steps. In both a formal, organizational sense and in a theoretical one, future community-based research should devote attention to what "the community" is, what it does, and how it functions, before considering what it *needs*.

The first aspect of this recasting of the idea of community in an urban context is quite obviously related to language loss and, in turn, to the ways in which collaborations are and could be formed to combat it. Because linguists are concerned, by definition, with language, the idea that focusing on an ethnolinguistic group is the most useful way of determining the boundaries of the research topic is almost tautological. While linguistic work is usually done with the recognition that the idea of bounded "cultures" is problematic, questions about the meaning of "language" – what should be documented, how and to whom a language should be taught, who is considered a speaker, how the boundaries between groups are determined – have not necessarily been taken up. The city of São Gabriel presents an opportunity to analyse multilingualism at work and to consider the role of multiple languages in the formation of group and individual identities; it also provides new avenues for exploring language-in-use that could enhance existing documentary work. For example, linguistic and linguistic anthropological work on the Tukano and Nheengatú languages – both of which serve as regional *linguas francas* – could benefit from an analysis of the ways in which these languages are used by members of different ethnic groups, especially in the contact environment of São Gabriel. The power and status relationships that play out among the city's language groups are significant aspects of this speech community, as Stenzel (2005) observes in her discussion of the impact of language shift and revitalization on multilingualism in the region. Considering the extent to which the city space changes or reinforces these cultural and sociolinguistic factors by examining patterns of discourse, interaction, and contact entails revisioning the boundaries of the "communities" we study and looking at their discontinuities, loose interconnections, and cross-linguistic overlaps.

A second way in which revitalization activists may need to reconsider their approach to "the community" as it relates to an urban centre has to do with addressing the disconnections in the ways people relate to one another. This factor is more urgent in a city like São Gabriel, where the term *urbanizing* still applies, for many of its people have only recently settled there from the rural territories and they face a major lifestyle shift. In leaving an environment that offers extended family support, including a speech community that for the most part uses the same Indigenous language in daily life, and entering a multilingual, multicultural space defined by a Brazilian non-Indigenous bureaucracy, Indigenous people find themselves disconnected from one another and from their emotional, social, and spiritual support systems. Members of extended families live across town and rarely see one another, while children attend school in Portuguese, in contexts dominated by non-Indigenous values, and are pulled away from their parents by television, the Internet, or soccer games with friends. Clearly, revitalizing Indigenous languages in the city will involve creating spaces in which they can be spoken, and part of the purpose of the co-officialization law, with its focus on valorization, is to provide such spaces as a means to reduce people's shame about speaking their languages in public spaces. But the ideal of "valorization" only goes so far in terms of increasing language use; and furthermore, the law, which targets only three of twenty-one languages, is limited in its efficacy with respect to the revitalization of the eighteen it does not target. To help create community, linguists need to consider ways to bring together speakers of these languages. Those speakers could then be divided into subgroups for conversation and cultural activity lessons, performance preparations, or food preparations. This would provide an opportunity outside the home for them to use their languages and express their cultures and expose their children and youth to both.

This effort, however, involves more than just working to create contexts in which the language might be spoken. It ties in with understandings of individual and group identity that are central to language revitalization. Besides having an impact on language use, community discontinuities and the changing nature of extended- and immediate-family relationships (particularly between parents and children) may be contributing to some of the serious social issues that face the city of São Gabriel. In considering what it means to be Indigenous in the city and why urbanization is so strongly associated with language loss, a common discursive theme has been that youth are losing respect for their rural, Indigenous parents as they come to place greater value on the markers of social capital that matter in non-Indigenous Brazilian society (such as the clothes they see on television programs). This disrespect, in turn, is perceived as heightening their risk of succumbing to destructive influences and behaviour (see above), for parents are less able to either understand their children's actions or to communicate effectively with them about their problems. So, reimagining language revitalization also involves examining the role of youth in these processes. In the current situation, the lack of interest among youth is often put forward as a reason for language loss; but at the same time, linguists' focus on language documentation has meant they have engaged little with youth and other non-speakers, or even passive speakers, of Indigenous languages. As Meek (2011) points out with respect to Kaska language revitalization efforts, respect for elders, and orientation towards their ways of speaking, together bring to the surface a number of ideological beliefs that discourage language use by the young and by language learners.

Among older adults involved in the Indigenous political movement and language revitalization, there is a persistent belief that youth are apathetic. Yet my own experiences with young people, including through the Municipal Youth Council (whose demographic includes fifteen- to twenty-nine-year-olds), contrasted sharply with this presumption, as I met several youth who were interested in their languages and cultures and who were deeply concerned about the future of their community and city. For the most part, these youth felt excluded from the conversation about language revitalization and were unsure how, as non-speakers, they might become involved. Gabriela Ferraz, a nineteen-year-old Kotiria woman who was born in São Gabriel and who had travelled all over Brazil as part of a network of youth activists, told me that when she was away from São Gabriel, she felt "ashamed" at being unable to speak her language:

> This leaves me ashamed to raise my flag and say that I am 100% Indigenous, I am the daughter of two Indigenous people, I am of the Wanano ethnicity. Fine, I can say that, pounding my chest, that I am. But it makes me sad, ashamed, because I don't know how to speak [my language], so I'm like – man, I have to learn, but – I haven't learned. (focus group conversation, 19 August 2012)

Gabriela's comments also reflect the sense among young people that they have no real opportunities to learn their own language in the city. Many of them have taken it upon themselves to form organizations based on their own interests, such as hip hop dance, theatre, and *capoeira* (the Brazilian martial art). Such groups double as means to create support in overcoming challenges such as trauma, family violence, and drug/alcohol dependency – exactly the kinds of challenges that their parents highlight as resulting from their lack of connection to their languages and cultures. Language revitalization work in other parts of the world has drawn productively on these kinds of activities and miniature "communities." They serve as places to meet people, including youth, on their own terms and to demonstrate the ongoing relevance of their languages and cultures in the contemporary world (Patrick and Tomiak 2008; Hornberger and Swinehart 2012). But this approach to collaborative linguistic relationships requires an unpacking of ideological disjunctures of the kind that Meek (2011) reveals to be central to continued language shift. For example, because of the strong connection between rural (agricultural) lifestyles and Indigenous languages, and the quite common prohibition on speaking a language unless one can speak it fluently, youth, especially urban-born youth, are immediately presented with barriers to entry into language revitalization and language-related activities. Revitalization work must engage with learners and potential learners of languages beyond the boundaries of institutionalized education, not only to transmit the language but also to strengthen community relationships that have been weakened as a result of urbanization.

Creating a Model for Urban Collaborations

In some ways, São Gabriel is a great place to conduct anthropological fieldwork, because the local population is extremely familiar with research methods and topics in this discipline. The make-up of the population is such that most outsiders who arrive in the city are easily classifiable, based on their style of dress and social habits, as either researchers or members of the military. At the same time, this means that academics are an important part of local political and social life, although their role in shaping ongoing cultural change, including language loss and/or revitalization, has been below the radar of most discussions of the region. Academics' successes and challenges, reflected both in my own fieldwork experiences and in examinations of the results of past collaborations, point first and foremost towards the need for a conversation about the purpose of linguistic study and language revitalization in the region. Analytical starting points for this type of work include Ahlers and Wertheim (2009), who encourage developing a "theory of fieldwork" for the discipline as a whole; Dauenhauer and Dauenhauer (1998), who emphasize active "ideological clarification"; and Leonard and Haynes (2010), who push for a renewed openmindedness about how to "make collaboration collaborative." There has been a trend towards co-theorization in collaborative ethnography, and this could provide a productive model, for it raises vital questions about what language is, what it means to be a speaker of a particular language, and what (or whom) revitalization is for (Shulist 2013).

An alternative model for collaborative work on Indigenous languages in São Gabriel would include examining how language – both its loss and and its revitalization – affects *all* aspects of urban Indigenous people's lives. Components of this new model might include:

- recognizing the link between documentary linguistics and rurality, and moving away from a fatalistic view of language loss as an inevitable part of urbanization to seriously consider how to address the concerns that urban people have for their languages;
- considering how to move outside the educational sector, and away from talking about language in objectified, Saussurean terms, to expand our view of collaboration and consider the broader impact of our discourses;
- addressing the idea of creating community as a significant part of revitalization work; *and*
- examining the work that has been done in other disciplines – notably in psychology and geography in Canada and the United States – regarding the conditions and experiences of urban Indigenous peoples.

When we treat language revitalization as mainly a matter of making sure the language doesn't disappear completely, we risk suggesting that we are not concerned about who is speaking it and what it means for the individuals who no longer speak it, or who see their children unable to speak it. Language work has become linked primarily to the formal educational sector, and as a result, other elements of socialization that had previously been embedded in language learning have become disconnected from it. Recognition of the social and spiritual consequences of this disjuncture may point the way towards new approaches to documentation and revitalization. First, though, we need to discuss the role (past and present) that academics have played in the politics and ideologies of revitalization linguistics. The situation in São Gabriel suggests that additional ideological clarification is especially needed in urban contexts, where relationships, ways of being, and social and institutional structures are inherently different from those in rural areas. Globally, Indigenous populations are increasingly urban, and in that context the theory and practice of language revitalization has been criticized as "reactionary, backward-looking," and "impossibly nostalgic" (quoted in Romaine 2006: 446). Language revitalization activists must reconcile their efforts with processes of cultural change;

they should also make explicit the degree to which they are embedded in shaping that cultural change. Becoming concerned with the community of (actual and potential) speakers as a whole – urban as well as rural – will change the dynamic of how we approach it, the goals that we establish through our collaborative consultations, and, ideally, the outcomes of our research.

7 Conclusions: Language Revitalization and Urban Indigeneity

Like any anthropological work, this book has considered the experiences of a specific group, at a certain moment in time, in a particular place – and São Gabriel is in many ways a *very* particular place. Because of the sheer number and concentration of Indigenous people, not to mention of languages, Indigenous languages and politics are prominent concerns in the municipality, even though the city is embedded in a settler state in which Indigenous people are a very small minority. For most Brazilians, Indigenous policy remains a marginal concern, and even during the relatively progressive Lula and Dilma governments, efforts to address marginalization and to reduce economic and educational inequality focused on non-Indigenous people. In Brazilian discourses about race, Indigenous people are an add-on (Warren 2001), and their cultural practices have little to no presence beyond the Amazon region. When Indigenous people do appear on the national radar, the challenges of cultural continuity are viewed largely through the lens of land rights and environmental preservation. Also, the urban area has become a space in which the material hardships of contemporary Indigenous lives come to the surface, given that for the most part, they migrate to cities in search of the quality of life they had been promised as an outcome of education and development. While some of the challenges that urban Indigenous people face in São Gabriel can also be seen in other Latin American cities, including Manaus and Belém, along with Cuzco, Asunción, and others, a multiplicity of marginalizations intersect in the Brazilian Amazon in ways that are unique. The geographic remoteness of the Amazon region, the minimal demographic presence of Indigenous people at the national level, and the highly territorialized politics of Indigenous rights movements have generated major challenges for Indigenous peoples' advocates. When we add in the quantity and variety of languages spoken, language advocates face a difficult battle.

Ethnographic examination renders the picture even more complicated. The debates and difficulties that have emerged in relation to language revitalization efforts in São Gabriel reflect the diversity of positions in the city. That diversity is not simply a matter of linguistic difference; it also reflects conflicting ideological positions that have emerged not only along ethnolinguistic lines but also between urban and rural Indigenous people, among different generations, and within different political-institutional frameworks (from FOIRN, to federal and municipal administrators, to church personnel, to those involved in formal commercial trade). The ideologies that emerge from different actors in different sociopolitical contexts reflect different beliefs about the role of each of the languages spoken in the city, about the significance of place, and about the complex relationship between language and identity. A wide variety of influences, including the state (in its various forms), anthropologists and linguists, the organized Indigenous political movement, and Indigenous people themselves as they go about their daily lives, have transformed the status of Indigenous people and their languages, and these influences continue to alter understandings of Indigenous identity and the meaning of associated symbolic representations.

The themes discussed here – language revitalization, Indigenous identity, urbanization – manifest themselves in unique ways in São Gabriel, given the social circumstances; but at the same time, those themes relate to a global context of social change and cultural activism. The analysis I have presented here reinforces the fact that the societies of the Northwest Amazon require us to reconsider our long-standing approaches to discussing culture, identity, and social change (Jackson 1983) – especially, in this case, when it comes to language revitalization work. But in addition to these theoretical concerns, the challenges in São Gabriel point to the possibility of reworking methodologies for language revitalization to better serve diasporic, multilingual communities. Taken together, these two lines of thought raise questions about the actual and potential role played by various parties interested in improving the conditions facing Indigenous and minority populations in urban and diasporic environments – parties that include, most notably, state agents and academic allies.

Transforming Indigeneity: The Changing Meaning of Culture and Identity

The Northwest Amazon of Brazil, Colombia, and Venezuela has long been recognized as a site that requires a radical reinterpretation of "culture" and, especially, of the politics of culture and Indigeneity (Jackson 1983; 1995; R. Wright 2009; Lasmar 2009). The practice of "cultural preservation" in particular has deepened the interactions between Indigenous people and external institutions, including the state, NGOs, and academic researchers, and these connections have led to new systems of meanings for symbols of Indigenous identity (Jackson 1995). Because symbolic presentations, including linguistic performances (both everyday speech and more ritualized interactions), were prominent ways in which Tukanoans in particular worked to constitute their social identities, it has been easy in some ways to make use of them for these new, state-level political purposes (Hugh-Jones 2010; Shulist 2016c). That is to say, given that language and linguistic products such as songs are a part of cultural property that was already being used to display membership in a particular ethnolinguistic group (in other words, to differentiate Tukano from Tuyuka, or Kotiria from Kubeu), using these same forms of property to demonstrate Indigeneity for state representatives makes sense. These conscious performances, then, simultaneously "revitalize" social practices and identities and transform their meanings in complex ways.

These transformations are experienced differently, of course, depending on the political context. Brazil's Indigenist policy (not to mention its educational and developmental policies) has been different from those of the neighbouring states in which these same groups can be found, and the priorities of the Venezuelan and Colombian governments have created different attitudes towards and challenges for Indigenous people. The legal framework has had a direct impact on the experiences of the urban population, as state classifications of Indigeneity are tightly bound to specific land bases. Another complicating factor emerging from the border region is that while the exodus of rural Indigenous people from Brazilian territories may have slowed, São Gabriel continues to grow rapidly in population. One reason for this growth is the increasing arrival of Kotiria, Waikhena, and Kubeu people from the Colombian side of the border. The influence of this population on the dynamics of language in São Gabriel remains to be determined.

In focusing on the urban population, the work presented here has examined divisions and exclusions among Indigenous Amazonians themselves as a primary topic of interest in understanding the politics of culture. New kinds of identity, community, and cultural practices are being created in São Gabriel, and language sits at the forefront of debates about the meaning of culture, the possibility of change, and the role of place in shaping identity.

The relationships among language, culture, and identity have been among the arguments brought forward by linguists working to generate interest in the issue of language loss (Hale et al. 1992; Krauss 1998; Grenoble and Whaley 2006; Evans 2010). An examination of revitalization, however, reveals that the equation of language with culture, and the implication that saving one is equivalent to saving the other, cannot be taken as a given, but is in fact based in semiotic processes of iconicization (Irvine and Gal 2000) to which language activists are contributing. In the Rio Negro region, language does, in many ways, embody cultural identity, but the inherently multilingual nature of the community complicates the meaning of both loss and revitalization practices. As Jackson (1983) pointed out thirty years ago, the boundaries between language and culture do not match up neatly in these societies; the discourses of revitalization that make use of these equations therefore fit awkwardly into this cultural group, for they separate the interrelated Indigenous linguistic groups from one another in defining project goals at the language-group level.

At the same time, the degree to which language serves as a symbol of Indigenous identity and as a performative political tool is often elided in linguistic discussions of revitalization (Ahlers 2006; Graham 2002). Urban Indigenous peoples further confound this equation, especially in terms of these symbolic uses of language. Many of the other frequently invoked symbols of Indigeneity – most notably territoriality – are not available to these urban populations. A debate therefore emerges about whether urban populations should be allowed to participate in revitalizationist politics or benefit from material support directed towards their language, when the need for such financial support is clearer in remote rural communities that are facing severe economic and environmental threats to their very existence. Furthermore, efforts directed purely at the preservation of languages are not generally oriented towards who speakers are, but rather at the continued maintenance or growth of a speaker base, and such a base is most often easiest to find and strengthen in more homogenous rural areas. Urban Indigenous people therefore struggle to convince both state agents and Indigenous rights advocates that their cultural distinctness remains meaningful even in the city, and that despite the inherent challenges, their connection to culture is one they wish to maintain.

Language can, in theory, be removed from the land base in a way that other cultural practices (such as swidden agriculture and communitarian living arrangements) cannot be. This mobility is, however, ideologically limited, both by legal and institutional contexts that cannot imagine Indigeneity detached from its land base (see Patrick 2005 for discussion of a similar phenomenon in Canada) and by Indigenous people's own attitudes regarding what constitutes the preservation of their culture. Efforts to create spaces for the use of Indigenous languages in the city of São Gabriel have proven extremely contentious. This contention has emerged not because urban people are placing less value on their Indigenous identities or their relationship to language, but because the iconicization of the language/culture connection has fostered an increasingly politicized notion of the holistic package that constitutes "Indigeneity" – a package that by its nature cannot be transferred to the urban area. In this regard, anthropologists must grapple with the role that global discourses and practices of language revitalization are playing in urban and diasporic contexts, which in turn means re-examining how we conceive the connections among language, culture, and identity (see, for example, Giles 2013; Davis 2013; Shulist 2016a). Indigenous people as well as anthropological theorists have critiqued the perception that "culture" is static and unchanging (Maybury-Lewis 2002; Henderson 2000; Alfred and Corntassel 2005); yet the idea that cultures are closed and fixed retains a powerful hold. Recall my description of watching a presentation of a *dabucuri* at the downtown *maloka*: the Indigenous people at that event took pains to ensure that I understood that what I was seeing was not "real." The reasons cited for its artificiality had largely to do with the mixing of dance forms – which were being drawn from different Tukanoan groups – and with the ethnic identities of the dancers themselves. The strict boundary policing that goes on among Tukanoan people with respect to languages and cultural practices has made the idea of a "closed" culture more salient in this context, even though the kinship relations and exogamous marital exchanges embedded in these practices make it clear, paradoxically, that the "cultures" are in fact part of an inseparable whole.

Clearly, urban language advocates in São Gabriel are setting themselves a challenge when they equate language with culture, given that

[margin note: making space in urban setting]

for many urban youth, some core features of the cultural system have become so strongly antiquated. Most notable among these features is the most frequently analysed aspect of Tukanoan social organization – linguistic exogamy. When I talked to young, unmarried Indigenous people in the city, I found that even those who were most interested in revitalizing and valorizing their culture balked at the notion of accepting a marriage based on the ethnolinguistic criteria that had been followed by their parents or grandparents. Two young women I knew, one Tariana and one Kotiria, joked with me about how such a practice might work in their own lives. What were they to do, they asked me – stop and ask every attractive young man they might want to date if he belonged to an appropriate group? In São Gabriel, young women, who had been influenced by non-Indigenous media and education to think in terms of both emotional security and romantic love in choosing a partner, thought it ridiculous to limit their options even further. Even the daughter of Max Menezes – whose leadership in revitalizationist politics has been mentioned several times in preceding chapters – was taken aback when I asked whether she would consider marrying a man who was Tukano. "Of course!" she told me. "And do you think your father would accept that?" I continued. She waved her hand dismissively – "My father is modern," she answered.

These statements point to the deep questioning that is taking place in São Gabriel about what it means to be Indigenous and what types of practices must be sustained and strengthened. At the same time, these questions of "Indigeneity" are complicated by the multiplicity of Indigenous identities present in the city. The Baré in particular are engaged in a discussion and debate about how to understand themselves as a cultural group, as well as how to demonstrate their Indigenous status in ways that are intelligible to the powerful outsiders who have made this label both symbolically and materially vital. The practices of language revitalization and the ideological position of the Nheengatú language within the politics of Indigeneity remain unsettled, and the debates surrounding that language are making important contributions to anthropological understandings of both ethnogenesis (Warren 1998; Wroblewski 2012) and the social status of contact languages, especially endangered ones (Garrett 2006; 2012). For the urban Indigenous population of São Gabriel, the abstract, nebulous concepts of "culture" and "identity" are directly related to the concrete, material realities of state recognition and competition for scarce resources from NGOs and other outside sources.

As Keesing (1987) points out, anthropology's "interpretive quest" has helped Indigenous intellectuals develop an elusive and temporary coherence in their descriptions and definitions of what constitutes "their culture." Given the political significance of Indigenous identity within the institutions of the Brazilian state – and those of other Latin American states – solidifying this coherence in order to create something stable and reliable has become vital to individual, physical survival and to the continuity of the group "culture." São Gabriel's urban Indigenous people are living squarely within "the house of transformation," with all motion, upheaval, and instability that metaphor implies. Their efforts to participate in existing forms of language revitalization – including the creation of alternative educational structures, the establishment of new language policies, and the valorization of languages as symbols of identity – take place within this shaky structure.

Their efforts, and the ideological challenges that confront them, demonstrate that "Indigenous culture" in the Northwest Amazon is concept that, while often used, is far from settled in its meaning. The question of who is entitled to define it, and to claim it or work for and with it in a political and social advocacy sense, is constantly debated among the city's Indigenous people. The role played by the state and its agents in these challenges has often been considered in sociocultural anthropology, but only recently have linguistic anthropologists turned to consider the broad implications of minority language policies, language revitalization projects, and other language planning endeavours in light of the changing role and status of the state within a globalized political economy (Patrick 2007; Heller 2009; Collins 2011). The complex situation of change, resistance, and adaptation among the Indigenous people of São Gabriel highlights questions that must be considered by anthropologists working in other contexts. How do the politics of revitalization, and anthropological interpretations of cultures-as-texts, contribute to Indigenous peoples' understandings of their own ways of being, of the boundaries of their cultures, and of the meaning of their identities? What forms of dispute and contestation are emerging from these groups that suggest further examination may be in order, particularly where the idea of wholesale "preservation" of cultural practices is clearly untenable, as in urban and diasporic contexts? The multilingual environment of São Gabriel demonstrates that insufficient attention has been devoted to the many possible roles that endangered and minority languages play in these sociopolitical debates.

Effective Engagement with Urban Language Revitalization

Language revitalization is a (relatively) new field of engagement with minority languages and the politics of culture; and especially in contexts where widespread social change (such as urbanization) is having a significant impact, it requires conscious attention to the shifting meanings of basic ideas about culture and identity. Revitalization practices and politics are particularly fruitful grounds for reconsidering the multiple meanings of "language." What *is* language? What are the boundaries between language and culture, and to what degree is language revitalization the same thing as cultural revitalization? Even while linguistic anthropologists have begun to wrestle with these questions (cf. Faudree 2013; Nevins 2013; Urla 2015), the practical approaches taken by many documentary linguists have facilitated the erasure of some of their implications. Given the degree of interest in language revitalization today, these questions require further theoretical consideration and cross-disciplinary conversation. These theoretical concerns also have direct implications for the practical approaches taken by those working to implement language revitalization programs.

Like other linguistic anthropologists (Hill 2002; Errington 2003), I have been critical of some of the discourses, ideologies, and practices surrounding language revitalization while at the same time supporting these efforts in a general sense. In São Gabriel, as in many parts of the world, the loss of Indigenous languages has resulted from, and continues to be experienced as part of, a system of colonial domination and institutional racism that ranges from assimilationist at best to genocidal at worst (Wright 2005). Efforts to reclaim and revitalize languages are therefore not merely a matter of academic interest; they also entail supporting Indigenous peoples' autonomy and respecting the value of a variety of cultural practices and belief systems, or ways of being and knowing in the world. In critiquing some aspects of revitalization practice and discourse in São Gabriel, then, my intention has been to draw attention to the consequences of some of these endeavours – specifically, to the experiences of urban Indigenous residents in relation to culture and language. These people have found themselves between a rock and a hard place: in effect, they have been presented with a choice between their cultural practices and their economic and material security.

São Gabriel's urban Indigenous residents are, of course, far from homogenous or uniform in their attitudes towards language revitalization, and the ideological perspectives and contradictions underlying existing language planning efforts reflect the depth of disagreements among them. As with many aspects of language ideology, however, these disagreements often remain below the surface (Silverstein 1979; Woolard and Schieffelin 1994), even though language is a frequent topic of political analysis among Indigenous and non-Indigenous leaders. One focal point of my analysis, then, has been how ideological clarification (Dauenhauer and Dauenhauer 1998; Kroskrity 2009) is necessary to meet the specific needs of this urban population.

While this analysis of ideologies has addressed political, cultural, and sociolinguistic circumstances unique to São Gabriel, the basic framework for analysis is equally relevant for other urban, diasporic minority-language populations. Global-level revitalization discourses continue to employ idealized, one-to-one equations between language and identity, along with ethnonationalist frames that do not necessarily align well within these social environments. Brazilian political structures are not the only ones that construct policies for Indigenous people in relation to territory and territorialization (Peters and Andersen 2013), and challenges to urban Indigenous peoples' "authenticity" relate directly to their ability to make claims for recognition of their rights. The Amazon and its inhabitants have been an especially rich political-economic symbol, not only in Brazil but also in the global environmentalist and Indigenous rights discourse, and the implications of urbanization and loss of "authenticity" are therefore potent. The deterritorialization of linguistic practices and their associated identities is a complex process that may offer insight into the situation facing heritage-language speakers or people engaged in language revitalization in diasporic contexts (Garrett, Bishop, and Coupland 2009).

This perspective presupposes not only that Indigenous and minority languages are worth preserving, but also that they are worth preserving in urban centres, for the sake of the speakers who live in those places and their children. So I dispute those arguments for language preservation that are grounded in "universal valorization" or in the possibility of abstract loss that is experienced with the loss of a language (Hill 2002), preferring instead to focus on what the loss of a language may mean to the individuals who experience it first-hand. Given the degree to which globalization, deterritorialization, and mobility are features of the contemporary linguistic reality, a full understanding of language loss and the possibilities for revitalization depends on recognizing their uniquely personal and localized implications. Language revitalization efforts in São Gabriel point towards fundamental questions about what "community" means and to the possibility that it must be *created* rather than merely *found* in urban contexts. The complex relationships among speakers of different languages – or even among different languages within the repertoire of one speaker – indicate that we must examine language revitalization beyond a binary between the Indigenous/local language and the colonizing/dominant language; and the multilayered multilingualism of urban centres (including, again, both Indigenous and non-Indigenous diasporas) must be understood as transforming the language hierarchies that perpetuate the threat of language loss.

Final Considerations

The situation in São Gabriel highlights the need to further investigate what it means to be Indigenous, who gets to decide, and how those decisions can be disputed or renegotiated. For various reasons, language sits at the heart of these questions in the Northwest Amazon, and this raises significant themes about the meaning of multilingualism for revitalizationist purposes, the goals and benefits of language revitalization projects, and the importance of ideological contestation in shaping the outcomes of such endeavours. Although these forms of language planning often invoke the ideal of preservation and maintenance of "traditional" Indigenous life ways, they cannot be disconnected from social change, for they are, fundamentally, efforts to control the direction of that change. On the one hand, then, language revitalization practices fit squarely within a globalized discourse of Indigenous rights and a changing politics of culture; on the other hand, the transformations these practices embody can be understood in direct relation to concepts of change that are already central to the peoples of the Northwest Amazon (Stephen Hugh-Jones 1979; Cerqueira 2008). Improving our understanding of what these practices and projects mean within the framework of local symbols, myths, practices, and politics, and using these projects to create positive change in the lives of marginalized peoples, depends on considering the impacts from a variety of angles and incorporating a range of voices. With the urban Indigenous population experiencing marginalization in two separate ways – both as Indigenous people in a world dominated by non-Indigenous ways of being, and as urban people in a context of an Indigenous politics in which a romanticized rural ideal has power – their voices become especially important ones to amplify.

Appendix: Text of São Gabriel's Language Legislation[1]

Law No. 145 – 11 December 2002

Pertaining to the co-officialization of the Nheêgatu, Tukano, and Baniwa languages along with the Portuguese language in the municipality of São Gabriel da Cachoeira, state of Amazonas, Brazil.

The President of the Municipal Council of São Gabriel da Cachoeira, AM:

Be it known to all that the Municipal Council of São Gabriel da Cachoeira, state of Amazonas, declares the following:

LAW:

Art. 1 The Portuguese language is the official language of the Federal Republic of Brazil.

Single paragraph – It is established that the municipality of São Gabriel da Cachoeira, state of Amazonas, will come to have as co-official languages Nheêgatu, Tukano, and Baniwa.

Art. 2 The status of co-official language, here conceived, obligates the municipality:

a. To provide basic services to the public in all public offices in the official language and in the three co-official languages, orally and in writing

b. To produce published documents, such as public information campaigns, in the official language and in the three co-official languages

c. To encourage and support the learning and use of the co-official languages in the schools and media

Art. 3 All administrative acts conducted in the official language or in any of the co-official languages are valid and effective.

Art. 4 In no case may anyone be discriminated against for reason of the official or co-official language used.

Art. 5 All corporate entities should have a body of translators available in the municipality, as established in the preceding article, under penalty of law.

Art. 6 The use of the other indigenous languages spoken in the municipality shall be assured in the indigenous schools, according to federal and state legislation.

Art. 7 Any decisions to the contrary are repealed.

Art. 8 This law comes into effect on the date of its publication.

Chamber of the Municipal Council of São Gabriel da
Cachoeira, State of Amazonas, 11 December 2001.
DIEGO MOTA SALES DE SOUZA
President of the Municipal Council

Law No. 210 – October 31, 2006

Pertaining to the regulation of the Co-Officialization of the **NHEEN-GATU**[1], **TUKANO**, and **BANIWA** languages, along with the Portuguese languages, in the municipality of São Gabriel da Cachoeira/state of Amazonas.

The President of the Municipal Council of São Gabriel da Cachoeira/AM,

Let it be known to all that the Municipal Council of São Gabriel da Cachoeira/state of Amazonas, declares the following:

LAW:

Art 1. The Portuguese language is the official language of the Federal Republic of Brazil;
   Single paragraph – It is established that the municipality of São Gabriel da Cachoeira/state of Amazonas, has as co-official languages Nheengatu, Tukano, and Baniwa.

Art 2. The status of co-official language, here conceived, obligates the municipality:
   1. To provide basic services to the public in all public offices in the official language and in the three co-official languages, orally and in writing;

A. The status of "co-officiality" is equivalent to the concept of "officiality," as such it is established that the municipality of São Gabriel da Cachoeira has, as of the publication of this law, four official languages.

B. The executive power of the municipality will conduct, within 60 days following the regulation of this law, a survey of the employees of its agencies that are proficient in the co-official languages and appoint them to provide the services of that agency in the co-official languages.

C. The executive power of the municipality shall have a period of 180 days following the regulation of this law to initiate the provision of services in these languages in their oral form

D. The executive power of the municipality shall have a period of one year following the regulation of this law to provide these services in written form.

E. Public municipal offices that do not have employees that are capable of providing services in the co-official languages among their staff will contract speakers who are proficient in the co-official languages in both oral and written form.

F. Public state and federal agencies in operation in the municipality are recommended to contract employees who are proficient in oral and written use of the co-official languages

G. Competitions for municipal public service positions for roles that include public service shall require proficiency in Portuguese as well as one of the three co-official languages.

H. All competitions for municipal public service positions shall offer candidates exams in the four official languages, and the candidate may choose the language in which the test will be conducted.

I. Any public institution should have a number of employees that speaks the co-official languages that is compatible with the demand.

2. To produce published documents, such as public information campaigns, in the official language and in the three co-official languages

A. Any documentation of public interest in the scope of the municipality, such as notices, warnings, announcements, including public signage within the city, traffic signs, names of public agencies, shall by systematically produced in the four official languages.

B. Birth certificates and other portable documents that imply tax payments shall be bilingual Portuguese/one of the co-official languages, by request of the holder. Exceptions shall be taken to the Municipal Council on Language Policy, according to Article 7.

C. The Municipal Secretary of Education will create an institutional network concerned with the formation of teaching staff, translators, and other professionals in various roles for the training and development of linguistic materials (toponomy, terminology, etc) with the active participation of the Municipal Council on Language Policy.

D. It is strictly prohibited to charge higher rates, or to double the payment requested, for any bilingual document produced according to the terms of Article 2, subsection B.

3. To encourage and support the learning and use of the co-official languages in schools and the media

A. The executive power shall designate funds in order to assure the availability of the co-official languages within the educational system: this includes the contracting and training of teachers of/in the three official languages, as well as the production of pedagogical material, etc.

B. Early childhood education will be conducted within a bilingual framework with the teaching of a co-official language and of Portuguese.

C. The offering of the three co-official languages is mandatory in all of the educational networks of the municipality and optional in the indigenous schools specifically for the *etnias* that speak other languages of the municipality, that have their ethnic language as the language of instruction.

D. All teaching establishments within the Municipal, State, and Federal spheres are subject to the co-officialization language policy prioritizing the teaching of the three languages within their respective places of learning within a period of two years.

E. Communication media (radio, newspaper, video, local writings, public events, publicity cars) will include the three co-official languages within their daily programming. On the radio, there will be at least one news program of significant public interest in each of the co-official languages presented on a daily basis. Within a period of three years, 10% of broadcast time should be dedicated to each of the three co-official languages on radio broadcasting within the municipality. State-run radio will reach 50% of broadcast time in the three co-official language within three years of the regulation of this law.

F. The executive power of the municipality will support the creation of community radio prioritizing transmission in the three co-official languages.

G. Television broadcast will include at least 10 minutes daily in each of the three co-official languages within a period of two years.

H. Public advertising, and private advertising of public interest, should be transmitted throughout the media in the four official languages of the municipality.

I. Services to the public by radiophone will prioritize transmission in the co-official languages when the transmission is directed at the specific linguistic territory of that language (Baniwa on the Rio Içana, Nheengatu on the Rio Negro, and Tukano in the Uaupés Basin).

Art 3. All administrative acts conducted in the official language or in any of the co-official languages are valid and effective.

Art 4. In no case may anyone be discriminated against for reason of the official or co-official language used.

1. Any discrimination based on language is a crime. Penalties may include the provision of services for those entities that implement language policy (schools, indigenous organizations, etc), or payment of fines to the Municipal Language Policy Fund for the teaching and promotion of the co-official languages

2. Complaints shall be communicated to the police under the governance of the federal and state authorities, with possible with guidance from the Municipal Council for Language Policy.

Art 5. All corporate entities should have a body of translators available in the municipality, as established in the preceding article, with a penalty of payment of a fine of 150 UFIR[1] for the first office and 450 UFIR for subsequence offenses, resources that should be directed to the Municipal Language Policy Fund (MLPF).

1. The operating license for private corporations within the municipality will be provided based on the presentation of certification of compliance with Article 5 of law 145-2001; this license will be renewed annually through a new certification process by the Municipal Council for Language Policy.
2. Business with few than five employees who do not provide services to the public will be exempt from this certification of compliance. Exceptions will be submitted to the Municipal Council for Language Policy.
3. Public authorities will prioritize bids for services within the municipality service providers who respect Law 145, offering services to the public in the co-official languages.
4. Private institutions with commercial or non-commercial interests (associations, churches etc) will also have the obligation to attend the public in the co-official languages.
5. Signs, billboards, flyers, and publicity pamphlets in public space should offer information in the three co-official languages. In addition, price lists and snack bar or restaurant menus will also be offered in the three languages.
6. Churches should offer religious services in the three co-official languages according to the languages of their membership and on a schedule to be determined by the congregational community for a period of one year.

Art 6. The use of the other indigenous languages spoken in the municipality shall be assured in the indigenous schools, according to federal and state legislation.

1. The additional languages shall be considered official in the context of their communities.

Art 7. The Municipal Council for Language Policy (MCLP) in the municipality of São Gabriel da Cachoeira is hereby established.

1. The Council will have a deliberative and consultative role, and should accompany, orient, and ensure accountability in the application of Law 145/2001, and administer the Municipal Language Policy Fund.
2. The Municipal Council for Language Policy will encourage efforts to promote the other languages of the municipality, through workshops, the publication of materials, the training of teachers, and audiovisual productions.
3. The Council will consist of institutions of public authority and institutions of civil society that function within the

municipality (FOIRN, town council, SEMEC [municipal department of education and culture], SEDUC [state department of education], UFAM [Federal University of Amazonas], FUNAI [National Indian Affairs Association], IPOL [Institute for Language Policy], COPIARN [association of Indigenous teachers within the state educational board], ISA [Socio-environmental institute], UEA [state university of Amazonas], Agrotechnical school [now IFAM, the federal institute of Amazonas], SSL [Health Without Limits, an NGO with limited current functioning], APIARN [association of Indigenous teachers within the municipal education board], religious institutions, business associations, a member of neighbourhood associations).

4. FOIRN will have four members, made up of one representative of each co-official language and one representative of the other languages, while the other institutions will have one representative with an alternate.

5. The initiation of the Council's work shall be 60 days following the regulation of this law.

Art 8. The Municipal Language Policy Fund [MLPF] shall be established in the municipality of São Gabriel da Cachoeira.

Art 9. Any decisions to the contrary are repealed.

Art 10. This law comes into effect on the day of its publication.

Chamber of the Municipal Council of São Gabriel da Cachoeira, state of Amazonas, October 31, 2006.
FRANCISCO ORLANDO DIOGENES NOGUEIRA
President of the Municipal Council

Notes

1. Playing Indian: The Politics of Language, Identity, and Culture in Urban Amazonia

1 Portions of Chapter 1 and Chapter 6 present revised versions of previously published material by the author. The original version was published as "Collaborating on Language: Contrasting the Theory and Practice of Collaboration in Linguistics and Anthropology," in *Collaborative Anthropologies* 6: 1–29 (copyright University of Nebraska Press).

2 Throughout this book, I have used real names in cases where a person's preference to be identified and acknowledged was clearly expressed and documented on consent forms, or for descriptions of public events and statements. In all other cases, I have changed names and other identifying details to preserve anonymity.

3 All quotations from interviews and conversations are my own translations of Portuguese originals.

4 The capitalization of the umbrella term "Indigenous" is used to indicate the degree to which my interlocutors in Brazil accepted and viewed this term as a descriptor of an identity category that was just as relevant to them as, for example, their tribal or national affiliation. That is to say, despite scholarly recognition of the fact that the concept of Indigenous identity is recent and supplemental to identities as members of particular Indigenous groups (Niezen 2003; Graham and Penny 2014), a central tenet of this book is that it is a significant identity category in itself and, as such, worthy of the capital letter. Occasional uses of the pejorative term "Indian" will also appear in this book but should not be taken as interchangeable with "Indigenous," since the connotations are fundamentally different. "Indian" has historically worked as a racializing construct, grouping all of the peoples of the

Americas into one "biological" unit, and ensuring their inferior placement on a hierarchical typology of humans (Forte 2013; Dunbar-Ortiz 2014). My uses of the heavily laden term "Indian," then, are part of an intentional effort to show how this version of Indigenous identity persists in complex ways and how Indigenous people themselves engage with it in their representations of themselves and others.

A full accounting of how this latter term has functioned as a racializing construct for all of the peoples of the Americas can be found in Graham and Penny (2014).

5 In 2000, 68 per cent of the population of the entire multinational region of Amazonia lived in areas defined as "urban"; by 2014 the proportion had increased to 75 per cent, and it is continuing to rise rapidly (Emperaire and Eloy 2015: 71).

6 See, for example, the recent edited volume of the Journal of Latin American and Caribbean Anthropology on Indigenous Urbanization in Lowland South America (Alexiades and Peluso 2015).

7 Counting languages, especially endangered ones, inevitably involves abstraction and debate, both about whether any fluent speakers of a given language remain and about the boundaries between language and dialect (Hill 2002; Dobrin, Austin, and Nathan 2007); as such, various sources offer different, and sometimes imprecise, counts of the total number of languages spoken in the Rio Negro region. For example, FOIRN/ISA (2006) places the count at "more than twenty," and Epps and Stenzel (2013) at "some two dozen," while Ana Carla Bruno (2010) gives a specific count at nineteen. These disputed numbers may also be the result of differing definitions of the boundaries of the region in question.

8 The Portuguese word *município* refers to the smallest administrative unit of governance in Brazil, below the level of the state. Brazilian *municípios* generally encompass a geographic territory that includes some rural areas in which small settlements are located, and an administrative seat (*sede*) in a city from which all services are coordinated and political decisions are made. While the political entity does not match up exactly to the North American concept of "municipality," for the sake of simplicity, I have used this term (and the adjectival form "municipal") as the translation.

9 The Brazilian Institute of Geography and Statistics estimates approximately 17,000 inhabitants as of 2015 (IBGE 2015).

10 This type of back-and-forth mobility has been discussed as typical of Indigenous urbanization processes, and of Amazonian cities in particular (Peters and Andersen 2013; Alexiades and Peluso 2015), despite the continued construction of a dichotomy between urban and rural peoples.

The specific dynamics of this mobility, however, vary from context to context; in the Upper Rio Negro region, some communities are relatively easy to access by boat, which allows for short visits to the city (or vice versa) several times a year. Other communities, however, such as the Kotiria and Kubeu villages on the Upper Uaupes near the Colombian border, are so difficult to access that most urban-dwelling members of these communities could count on one hand the total number of times they had returned to their villages after settling in the city.

11 See Emperaire and Eloy (2015) and Eloy (2015) for extensive discussion of urbanization and the social meaning of agricultural practices for Indigenous people living in and around the city of São Gabriel.

12 This calculation is based on interviews and consultations conducted by Janet Chernela (personal communication).

13 A counterpoint to this assumption can be found in Sobreiro (2015), who offers an interpretation of the rise of a territorialized claim to identity and political authority in the Middle Rio Negro region that places urbanization at the centre. She points out that Indigenous rural peoples remained invisible to the structures of governance and international activism until their presence in the urban area created both a consciousness of their difference and a way of linking to the political bodies that could be used to build a "movement."

14 The "Milk River" (*Lago da Leite*) is identified in Tukanoan cosmology as the source water from which the anaconda-canoe emerged; contemporary Tukanoans have identified this body of water as Guanabara Bay in Rio de Janeiro (Lasmar 2005).

15 See Andrello (2006) for a corresponding analysis applied to the context of Iauaratê, the next-largest settlement in the municipality of São Gabriel.

16 French's discussion of Maya ethnolinguistic identity also productively engages with the way that revitalization and resistance politics themselves reiterate and reify the essential nature of this opposition, but reframe it in positive terms as a means to promote programs that protect Mayan languages in order to preserve this inherent difference.

17 This concern about linguistic difference within a pan-Indigenous social movement is heightened by the fact that, in contrast to some other Indigenous communities in Latin America, many of the languages do not even belong to the same family. This differs, for example, from the Mayan context in Central America discussed by Nora England (2003), Brigittine French (2010), and others.

18 Reasons offered for combatting this crisis include the preservation of the full range of human knowledge (Nettle and Romaine 2000), the

relationship between linguistic and ecological diversity (Maffi 2005), the protection of human rights (May 2003), and the struggles of Indigenous people for autonomy (Skutnabb-Kangas 2000; Battiste 2000).

19 See Perley (2011) for a thorough discussion of the complexities of causality and responsibility in a Canadian Indigenous community.

20 The condition that creates this sense that Indigeneity is "out of place" in the modern city constitutes a pattern with few exceptions throughout the Americas (e.g., in Oaxaca and Bolivia), and relates to discursive patterns that situate Indigeneity within the past. The framework, in other words, is one that functions through distancing in both time and space.

21 Perley (2011) and Davis (2016) are noteworthy exceptions, especially in their engagements with projects of language revitalization both as anthropologists/linguists and as concerned members of their respective Indigenous communities.

22 Other linguistic anthropological research that examines similar processes in different social contexts includes Faudree (2013), Debenport (2014), and Nevins (2013). Each of these texts provocatively contrasts the stated goals of language revitalization activists with the linguistic practices they employ, showing how "disjunctures" appear to go unnoticed and ultimately weaken their efforts.

23 These publications include several volumes by Henri Ramirez on languages from three of the different families of the region (Ramirez 1994 on Yamonami; Ramirez 1997 on Tukano; Ramirez 2001 on Baniwa), Alexandra Aikhenvald's work on the Tariana language (2003c), Patience Epps's analysis of Hup (2008), Kristine Stenzel's documentation of Kotiria (2013), and doctoral dissertations by Wilson Silva on Dessana (2012), Aline da Cruz on Nheengatú (2011), and Thiago Chacon on Kubeu (2012) .

24 Nancy Dorian (1998) describes these attitudes as an overall "ideology of contempt" held by European colonizers; additional examples of these widespread shaming practices can be found in Battiste (2000) and, for examples specific to the Rio Negro region, in Cabalzar (2012).

25 Indigenous scholars Audra Simpson (2014) and Glen Coulthard (2014) demonstrate the ways in which "recognition" continues to function as a process of discrimination and violence, and put forward analyses that reject the idea both politically and ethnographically. These refusals of recognition can also be seen in the ways in which urban Amazonians are redefining the conditions around which they express their identities outside of, rather than in response to, colonial categorizations (Shulist 2016c).

26 See also Muehlmann (2013) for discussion of these concerns with specific reference to hunting and fishing rights.

27 See, for example, Wroblewski (2012) for discussion of Kichwa in the
Ecuadoran Amazon, including consideration of how the national
relationship to the (highland) variety of this language affects the
perception of its role in lowland identities. For additional discussion of
the changing shape of Indigeneity in Brazil in relation to non-Amazonian
populations, see Warren (1999; 2001).

28 Additional literature that examines urban contexts and that contests this
kind of essentialism (Daveluy and Ferguson 2009; French 2010; Urla 2015)
generally focuses on the experiences of speakers of one language. As the
analysis in this book will show, the multilingualism of the Northwest
Amazon creates additional complications and points of dispute about how
best to represent and promote Indigenous identities and interests.

29 In addition to São Gabriel itself, there are a few large settlements with
more town-like structures throughout the municipality, including Iauaratê,
Taracuá, Pari-Cachoeira, and Acunção da Içana. While these spaces
may be worth analysing in their own right for the relationship between
Indigeneity and urbanization – and Iauaratê has been, in Andrello (2006) –
São Gabriel itself is further distinguished by the fact that it lies outside of
demarcated territories, as well as by a pattern in local discourse that draws
a boundary between it, "the city," and all other parts of the municipality,
"the communities." While the accuracy of this binary is questionable
for many reasons, it remains a relevant one to local perceptions. Lasmar
(2005) also discusses the binary of "city" and "community" as a locally
constructed discursive contrast that helps shape the social realities of each
of the two categories.

30 The practice of language-based exogamy means, of course, that all
Tukanoan communities are multilingual, since all of the in-marrying
women must speak primary languages that differ from those of their
husbands; patrilocality and socialization processes, however, mean that
women's languages are systematically excluded from public spaces and
that the community is defined according to the use of the (uniform) men's
language (Chernela 2003; 2004)

31 While "Wanano" (sometimes spelled "Guanano") is the more commonly
used ethnonym, this term comes from the Nheengatú language, and
members of the group with whom I worked have come to prefer to use
"Kotiria." Originally assigned to them by the neighbouring Kubeu people,
this name comes from the group's origin myth and means "water people"
(Stenzel 2013). The meaning of the word "Wanano" is not clear, but it may
be a translation of this term and a cognate of the Nheengatú word
anana, rain.

2. City of Transformation: Ethnography and History of a Multilingual Amazon Town

1 By the mid-eighteenth century, the lower and middle Rio Negro regions had been nearly completely depopulated and several Indigenous groups had been decimated (Wright 1992)

2 São Gabriel began its official existence as a small military fort shortly after the signing of this treaty.

3 Many of the non-Indigenous inhabitants of São Gabriel come specifically from the Northeast region, which is among the more heavily populated and impoverished areas of Brazil, and which was targeted for this kind of relocation to the more sparsely populated North, using the slogan "Men without land in the Northeast, land without men in the North" (Reid 2014).

4 This example came to my attention because it was an oddly fortuitous situation for me, personally, as I was pregnant during my first field visit and had an infant with me during the second. While many other imbalances and uncertainties in medical specialization certainly exist, this is also an important one to note given that ensuring the safety of women in childbirth and combatting infant mortality are among the specific concerns cited by Indigenous health advocates.

5 For extensive analysis, see Jonathan Hill (2008) and Alexandra Aikhenvald (2003a; 2001).

6 An additional, contrasting example can be seen in the case of the Kubeu. The Kubeu language is a member of the Eastern Tukanoan family, but the cultural practices and beliefs of this group, including its definitions of group membership and kinship, differ from those of the rest of the Tukanoan peoples (Chacon 2012). While present in São Gabriel and occasionally figuring among my research participants, Kubeu people are not as prominent, politically or demographically, as groups such as the Tariana.

7 Sibs in the Northwest Amazon are "named, ranked, exogamous, localized patrilineal descent groups" (Jackson 1983: 71). Sibs are defined, in Tukanoan understandings, as descendants of a single parent (the ancestor sibling who emerged from the anaconda-canoe). While sib boundaries are fluid and imprecise in many cases, they remain an important category for social organization (Ibid.: 72–75).

8 See Vilaca (2016) for an account of evangelism and Christianity in the Amazon region that addresses the complexities of the relationship between Indigenous and Christian identities and practices.

9 Roussef was impeached in May 2016; the research for this book, and the vast majority of its writing, took place prior to these major political shifts, so that change does not figure into the analysis presented here.

10 As more and more Indigenous women choose to come to the city to give
birth in order to have access to health care professionals, these connections
are not necessarily established at birth, but neither are they completely
lost – naming and other ceremonies may be performed later to offer this
kind of rooting in the territory.

3. Language Policy on Paper and in Practice

1 Formal education in the region was initially the result of the efforts
of Catholic missionaries, who founded schools in some of the larger
communities and expanded their efforts by sending students who had
completed primary school (eighth grade) back to their home communities
to teach younger children. As a result, many people who have been
teaching in rural areas for years have never gone beyond this level
of education, and improving their credentials has been an important
goal of the Indigenous movement. The importance of this program has
further increased since the Worker's Party (*Partido dos Trabalhadores*, PT)
governments of Luiz Ignácio da Silva (Lula) and Dilma Rousseff began
emphasizing quality education in Brazil; these governments passed
legislation requiring all teachers in Brazil to have enrolled in post-
secondary education by 2015.

2 These discussions took place in 2000, before I began my work in São
Gabriel. This recounting is based on the recollections of Maximiliano
Menezes, the second student in the story, as he offered them at the event
commemorating the tenth anniversary of this law, held at the São Gabriel
campus of the Universidade Estadual de Amazonas in February 2012,
which I will discuss in more detail later in this chapter.

3 The most prominent examples during my fieldwork were the mayor and
deputy mayor (*prefeito* and *vice-prefeito*), Pedro Garcia (Tariana) and André
Fernando (Baniwa), both of whom are Indigenous men who began their
political careers in FOIRN and who were elected to office with the strong
support of the Indigenous movement. Their status as the first Indigenous
governors of the municipality led to a lot of excitement following their
victory, but by the time of my fieldwork (towards the end of their
administration), that excitement had turned into a powerful and almost
universal sense of disappointment and betrayal among the Indigenous
people of the region. The reasons for this shift in perspective are complex
and beyond the scope of this chapter, but it must be noted that the two
men ran against each other in the 2012 election, that both were defeated
by a wide margin, and that a non-Indigenous mayor (with an Indigenous
deputy) took power in 2013.

4 In older linguistic and anthropological literature, "Maku" refers to the language family that includes four of the languages spoken in the Rio Negro region – Hup, Dâw, Nadëb, and Yehupdah (Epps 2008). Current nomenclature for the group usually favours "Nadahup," since the term "Maku" is considered pejorative, indicating a degree of extreme "backwardness" and lack of civilization. This use has come about as a result of the pre-contact status of these peoples, whose presence in the region pre-dates the arrival of any other language family, but who were considered inferior by these other groups. They have never been included in the system of linguistic exogamy, and were in fact enslaved by Tukanoans once they came to inhabit the region (Aikhenvald 2003b).

4. Education in the City: Defining Urban Indigeneity

1 As noted in chapter 3, these data remain unpublished, and I am grateful to Kristine Stenzel for providing me with access to these results.
2 See Andersen and Peters (2013) for discussion of this contrast.
3 São Gabriel has consistently been ranked among the lowest municipalities in Brazil according to the human development index (Atlas of Human Development in Brazil 2013).

5. Making an Indigenous Public: A Perspective from the Non-Official Languages

1 The Portuguese term *minoritario* was consistently used to refer to the non-official Indigenous languages, and my interlocutors would refer to the language policy as the means by which this formalized "minority" status was created.
2 The publication of a series of Kotiria narratives, edited by Janet Chernela and authored by several association members, is one of these projects; proceeds from the sales will generate some income for the association.
3 See Shulist (2016b) for a critical evaluation of ethnolinguistic identity as a concept in language revitalization.
4 This is, it is worth noting, possibly more of a discursive limitation than a pragmatic one, as research on Rio Negro foodways demonstrates that, even in the cities of São Gabriel and Santa Isabel, Indigenous people produce and consume foods according to distinctive cultural patterns (Eloy and Lasmar 2011; Emperaire and Eloy 2015; Sobreiro 2015a).
5 *Dabucuri* is the Nheengatú term for a ceremonial exchange ritual used by many of the Indigenous peoples of the region, including both Tukanoan and some Arawakan groups. It is characterized by a series of dances and chants

during which gifts (generally food, including fruit, manioc bread, and fish, or artesanal products) are offered from one group of relatives to another.

6. Revising Expectations: Reflections on the Research Process

1 Examples of linguists' pragmatic approach can be seen in Czaykowska-Higgins (2009) and in Rice (2009), each of which works to construct a solid base for the practice of linguistic collaborations and makes a strong case for the value this type of work has for the discipline of linguistics and its practitioners. Anthropologists' more critical approach to discussing revitalization and collaboration can be seen in Hill (2002), Errington (2003), Whiteley (2003), and Heller and Duchene (2007).

2 Tukano was the only Indigenous language included on the sign because it was the first one for which I was able to find a written translation, and my friend had already cut letters of a size that meant there would not be enough space for more than three languages (English, Portuguese, and Tukano).

3 Ramirez has written grammars of several of the Indigenous languages of the region, including Yanomami (Ramirez 1994) and Baniwa (Ramirez 2001) as well as Tukano (Ramirez 1997). His work and publications were sponsored by the Salesian missionaries of the Catholic Church, and the orthography he developed for the Tukano language in particular remains extremely controversial among the Indigenous population. While his status as a respected academic linguist has led some people to view him as the most authoritative source of a "correct" writing system, others feel that the complexity of his orthographic choices is not appropriate for the needs of speakers and is only suitable for linguistic analysis.

4 The traditional meaning of *maloka* as a communal living structure, and the significance of using this form as a place for political meetings and ceremonial gatherings in a revitalizationist context, is discussed in the introduction. Although the one that was located in the town centre is sometimes called a *maloka*, several of the features that characterize the original form are not present, and some Indigenous people refuse to use this name to refer to it. Colloquially, however, it is known as "the *maloka*," and given the motivation for its construction discussed here, I have chosen to retain that phrasing.

Appendix

1 English translations mine.

Bibliography

Abadian, Sousan. 2006. "Cultural Healing: When Cultural Renewal Is Reparative and When It Is Toxic." *Pimatisiwin: A Journal of Aboriginal and Indigenous Community Health* 4(2): 5–27.

Ahlers, Jocelyn C. 2006. "Framing Discourse: Creating Community through Native Language Use." *Journal of Linguistic Anthropology* 16(1): 58–75.

– 2009. "The Many Meanings of Collaboration: Fieldwork with the Elem Pomo." *Language and Communication* 29(3): 230–43.

– 2012. "Two Eights Make Sixteen Beads: Historical and Contemporary Ethnography in Language Revitalization." *International Journal of American Linguistics* 78(4): 533–55.

Ahlers, Jocelyn C., and Suzanne A. Wertheim. 2009. "Introduction: Reflecting on Language and Culture Fieldwork in the Early 21st Century." *Language and Communication* 29(3): 193–8.

Aikhenvald, Alexandra Y. 2001. "Language Awareness and Correct Speech among the Tariana of Northwest Amazonia." *Anthropological Linguistics* 43(4): 411–30.

– 2003a. "Multilingualism and Ethnic Stereotypes: The Tariana of Northwest Amazonia." *Language in Society* 32(1): 1–21.

– 2003b. *Language Contact in Amazonia*. Oxford: Oxford University Press.

– 2003c. *A Grammar of Tariana, from Northwest Amazonia*. Cambridge: Cambridge University Press.

– 2012. *The Languages of the Amazon*. Oxford: Oxford University Press.

Akkari, Abdeljalil. 2012. "Intercultural Education in Brazil: Between Conservatism and Radical Transformations." *Prospects* 42(2): 161–75.

Albert, Bruce, and Alcida Rita Ramos. 1989. "Yanomami Indians and Anthropological Ethics." *Science* 244(4905): 632.

Alexiades, Miguel N., and Daniela M. Peluso. 2015. "Introduction: Indigenous Urbanization in Lowland South America." *Journal of Latin American and Caribbean Anthropology* 20(1): 1–12.

Alfred, Taiaiake, and Jeff Corntassel. 2005. "Being Indigenous: Resurgences against Contemporary Colonialism." *Government and Opposition* 40(4): 597–614.

Andersen, Chris, and Evelyn Peters. 2013. "Conclusion: Indigenizing Modernity or Modernizing Indigeneity?" In *Indigenous in the City: Contemporary Identities and Cultural Innovation*, ed. Evelyn Peters and Chris Andersen, 377–87. Vancouver: UBC Press.

Andrello, Geraldo. 2006. *Cidade do índio: transformações e cotidiano em Iauaretê*. São Paulo and Rio de Janeiro: Editora Unesp: Instituto Socioambiental; NUTI, Núcleo Transformações Indígenas.

– 2010. "Falas, Objetos E Corpos: Autores Indígenas No Alto Rio Negro." *Revista Brasileira de Ciências Sociais* 25(73): 5–26.

Atlas of Human Development in Brazil 2013. http://www.atlasbrasil.org.br/2013/en/perfil_m/sao-gabriel-da-cachoeira_am

Avineri, Netta, and Paul V. Kroskrity. 2014. "On the (Re-)Production and Representation of Endangered Language Communities: Social Boundaries and Temporal Borders." *Language and Communication* 38(1): 1–7.

Azevedo, Miguel, and Antenor Nascimento Azevedo. 2003. *Dahsea Hausirõ Porã ukushe wiophesase merã bueri turi: mitologia sagrada dos Tukano Hausirõ Porã*, ed. Aloisio Cabalzar. São Paulo: UNIRT.

Battiste, Marie, ed. 2000. *Reclaiming Indigenous Voice and Vision*. Seattle: University of Washington Press.

Bauman, Richard, and Charles L. Briggs. 2003. *Voices of Modernity: Language Ideologies and the Politics of Inequality*. Cambridge: Cambridge University Press.

Biolsi, Thomas, and Larry Zimmerman, eds. 1997. *Indians and Anthropologists: Vine Deloria, Jr, and the Critique of Anthropology*. Tucson: University of Arizona Press.

Blommaert, Jan. 1999. *Language Ideological Debates*. Berlin and New York: Mouton de Gruyter.

Bourdieu, Pierre. 1991. *Language and Symbolic Power*. Cambridge, MA: Harvard University Press.

Bruno, Ana Carla dos Santos. 2010. "Multilinguismo no Alto Rio Negro: Uma Interação entre Língua, Cultura e Sociedade." In *Mobilizações Étnicas e Transformações Sociais no Rio Negro*, ed. Alfredo Wagner Berno de Almeida and Emmanuel de Almeida Farias Júnior. 96–104. Manaus: UEA Edições.

Cabalzar, Flora Dias, ed. 2012. *Educação Escolar Indígena do Rio Negro 1998–2011*, 1st ed. São Paulo: Instituto Socioambiental.

Cerqueira, Felipe Agostini. 2008. "A Viagem Da Gente de Transformação: Uma Exploração Do Universo Semântico Da Noção de Transformação Em Narrativas Míticas Do Noroeste Amazônico." PhD diss., Universidade Federal Fluminense, Niterói, Brazil.

Chacon, Thiago Costa. 2012. "The Phonology and Morphology of Kubeo: The Documentation, Theory, and Description of an Amazonian Language." PhD diss., University of Hawai'i at Manoa. http://scholarspace.manoa. hawaii.edu/handle/10125/101344

Chandler, Michael J., and Christopher Lalonde. 1998. "Cultural Continuity as a Hedge against Suicide in Canada's First Nations." *Transcultural Psychiatry* 35(2): 191–219.

Chernela, Janet M. 1993. *The Wanano Indians of the Brazilian Amazon: A Sense of Space*. Austin: University of Texas Press.

– 2003. "Language Ideology and Women's Speech: Talking Community in the Northwest Amazon." *American Anthropologist* 105(4): 794–806.

– 2004. "The Politics of Language Acquisition: Language Learning as Social Modeling in the Northwest Amazon." *Women and Language* 27(1): 13–21.

– 2013. "Toward an East Tukano Ethnolinguistics: Metadiscursive Practices, Identity, and Sustained Linguistic Diversity in the Vaupés Basin of Brazil and Colombia. In *Upper Rio Negro: Cultural and Linguistic Interaction in Northwestern Amazonia*, ed. Patience Epps and Kristine Stenzel. 197–244. Rio de Janeiro: Museu Nacional, Museu do Índio/FUNAI.

– 2015. "Directions of Existence: Indigenous Women Domestics in the Paris of the Tropics." *Journal of Latin American and Caribbean Anthropology* 20(1): 201–29.

Chernela, Janet M., and Sarah A. Shulist. 2014. "Designing Difference: Ideology and Language Change in the Northwest Amazon of Brazil." Paper Presented at the 115th Annual Meeting of the American Anthropological Association, 3 December 2014, Washington D.C.

Collins, James. 1998. "Our Ideologies and Theirs." In *Language Ideologies: Practice and Theory,* ed. Bambi B. Schieffelin, Kathryn A. Woolard, and Paul V. Kroskrity. 256–70. New York and Oxford: Oxford University Press.

– 2011. "Language, Globalization, and the State: Issues for the New Policy Studies." In *Ethnography and Language Policy*, ed. Teresa L. McCarty. 128–35. New York: Routledge.

Conklin, Beth A. 1997. "Body Paint, Feathers, and VCRs: Aesthetics and Authenticity in Amazonian Activism." *American Ethnologist* 24(4): 711–37.

– 2002. "Shamans versus Pirates in the Amazonian Treasure Chest." *American Anthropologist* 104(4): 1050–61.

Conklin, Beth A., and Laura R. Graham. 1995. "The Shifting Middle Ground: Amazonian Indians and Eco-Politics." *American Anthropologist* 97(4): 695–710.

Coulthard, Glen Sean. 2014. *Red Skin, White Masks: Rejecting the Colonial Politics of Recognition*. Minneapolis: University of Minnesota Press.

Coupland, Nikolas. 2012. "Bilingualism on Display: The Framing of Welsh and English in Welsh Public Spaces." *Language in Society* 41(1): 1–27.

Crawford, James. 1989. *Bilingual Education: History, Politics, Theory, and Practice*. Trenton: Crane Publishing.

– 1995. "Endangered Native American Languages: What Is to Be Done, and Why?" *Bilingual Research Journal* 19(1): 17–38.

Czaykowska-Higgins, Ewa. 2009. "Research Models, Community Engagement, and Linguistic Fieldwork: Reflections on Working within Canadian Indigenous Communities." *Language Documentation and Conservation* 3(1): 15–50.

da Cruz, Aline. 2011. "Fonologia e Gramática do Nheengatú: A língua geral falada pelos povos Baré, Warekena, e Baniwa." PhD diss., Vrije Universiteit Amsterdam.

Dauenhauer, Nora Marks, and Richard Dauenhauer. 1998. "Technical, Emotional, and Ideological Issues in Reversing Language Shift: Examples from Southeast Alaska." In *Endangered Languages: Language Loss and Community Response*, ed. Lenore A. Grenoble and Lindsay J. Whaley. 57–98. Cambridge: Cambridge University Press.

Daveluy, Michelle, and Jenanne Ferguson. 2009. "Scripted Urbanity in the Canadian North." *Journal of Linguistic Anthropology* 19(1): 78–100.

Davis, Jenny L. 2013. "Learning to 'Talk Indian': Ethnolinguistic Identity and Language Revitalization in the Cherokee Rennaissance." PhD diss., University of Colorado, Boulder.

– 2016. "Language Affiliation and Ethnolinguistic Identity in Chickasaw Language Revitalization." *Language and Communication* 47: 100–11.

de la Cadeña, Marisol. 2010. "Indigenous Cosmopolitics in the Andes: Conceptual Reflections beyond 'Politics.'" *Cultural Anthropology* 25(2): 334–70.

Debenport, Erin. 2015. *Fixing the Books: Secrecy, Literacy, and Perfectibility in Indigenous New Mexico*. Santa Fe: School for Advanced Research.

Dobrin, Lise M., Peter K. Austin, and David Nathan. 2007. "Dying to Be Counted: The Commodification of Endangered Languages in Documentary Linguistics." In *Proceedings of Conference on Language Documentation and Linguistic Theory*, ed. Peter K. Austin, Oliver Bond, and David Nathan. London: SOAS.

Dorian, Nancy C. 1987. "The Value of Language-Maintenance Efforts Which Are Unlikely to Succeed." *International Journal of the Sociology of Language* (68): 57–67.

— 1998. "Western Language Ideologies and Small Language Prospects." In *Endangered Languages: Language Loss and Community Response*, ed. Lenore A. Grenoble and Lindsay J. Whaley. 3–21. Cambridge: Cambridge University Press.

— 2010. "Documentation and Responsibility." *Language and Communication* 30(3): 179–85.

Dove, Michael R. 2006. "Indigenous People and Environmental Politics." *Annual Review of Anthropology* 35(1): 191–208.

Dunbar-Ortiz, Roxanne. 2014. *An Indigenous Peoples' History of the United States*. Boston: Beacon Press.

Duranti, Alessandro. 2006. "Agency in Language." In *A Companion to Linguistic Anthropology*, ed. Alessandro Duranti. 451–73. Oxford: Blackwell.

Eisenlohr, Patrick. 2004. "Language Revitalization and New Technologies: Cultures of Electronic Mediation and the Refiguring of Communities." *Annual Review of Anthropology* 33: 21–45.

Eloy, Ludivine. 2015. "Urbanisation and Resource Management in Riverine Amazônia." *Bulletin of Latin American Research* 34(1): 1–2.

Eloy, Ludivine, and Cristiane Lasmar. 2011. "Urbanização e Transformação dos Sistemas Indígenas de Manejo de Recursos Naturais: O Caso do Alto Rio Negro (Brasil)." *Acta Amazonica* 41(1): 91–102.

Emperaire, Laure, and Ludivine Eloy. 2015. "Amerindian Agriculture in an Urbanising Amazonia (Rio Negro, Brazil)." *Bulletin of Latin American Research* 34(1): 70–84.

England, Nora C. 2003. "Mayan Language Revival and Revitalization Politics: Linguists and Linguistic Ideologies." *American Anthropologist* 105(4): 733–43.

Epps, Patience. 2008. *A Grammar of Hup*. Berlin: Walter de Gruyter.

Epps, Patience, and Kristine Stenzel, eds. 2013. *Upper Rio Negro: Cultural and Linguistic Interaction in Northwestern Amazonia*. Rio de Janeiro: Museu Nacional, Museu do Índio/FUNAI.

Errington, Joseph. 2003. "Getting Language Rights: The Rhetorics of Language Endangerment and Loss." *American Anthropologist* 105(4): 723–32.

Evans, Nicholas. 2010. *Dying Words: Endangered Languages and What They Have to Tell Us*. West Sussex: Wiley-Blackwell.

Faudree, Paja. 2013. *Singing for the Dead: The Politics of Indigenous Revival in Mexico*. Durham: Duke University Press.

Field, Les W. 1999. "Complicities and Collaborations: Anthropologists and the 'Unacknowledged Tribes' of California." *Current Anthropology* 40(2): 193–210.

Fishman, Joshua A. 1991. *Reversing Language Shift: Theoretical and Empirical Foundations of Assistance to Threatened Languages*. Multilingual Matters, 76. Philadelphia: Multilingual Matters.

_ ed. 2001. *Can Threatened Languages Be Saved? Reversing Language Shift, Revisited: A 21st Century Perspective*. Philadelphia: Multilingual Matters.

Fleming, Luke. 2009. "Indigenous Language Literacies of the Northwest Amazon." *Working Papers in Educational Linguistics* 24(1): 35–59.

– 2010. "From Patrilects to Performatives: Linguistic Exogamy and Language Shift in the Northwest Amazon." PhD diss., University of Pennsylvania, Philadelphia.

Fluehr-Lobban, Carolyn. 2008. "Collaborative Anthropology as Twenty-First-Century Ethical Anthropology." *Collaborative Anthropologies* 1(1): 175–82.

FOIRN/ISA. 2006. *Mapa-livro Povos Indígenas do Rio Negro: Uma Introdução à Diversidade Socioambiental do Noroeste da Amazônia Brasileira*. São Paulo.

Forte, Maximilian C. 2013. *Who Is an Indian?: Race, Place, and the Politics of Indigeneity in the Americas*. Toronto: University of Toronto Press.

Franchetto, Bruna. 2006. "Ethnography in Language Documentation." In *Essentials of Language Documentation*, ed. Jost Gippert, Nikolaus P. Himmelmann, and Ulrike Mosel. 183–212. Berlin: Mouton de Gruyter.

Freire, José Ribamar Bessa. 2004. "A Extensão Da Língua Geral Amazônica No Século XIX E a Política de Línguas." *Revista Internacional de Lingüística Iberoamericana* 2 (1): 9–22.

Freire, José Ribamar Bessa, and Maria Carlota Rosa, eds. 2003. *Linguas Gerais: Politica Linguistica E Catequese Na America Do Sul No Periodo Colonial*. Rio de Janeiro: Editora da Universidade do Estado do Rio de Janeiro.

French, Brigittine M. 2010. *Maya Ethnolinguistic Identity: Violence, Cultural Rights, and Modernity in Highland Guatemala*. Tucson: University of Arizona Press.

Froerer, Peggy, and Anna Portisch. 2012. "Introduction to the Special Issue: Learning, Livelihoods, and Social Mobility." *Anthropology and Education Quarterly* 43(4): 332–43.

Gagné, Natacha. 2013. *Being Māori in the City: Indigenous Everyday Life in Auckland*. Toronto: University of Toronto Press.

Gal, Susan. 1998. "Multiplicity and Contention among Language Ideologies: A Commentary." In *Language Ideologies: Practice and Theory*, ed. Bambi B. Schieffelin, Kathryn A. Woolard, and Paul V. Kroskrity. 317–31. New York and Oxford: Oxford University Press.

– 2005. "Language Ideologies Compared: Metaphors of Public/Private." *Journal of Linguistic Anthropology* 15(1): 23–37.

Gal, Susan, and Judith T. Irvine. 1995. "The Boundaries of Languages and Disciplines: How Ideologies Construct Difference. (Defining the Boundaries of Social Inquiry)." *Social Research* 62(4): 967–1001.

Galvão, Eduardo. 1979. *Encontro de Sociedades. Índios E Brancos No Brasil.* São Paulo: Paz e Terra.

Garcia, MaryEllen. 2003. "Recent Research on Language Maintenance." *Annual Review of Applied Linguistics* 23: 22–43.

Garcia, Ofelia. 2012. "Ethnic Identity and Language Policy." In *The Cambridge Handbook of Language Policy*, ed. Bernard Spolsky. 79–99. Cambridge: Cambridge University Press.

Garnelo, Luiza. 2003. *Poder, Hierarquia, E Reciprocidade: Saúde E Harmonia Entre Os Baniwa Do Alto Rio Negro.* Rio de Janeiro: Editora Fiocruz.

Garnelo, Luiza, and Dominique Buchillet. 2006. "Taxonomias Das Doenças Entre Os Índios Baniwa (Arawak) E Desana (Tukano Oriental) Do Alto Rio Negro (Brasil)." *Horizontes Antropológicos* 12(26): 231–60.

Garrett, Paul B. 2006. "Contact Languages as 'Endangered' Languages: What Is There to Lose?" *Journal of Pidgin and Creole Languages* 21(1): 175–90.

– 2012. "Dying Young: Pidgins, Creoles, and Other Contact Languages as Endangered Languages." In *The Anthropology of Extinction: Essays on Culture and Species Death*, ed. Genese Marie Sodikoff. Bloomington: Indiana University Press.

Garrett, Peter, Hywel Bishop, and Nikolas Coupland. 2009. "Diasporic Ethnolinguistic Subjectivities: Patagonia, North America, and Wales." *International Journal of the Sociology of Language* 195: 173–99.

Giles, Jonathan. 2013. "The Call of the Wild Geese: An Ethnography of Diasporic Irish Language Revitalization in Southern and Eastern Ontario." MA thesis, University of Western Ontario, London.

Gippert, Jost, Nikolaus P. Himmelmann, and Ulrike Mosel. 2006. *Essentials of Language Documentation.* Berlin: Mouton de Gruyter.

Gomez-Imbert, Elsa. 1991. "Force des Langues Vernaculaires en Situation D'exogamie Linguistique: Le Cas Du Vaupès Colombien, Nord-Ouest Amazonien." ResearchGate 27. https://www.researchgate. net/publication/32978895_Force_des_langues_vernaculaires_en_ situation_d'exogamie_linguistique_le_cas_du_Vaupes_colombien_Nord-Ouest_amazonien

Gone, Joseph P. 2008. "Introduction: Mental Health Discourse as Western Cultural Proselytization." *Ethos* 36(3): 310–15.

Gorter, Durk. 2006. *Linguistic Landscape: A New Approach to Multilingualism.* Philadelphia: Multilingual Matters.

Graham, Laura R. 2002. "How Should an Indian Speak? Amazonian Indians and the Symbolic Politics of Langauge in the Global Public Sphere." In *Indigenous Movements, Self-Representation, and the State in Latin America*, ed. Kay B. Warren and Jean E. Jackson. Austin: University of Texas Press.

Graham, Laura R., and H. Glenn Penny. 2014. *Performing Indigeneity: Global Histories and Contemporary Experiences*. Lincoln: University of Nebraska Press.

Granadillo, Tania. 2006. "An Ethnographic Account of Language Documentation among the Kurripako of Venezuela." PhD diss., University of Arizona, Tucson.

Granadillo, Tania, and Heidi A. Orcutt-Gachiri, eds. 2011. *Ethnographic Contributions to the Study of Endangered Languages*. Tucson: University of Arizona Press.

Grenoble, Lenore A., and Lindsay J. Whaley. 2006. *Saving Languages: An Introduction to Language Revitalization*. Cambridge: Cambridge University Press.

Hale, Ken, Michael Krauss, Lucille J. Watahomigie, et al. 1992. "Endangered Languages." *Language* 68(1): 1–42.

Hallett, Darcy, Michael J. Chandler, and Christopher E. Lalonde. 2007. "Aboriginal Language Knowledge and Youth Suicide." *Cognitive Development* 22(3): 392–9.

Harmon, David. 2001. "On the Meaning and Moral Imperative of Diversity." In *On Biocultural Diversity: Linking Language, Knowledge and the Environment*, ed. Luisa Maffi. 53–71. Washington: Smithsonian Institution Press.

Heller, Monica. 2009. "Colonialism and Re-Imaging Minority Language Management." *Journal of Multicultural Discourses* 4(2): 103–6.

Heller, Monica, and Alexandre Duchêne. 2007. *Discourses of Endangerment: Ideology and Interest in the Defence of Languages*. London: Continuum.

Henderson, James (Sakéj) Youngblood. 2000. "Postcolonial Ledger Drawing: Legal Reform." In *Reclaiming Indigenous Voice and Vision*, ed. Marie Battiste. 161–71. Vancouver: UBC Press.

Henze, Rosemary, and Kathryn A. Davis. 1999. "Introduction: Authenticity and Identity: Lessons from Indigenous Language Education." *Anthropology and Education Quarterly* 30(1): 3–21.

Hill, Jane H. 1998. "Language, Race, and White Public Space." *American Anthropologist* 100(3): 680–9.

– 2002. "'Expert Rhetorics' in Advocacy for Endangered Languages: Who Is Listening, and What Do They Hear?" *Journal of Linguistic Anthropology* 12(2): 119–33.

– 2006. "The Ethnography of Language and Language Documentation." In *Essentials of Language Documentation*, ed. Jost Gippert, Nikolaus P. Himmelmann, and Ulrike Mosel. 113–28. Berlin: Mouton de Gruyter.

Hill, Jonathan D. 1984. "Social Equality and Ritual Hierarchy: The Arawakan Wakuénai of Venezuela." *American Ethnologist* 11(3): 528–44.
– 2008. *Made-from-Bone: Trickster Myths, Music, and History from the Amazon.* Champagne: University of Illinois Press.
Hill, Jonathan D., and Fernando Santos-Granero. 2002. "Comparative Arawakan Histories: Rethinking Language Family and Culture Area in Amazonia." Champagne: University of Illinois Press.
Hinton, Leanne. 2003. Language Revitalization. *Annual Review of Applied Linguistics* 23: 44–57.
Hinton, Leanne, and Ken Hale. 2001. *The Green Book of Language Revitalization in Practice.* San Diego: Academic Press.
Hornberger, Nancy. 2000. "Bilingual Education Policy and Practice in the Andes: Ideological Paradox and Intercultural Possibility." *Anthropology and Education Quarterly* 31(2): 173.
– 2008. *Can Schools Save Indigenous Languages? Policy and Practice on Four Continents.* New York: Palgrave Macmillan.
Hornberger, Nancy, and Karl F. Swinehart. 2012. "Bilingual Intercultural Education and Andean Hip Hop: Transnational Sites for Indigenous Language and Identity." *Language in Society* 41(04): 499–525.
Hugh-Jones, Christine. 1979. *From the Milk River: Spatial and Temporal Processes in Northwest Amazonia.* Cambridge: Cambridge University Press.
Hugh-Jones, Stephen. 1979. *The Palm and the Pleiades: Initiation and Cosmology in Northwest Amazonia.* Cambridge: Cambridge University Press.
– 2006. "The Substance of Northwest Amazonian Names." In *The Anthropology of Names and Naming,* ed. Gabriele Vom Bruck and Barbara Bodenhorn. 74–97. Cambridge: Cambridge University Press.
– 2010. "Entre l'image et l'écrit. La politique tukano de patrimonialisation en Amazonie," trans. Pierre Déléage. *Cahiers des Amériques latines* 1–2(63–64): 195–227.
Instituto Brasileiro de Geografia e Estatística 2010 Censo 2010: Resultados. http://censo2010.ibge.gov.br/resultados
Instituto Socioambiental 2010. Introdução: Tukano. Povos Indígenas No Brasil. http://pib.socioambiental.org/pt/povo/tukano
Irvine, Judith T. 1989. "When Talk Isn't Cheap: Language and Political Economy." *American Ethnologist* 16(2): 248–67.
Irvine, Judith T., and Susan Gal. 2000. "Language Ideology and Linguistic Differentiation." In *Regimes of Language: Ideologies, Polities, and Identities,* ed. Paul V. Kroskrity. 35–84. Santa Fe: School of American Research Press.
Iwasaki, Yoshitaka, and Namorah Gayle Byrd. 2010. "Cultural Activities, Identities, and Mental Health among Urban American Indians with Mixed Racial/Ethnic Ancestries." *Race and Social Problems* 2(2): 101–14.

Jackson, Jean E. 1983. *The Fish People: Linguistic Exogamy and Tukanoan Identity in Northwest Amazonia.* Cambridge: Cambridge University Press.

– 1989. "Language Identity of the Colombian Vaupés Indians." In *Explorations in the Ethnography of Speaking,* 2nd ed., ed. Richard Bauman and Joel Sherzer.50–64. Cambridge: Cambridge University Press.

– 1995. "Culture, Genuine and Spurious: The Politics of Indianness in the Vaupés, Columbia." *American Ethnologist* 22(1): 3–27.

Jaworski, Adam, and Crispin Thurlow, eds. 2010. *Semiotic Landscapes: Language, Image, Space. Advances in Sociolinguistics.* London and New York: Continuum.

Keesing, Roger M. 1987. "Anthropology as Interpretive Quest." *Current Anthropology* 28(2): 161–76.

Koch-Grünberg, Theodor. 2005. *Dois anos entre os indígenas: viagens no noroeste do* Brasil (1903/1905). Manaus: Editora da Universidade Federal do Amazonas.

Krauss, M. 1998. "The Condition of Native North American Languages: The Need for Realistic Assessment and Action." *International Journal of the Sociology of Language* (132): 9–21.

Kroskrity, Paul V. 2009. "Language Renewal as Sites of Language Ideological Struggle: The Need for 'Ideological Clarification.'" In *Indigenous Language Revitalization: Encouragement, Guidance, and Lessons Learned,* ed. Jon Reyhner and Louise Lockard. 71–83. Flagstaff: Northern Arizona University Press.

Kymlicka, Will, and Alan Patten. 2003. "Language Rights and Political Theory." *Annual Review of Applied Linguistics* 23: 3–21.

Landry, Rodrigue, and Richard Bourhis. 1997. "Linguistic Landscape and Ethnolinguistic Vitality." *Journal of Language and Social Psychology* 16(1): 23–49.

Lasmar, Cristiane. 2005. *De Volta ao Lago da Leite: Gênero e Transformação no Alto Rio Negro.* São Paulo: Editora da Universidade do Estado de São Paulo.

– 2009. *Irmã de Índio, Mulher de Branco: Perspectivas Femininas No Alto Rio Negro. Estudos de Antropologia Social* 14(2): 429–54.

Leonard, Wesley Y. 2012. "Framing Language Reclamation Programs for Everybody's Empowerment." *Gender and Language* 6(2): 339–67.

Leonard, Wesley Y., and Erin Haynes. 2010. "Making 'Collaboration' Collaborative: An Examination of Perspectives That Frame Linguistic Field Research." *Language Documentation and Conservation* 4: 268–93.

López, Luis Enrique, and Inge Sichra. 2008. "Intercultural Bilingual Education among Indigenous Peoples in Latin America." In *Encyclopedia of Language and Education,* ed. Nancy Hornberger. 1732–46. New York: Springer US.

Luciano, Gersem José dos Santos. 2012. "Educação para Manejo e Domesticação do Mundo entre a Escola Ideal e a Escola Real: Os Dilemas da Educação Escolar Indígena no Alto Rio Negro." PhD diss., Universidade de Brasilia.

Maffi, Luisa. 2005. "Linguistic, Cultural. and Biological Diversity." *Annual Review of Anthropology* 34: 599–617.

Maia, Paulo. 2009. "'Desequilibrando O Convencional': Estética E Ritual Com Os Baré (Amazonas, Brasil) – Paulo Roberto Maia Figueiredo." PhD diss., Universidade Federal de Rio de Janeiro.

May, Stephen. 2003. "Rearticulating the Case for Minority Language Rights." *Current Issues in Language Planning* 4(2): 95–125.

Maybury-Lewis, David, ed. 2002. *The Politics of Ethnicity: Indigenous Peoples in Latin American States.* Cambridge, MA; London: Harvard University/David Rockefeller Center for Latin American Studies.

McCarty, Teresa L. 2003. "Revitalising Indigenous Languages in Homogenising Times." *Comparative Education* 39(2): 147–63.

– ed. 2011. *Ethnography and Language Policy.* New York: Routledge.

McCarty, Teresa L., Mary Eunice Romero, and Ofelia Zepeda. 2006. "Reclaiming the Gift: Indigenous Youth Counter-Narratives on Native Language Loss and Revitalization." *American Indian Quarterly* 30(1–2): 28–48.

Meek, Barbra A. 2011. *We Are Our Language: An Ethnography of Language Revitalization in a Northern Athabaskan Community.* Tucson: University of Arizona Press.

Meira, Márcio. 1996. "O Tempo dos Patrões: Extrativismo, Comerciantes e Historia Indigena no Noroeste da Amzonia." In *Historia y Etnicidad en el Noroeste Amazónico,* ed. Alberta Zucchi and Silvia M. Vidal. 121–42. Mérida: Universidad de Los Andes Consejo de Publicaciones.

Melgueiro, Zilma Henrique. 2012. "A Situação Sociolingüística nas Escolas Indígenas Irmã Inês Penha e Dom Miguel Alagna na Cidade de São Gabriel da Cachoeira." MA thesis, Universidade Federal de Pernambuco, Brazil.

Michael, Lev, and Tania Granadillo. 2014. *Negation in Arawak Languages.* Leiden: Brill.

Muehlmann, Shaylih. 2013. *Where the River Ends: Contested Indigeneity in the Mexican Colorado Delta.* Durham: Duke University Press.

Mühlhäusler, Peter. 2001. "Ecolinguistics, Linguistic Diversity, Ecological Diversity." In *On Biocultural Diversity: Linking Language, Knowledge and the Environment,* ed. Luisa Maffi. 133–44. Washington, DC: Smithsonian Institution Press.

Nettle, Daniel, and Suzanne Romaine. 2000. *Vanishing Voices: The Extinction of the World's Languages.* New York: Oxford University Press.

Nevins, M. Eleanor. 2013. *Lessons from Fort Apache: Beyond Language Endangerment and Maintenance*. New York: John Wiley and Sons.

Niezen, Ronald. 2003. *The Origins of Indigenism: Human Rights and the Politics of Identity*. Berkeley: University of California Press.

Nimunedajú, Curt. 1982 "Reconhecimento dos Rios Içana, Ayari e Uaupés." In *Curt Nimuendajú. Textos Indigenistas*, ed. C. de Araújo Moreira Neto. 123–91. São Paulo: Edições Loyola.

Oakdale, Suzanne. 2004. "The Culture-Conscious Brazilian Indian: Representing and Reworking Indianness in Kayabi Political Discourse." *American Ethnologist* 31(1): 60–75.

Oliveira, Gilvan Müller de, and Alfredo Wagner Berno de Almeida. 2007. *Terra das Línguas: Lei Municipal de Oficialização de Línguas Indígenas, São Gabriel da Cachoeira, Amazonas*. Manaus: PPGSCA-UFAM/Fundação Ford.

Page, Helán, and R. Brooke Thomas. 1994. "White Public Space and the Construction of White Privilege in US Health Care: Fresh Concepts and a New Model of Analysis." *Medical Anthropology Quarterly* 8(1): 109–16.

Patrick, Donna. 2003. *Language, Politics, and Social Interaction in an Inuit Community*, vol. 8. Berlin and New York: Mouton de Gruyter.

– 2005. "Language Rights in Indigenous Communities: The Case of the Inuit of Arctic Quebec."
Journal of Sociolinguistics 9(3): 369–89.

– 2007. "Indigenous Language Endangerment and the Unfinished Business of Nation-States." In *Discourses of Endangerment: Ideology and Interest in the Defense of Languages*, ed. Alexandre Duchêne and Monica Heller. 35–56. London and New York: Continuum.

Patrick, Donna, and Julie-Ann Tomiak. 2008. "Language, Culture, and Community among Urban Inuit in Ottawa." *Etudes / Inuit / Studies* 32(1): 55–72.

Patten, Alan. 2009. "Survey Article: The Justification of Minority Language Rights." *Journal of Political Philosophy* 17(1): 102–28.

Peluso, Daniela M., and Miguel N. Alexiades. 2005. "Urban Ethnogenesis Begins at Home: The Making of Self and Place amidst Amazonia's Environmental Economy." *Traditional Dwellings and Settlements Review* 16(2): 1–10.

Perley, Bernard C. 2011. *Defying Maliseet Language Death: Emergent Vitalities of Language, Culture, and Identity in Eastern Canada*. Lincoln: University of Nebraska Press.

Peters, Evelyn J., and Chris Andersen, eds. 2013. *Indigenous in the City: Contemporary Identities and Cultural Innovation*. Vancouver: UBC Press.

Postero, Nancy. 2013. "Introduction: Negotiating Indigeneity." *Latin American and Caribbean Ethnic Studies* 8(2): 107–21.

Programa das Nações Unidos para o Desenvovimento. 2013. "O Índice de Desenvovimento Humano Municipal Brasileiro." *Atlas Do Desenvolvimento Humano no Brasil 2013*. Brasilia.

Ramirez, Henri. 1994. Iniciação à língua Yanomami. PhD diss., Université Aix-Marseille, Provence.

– 1997. *A fala Tukano dos Ye'pâ-Masa*. Manaus: Inspectoria Salesiana Missionária de Amazônia.

– 2001. *Dicionário da Língua Baniwa*. Manaus: Editora da Universidade Federal do Amazonas.

Ramos, Alcida Rita. 1998. *Indigenism: Ethnic Politics in Brazil*. Madison: University of Wisconsin Press.

– 2000. "Anthropologist as Political Actor." *Journal of Latin American Anthropology* 4(2): 172–90.

– 2003. "The Special (or Specious?) Status of Brazilian Indians." *Citizenship Studies* 7(4): 401–20.

Rappaport, Joanne. 2007. "Anthropological Collaborations in Colombia." In *Anthropology Put to Work*, ed. Les Field and Richard G. Fox. 21–44. Oxford and New York: Berg.

Réaume, Denise, and Meital Pinto. 2012. "Philosophy of Language Policy." In *The Cambridge Handbook of Language Policy*, ed. Bernard Spolsky. 37–58. Cambridge: Cambridge University Press.

Rede Globo. 2012. "Estudantes Indígenas Têm Direito à Educação Multicultural e Bilíngue: Novas Diretrizes para uma Educação Diferenciada Foram Aprovadas em 2012, Mas Especialistas Ressaltam Que Ainda é Difícil Aplicar as Leis na Prática." *Rede Globo*, 23 June. http://redeglobo.globo.com/globoeducacao/noticia/2012/06/estudantes-indigenas-tem-direito-educacao-multicultural-e-bilingue.html

Reid, Michael. 2014. *Brazil: The Troubled Rise of a Global Power*. New Haven: Yale University Press.

Rezende, Justino Sarmento. 2010. *A Educação na Visão de um Tuyuka*. Manaus: Faculdade Salesiana Dom Bosco.

Rice, Keren. 2006. "Ethical Issues in Linguistic Fieldwork: An Overview." *Journal of Academic Ethics* 4(1–4): 123–55.

– 2009. "Must There Be Two Solitudes? Language Activists and Linguists Working Together." In *Indigenous Language Revitalization: Encouragement, Guidance, and Lessons Learned*, ed. Jon Reyhner and Louise Lockard. Flagstaff: Northern Arizona University Press.

Rocha, Pedro. 2012. "Antes os brancos não existiam: corporalidade e política entre os Kotiria (Wanano) do Alto Uaupés." PhD diss., Universidade Federal de Rio de Janeiro.

Rockwell, Elsie, and Ana Maria R. Gomes. 2009. "Introduction to Special Issue: Rethinking Indigenous Education from a Latin American Perspective." *Anthropology and Education Quarterly* 40(2): 97–109.

Rodrigues, Aryon Dall'igna, and Ana Suelly Arruda Câmara Cabral. 2011. "A Contribution to the Linguistic History of the Língua Geral Amazônica." *Alfa: Revista de Linguística* 55(2): 613–39.

Romaine, Suzanne. 2002. "The Impact of Language Policy on Endangered Languages." *International Journal on Multicultural Societies* 4(2):1–28.

– 2006. "Planning for the Survival of Linguistic Diversity." *Language Policy* 5(4): 443–75.

Sarges, Fabiana. 2013. "A Lei da Cooficialização das Línguas Tukano, Nheengatu E Baniwa em São Gabriel da Cachoeira: Questões Sobre a Política Lingüística em Contexto Multilingüe." MA thesis, Universidade Federal da Amazonas, Manaus.

Scheper-Hughes, Nancy. 2000. "Ire in Ireland." *Ethnography* 1(1): 117–40.

Shankland, Alex, and Renato Athias. 2007. "Decentralisation and Difference: Indigenous Peoples and Health System Reform in the Brazilian Amazon." *IDS Bulletin* 38(1): 77–88.

Shulist, Sarah. 2013. "Collaborating on Language: Contrasting the Theory and Practice of Collaboration in Linguistics and Anthropology." *Collaborative Anthropologies* 6(1): 1–29.

– 2016a. "'Graduated Authenticity': Multilingualism, Revitalization, and Identity in the Northwest Amazon." *Language and Communication* 47: 112–23.

– 2016b. "Language Revitalization and the Future of Ethnolinguistic Identity." *Language and Communication* 47: 94–9.

– 2016c. "Indigenous Names, Revitalization Politics, and Regimes of Recognition in the Northwest Amazon." *Journal of Latin American and Caribbean Anthropology* 21(2): 336–54.

Silva, Wilson. 2012. "A Descriptive Grammar of Desano." PhD diss., University of Utah.

Silverstein, Michael. 1979. "Language Structure and Linguistic Ideology." In *The Elements: A Parasession on Linguistic Units and Levels*, ed. Paul R. Clyne, William F. Hanks, and Carol L. Hofbauer. 193–247. Chicago: Chicago Linguistic Society.

– 2000. "Whorfianism and the Linguistic Imagination of Nationality." In *Regimes of Language: Ideologies, Polities, and Identities*, ed. Paul V. Kroskrity. 85–138. Santa Fe: School of American Research Press.

Simpson, Audra. 2014. *Mohawk Interruptus: Political Life across the Borders of Settler States*. Durham: Duke University Press.

Skutnabb-Kangas, Tove. 2000. *Linguistic Genocide in Education, or Worldwide Diversity and Human Rights?* New York: Routledge.

Smith, Linda Tuhiwai Te Rina. 1999. *Decolonizing Methodologies: Research and Indigenous Peoples*. London: Zed Books.

Sobreiro, Thaissa. 2015. "Urban–Rural Livelihoods, Fishing Conflicts, and Indigenous Movements in the Middle Rio Negro Region of the Brazilian Amazon." *Bulletin of Latin American Research* 34(1): 53–69.

Sorensen, Arthur P. 1967. "Multilingualism in the Northwest Amazon." *American Anthropologist* 69(6): 670–84.

Souza, Maximiliano Loyola Pontes, and Luiza Garnelo. 2007. "When, How, and What to Drink: Alcoholism among Indian Peoples in the Upper Rio Negro, Brazil." *Cadernos de Saúde Pública* 23(7): 1640–8.

Spolsky, Bernard. 2003. "Reassessing Māori Regeneration." *Language in Society* 32(4): 553–78.

– ed. 2012. *The Cambridge Handbook of Language Policy*. Cambridge Handbooks in Language and Linguistics. Cambridge: Cambridge University Press.

Stenzel, Kristine. 2004. "A Reference Grammar of Wanano." PhD diss., University of Colorado.

– 2005. "Multilingualism in the Northwest Amazon, Revisited." In *Memorias Del Congreso de Idiomas Indígenas de Latinoamérica*. Austin: University of Texas Press.

– 2013. *A Reference Grammar of Kotiria (Wanano)*. Lincoln: University of Nebraska Press.

Swinehart, Karl F., and Kathryn Graber. 2012. "Tongue-Tied Territories: Languages and Publics in Stateless Nations." *Language and Communication* 32(2): 95–7.

Umúsin, Panlõn Kumu, and Kenhíri Tolamãn. 1995. *Antes o Mundo não Existia. Narradores Indígenas do Rio Negro*. São Gabriel da Cachoeira: FOIRN.

Urban, Greg. 1993. *A Discourse-Centered Approach to Culture: Native South American Myths and Rituals*. Austin: University of Texas Press.

Urla, Jacqueline. 2015. *Reclaiming Basque: Language, Nation, and Cultural Activism*. Reno: University of Nevada Press.

Vilaca, Aparecida. 2016. *Praying and Preying: Christianity in Indigenous Amazonia*. Berkeley: University of California Press.

Virtanen, Pirjo Kristiina. 2010. "Amazonian Native Youths and Notions of Indigeneity in Urban Areas." *Identities* 17(2): 154–75.

– 2012. *Indigenous Youth in Brazilian Amazonia: Changing Lived Worlds*. New York: Palgrave Macmillan.

Wallace, Anthony F.C. 1956. "Revitalization Movements." *American Anthropologist* 58(2): 264–81.

Warren, Jonathan W. 1999. "The Brazilian Geography of Indianness." *Wicazo Sa Review* 14(1): 61–86.

– 2001. *Racial Revolutions: Antiracism and Indigenous Resurgence in Brazil.* Durham: Duke University Press.

Warren, Kay B. 1998. *Indigenous Movements and Their Critics: Pan-Maya Activism in Guatemala.* Princeton: Princeton University Press.

Warren, Kay B., and Jean E. Jackson, eds. 2002. *Indigenous Movements, Self-Representation, and the State in Latin America,* 1st ed. Austin: University of Texas Press.

Weigel, Valéria Augusta. 2003. "Os Baniwa e a Escola: Sentidos e Repercussões." *Revista Brasileira de Educação* (22): 5–13.

Whiteley, Peter. 2003. "Do 'Language Rights' Serve Indigenous Interests? Some Hopi and Other Queries." *American Anthropologist* 105(4): 712–22.

Woolard, Kathryn A., and Bambi B. Schieffelin. 1994. "Language Ideology." *Annual Review of Anthropology* 23: 55–82.

Wortham, Stanton. 2008. "Linguistic Anthropology of Education." *Annual Review of Anthropology* 37: 37–51.

Wright, Robin. 1992. "História Indígena do Noroeste da Amazônia: Hipóteses, Questões, e Perspectivas. In *História Dos Índios No Brasil,* ed. Manuela Carneiro da Cunha. 253–65. São Paulo: Companhia das Letras.

– 1998. *Cosmos, Self, and History in Baniwa Religion: For Those Unborn.* Austin: University of Texas Press.

– 2005. *Historia Indigena e do Indigenismo no Alto Rio Negro,* 1st ed. Campinas: FAEP - Universidade Estadual de Campinas.

– 2009. "The Art of Being Crente: The Baniwa Protestant Ethic and the Spirit of Sustainable Development." *Identities* 16(2): 202–26.

Wright, Robin, and Jonathan D. Hill. 1986. "History, Ritual, and Myth: 19th Century Millenarian Movements in the Northwest Amazon." *Ethnohistory* 33(1): 31–54.

Wroblewski, Michael. 2012. "Amazonian Kichwa Proper: Ethnolinguistic Domain in Pan-Indian Ecuador." *Journal of Linguistic Anthropology* 22(1): 64–86.

Zellen, Barry. 1998. "Introduction: Media and Aboriginal Culture: An Evolving Relationship." *Cultural Survival Quarterly,* 31 July, 25.

Index

ANTHROPOLOGICAL HORIZONS

Editor: Michael Lambek, University of Toronto

Published to date: